A note on the Exceeding the Common Core State Standards series:

We undertook this series of three books (*Get It Done! Writing and Analyzing Informational Texts to Make Things Happen*; *Oh, Yeah?! Putting Argument to Work Both in School and Out*; *So, What's the Story? Teaching Narrative to Understand Ourselves, Others, and the World*) as a collaborative project designed to share our ideas on how to teach the three types of writing addressed by the Common Core State Standards in such a way that students will develop the knowledge they need to do important work both in and out of school. Each of us took the lead in writing one volume; the other two made or suggested a variety of revisions. We are able to work together because we share so much about what we think makes good writing and good teaching, so you'll see many, many similarities across the books, especially in the central principles we use to organize them. But you'll also see some differences in our approaches and in our points of emphasis. To paraphrase Mark Twain, we make this explanation for the reason that without it many readers would suppose that all three authors were trying to talk alike and not succeeding.

Get It Done!

Writing and Analyzing Informational Texts to Make Things Happen

Jeffrey D. Wilhelm

Michael W. Smith

James E. Fredricksen

HEINEMANN
Portsmouth, NH

Heinemann
361 Hanover Street
Portsmouth, NH 03801–3912
www.heinemann.com

Offices and agents throughout the world

The authors and publisher wish to thank those who have generously given permission to reprint borrowed material:

Excerpts from *Common Core State Standards* © Copyright 2010. National Governors Association Center for Best Practices and Council of Chief State School Officers. All rights reserved.

Excerpt from *Improving Comprehension with Think-Aloud Strategies: Modeling What Good Readers Do* by Jeffrey D. Wilhelm, Ph.D. Copyright © 2001 by Jeffrey D. Wilhelm. Published by Scholastic Inc. Reprinted by permission of the publisher.

Excerpt from the article *"Causes and Effects of Poverty"* appearing in *CliffsQuickReview*™ *Sociology* by George D. Zgourides and Christie S. Zgourides. Copyright © 2000 by John Wiley & Sons, Inc. Published by John Wiley & Sons, Inc. Reprinted by permission of the publisher.

Library of Congress Cataloging-in-Publication Data
Wilhelm, Jeffrey D.
    Get it done! : writing and analyzing informational texts to make things happen / Jeffrey D. Wilhelm, Michael W. Smith, James E. Fredricksen.
        p.   cm. – (Exceeding the common core state standards)
    Includes bibliographical references and index.
    ISBN-13: 978-0-325-04291-6
    ISBN-10: 0-325-04291-8
    1. English language—Composition and exercises—Study and teaching (Secondary).   2. Exposition (Rhetoric).
I. Smith, Michael W. (Michael William).   II. Fredricksen, James E.   III. Title.

LB1631.W394 2012
428.0071'2—dc23   2012021742

Editor: Samantha Bennett
Production: Vicki Kasabian
Interior and cover designs: Monica Crigler
Typesetter: Kim Arney
Manufacturing: Steve Bernier

Printed in the United States of America on acid-free paper
16 15 14 13 12 ML 1 2 3 4 5

To Connie Bates
For friendship beyond all calls of duty
You fill our hearts

Contents

Acknowledgments

This book could not have been written without the cheerful help of Jeff and Peggy's friend Connie Bates. As she has done on several occasions, Connie flew to Idaho to take care of Peggy as she dealt with the consequences of an undiagnosed vascular disorder—and she took care of Jeff too as he recovered from emergency knee surgery during the writing of this book.

Jeff also gives a tip of the hat and a twenty-one-gun salute to all his rafting buddies: the Foster/Sears family, the Greenburg clan, and the Lambeks for a great trip down the Grand Canyon that features prominently in this book.

Especially deserving of salutation includes Rachel Bear, head of the Boise State Writing Project (BSWP) Common Core State Standards Implementation Team, for reading numerous drafts and providing many helpful insights and CCSS connections. Rachel also led the team that composed the reader's study guide for this text, which we hope will prove useful to both individuals and study groups making use of the ideas presented here. Anna Daley not only read the manuscript and provided useful feedback but also developed the unit in the appendix that exemplifies the principles and features many of the ideas presented here. BSWP fellows Angie Young and Erika Boas also read and responded to drafts with their typical incisive commentary and offer of various resources. Thanks too to Cecilia Soto-Pattee, Brandon Bolyard, and other members of the BSWP CCSS Implementation Team for their help with this project. Stan Steiner, children's literature aficionado and expert, provided suggestions for mentor texts.

The Boise State Writing Project and the Rethinking Teaching Team provided ongoing professional resources and support that were and continue to be invaluable. Jeff particularly thanks Paula Uriarte and Jess Westhoff in this regard. Brian White is always a salutary and supportive influence on all professional and personal matters and gets Jeff's continuous gratitude.

Thanks, too, to teachers Terry Quain, Christine Tarchinski, and Blair Covino for their creation of content-area exhibits.

For personal and professional support, Jeff thanks his courageous wife Peggy Jo, who also offered many ideas about formative assessment and composing to transfer. Thanks always to his amazing daughters Fiona Luray and Jasmine Marie for keeping him humble and providing unfiltered feedback on and assistance with difficult sections of the book.

For continuous and meritorious personal support: One-armed Willie Stewart, the oh-so-French Dale Reynolds, the most-helpful-even-at-a-moment's-notice Todd Fischer, Commander Bob White, the oversized leprechaun Patrick Harren, the northern Italians Michael Lanza and Mike Weber-letti, that unabashed Hoosier Clyde Cody, the rollicking Ralph Comstock and mentor to all Raleigh Jensen, the old animal Paul Corrigan, teachers, colleagues, and friends extraordinaire Brian and Anne Ambrosius, Cary James, Jerry Hendershot, Frank Dehoney, Melissa Newell, and Audrey Linville, the entire Idaho Nordic crew, and many others too numerous to mention. Jeff is grateful to you all for friendship and support.

Michael thanks his colleagues from the University of Chicago, with whom he's worked so closely over the years that it's sometimes hard to remember whose idea is whose, especially George Hillocks Jr., Steve Gevinson, the late Larry Johannessen, Betsy Kahn, Carol Lee, Steve Littell, Tom McCann, Peter Smagorinsky, and Carolyn Calhoun Walter. Thanks, too, to Brian White for always providing a calming and supportive voice and to his colleagues at the College of Education at Temple University for making the College such a congenial environment. Finally, thanks to his wonderfully supportive wife, Karen Flynn, his daughters Catherine and Rachel, and his granddaughter Gabrielle who gives meaning to all that he does.

Jim thanks members of his writing group, Anne Whitney, Troy Hicks, and Leah Zuidema, who provide much-needed and timely support, as well as many thoughtful comments and questions. Thanks also to Boise State Writing Project colleagues, including Rachel Bear, Paula Uriarte, Jess Westhoff, and Angie Young, who read drafts, provided suggestions, offered supportive comments, and asked questions to keep the thinking headed in the right direction during this project. Jim would also like to thank the members of the National Writing Project's Literacy in the Common Core Leadership Team—Tanya Baker, Rebeca Garcia-Gonzalez, Elyse Eidman-Aadahl, Michael Thompson, Cindy O'Donnell-Allen, Marcie Wolfe, Linda Denstaedt, Laura Schiller, Jean Wolph, and Rachel Bear—who provide an intellectual home and practical suggestions in helping people create curriculum in thoughtful ways. Thanks also to the many teachers across a whole host of states and writing project sites who were and are involved in NWP's LCC work, including Boise State Writing Project's Anna Daley, Cecilia Pattee, Sarah Veigel, Andrew Porter, and James LeDoux, who originally broke ground and led the charge in helping teachers at our site and in our state work with the CCSS in ways that honor teachers' expertise and experience. Finally, Jim would like to thank family, friends, students, and colleagues, who make this life and work as a teacher a great gig.

Laying the Foundation

In this book we explore how to teach the composing—and also the reading—of informational texts. Our goal is to develop both real-world expertise in the reading and writing of these text structures, and the capacity to gain and express disciplinary understanding of the content embedded in informational text so that what students learn through the instruction we propose can help them not only in their academic pursuits but also in their daily lives.

Our great mentor is the famed researcher George Hillocks. While many well-known writing instructors seem to want to help students become highly accomplished writers, George's ultimate end, or *telos*, is more nuanced: he wants students to do intellectual and democratic work—both inside of school and outside of it—through their reading and composing. That's the reason for our title, *Get It Done!*

Though we were planning to write this book anyway, the wide-scale implementation of the Common Core State Standards (CCSS) makes it exceptionally timely, since these standards designate informational/explanatory texts as one of the three major types to be taught across grade levels and disciplines. In fact, informational/explanatory texts get some special privileging: in high school content-area classes and even in English classes, teaching informational/explanatory texts, along with argument, is supposed to predominate. The introductory CCSS documents state: "Evidence concerning the demands of college and career readiness gathered during development of the CCSS concurs with NAEP's [the National Assessment of Educational Progress] shifting emphases: standards for grades 9–12 describe writing in all three forms (narrative, argument, informational/explanatory), but, consistent with NAEP, the overwhelming focus of writing throughout high school should be on arguments and informative/explanatory texts" (retrieved from the CCSS Initiative website, 8/11/11).

➤ *CCSS connection*

1

The CCSS are vertically aligned and include standards for literacy in the disciplines and a focus on reading and writing informational texts in all content areas. Standards in the early grades clearly lead toward this end by emphasizing gathering evidence and structuring texts in various ways for various purposes and effects. (The notion of *rhetorical stance*, or a consideration—in one's reading and writing—of the author's "purpose, task, and audience" in achieving particular effects is emphasized throughout the CCSS.) Throughout this book, we accommodate the emphasis on comprehending and composing informational text structures by exploring two questions: Why think and write in informational/explanatory thought patterns? How can we leverage the special opportunity of the CCSS for the most vital kinds of teaching and learning?

➤ *CCSS connection*

This emphasis on informative/explanatory texts will require all teachers in all subjects to deeply understand how these structures work, how to teach them, and how to help students use them to get real work done. Let's get started!

What Is Informative/Explanatory Writing?

Let's take a look at how the kinds of texts the CCSS identify as informative/explanatory play out in life and help people get things done. What real-world purposes are served when we teach these kinds of thought patterns?

At this writing, Jeff has just returned from a lifelong dream adventure. He first developed a desire to float down the Colorado River through the Grand Canyon when he was a twelve-year-old Boy Scout reading about the river explorations of John Wesley Powell. Forty years later, this dream came true in the most spectacular way: he spent three weeks on a private raft and kayak trip with his daughter Jasmine and fourteen other friends. Planning this exciting trip took years.

It began with a lot of emailing among the participants. The first text type seemed to be mostly *naming* and *listing*: the group members named what they thought they would need and made lists of meals, snacks, and cooking equipment; emergency and rescue gear; and so on. The items the group eventually took varied substantially from these early lists, but the lists acted as placeholders so nothing important would be forgotten.

Next, there seemed to be a lot of *summaries*: of gear organization, the trip itinerary, training regimens, and the like. The summaries ensured everyone was informed, up-to-date, and on the same page.

Since the Glen Canyon Dam was emitting the maximum flow of 26,000 cubic feet per second, Jeff began writing to friends who had kayaked down the canyon for *process descriptions* of how to run particular rapids in the big water. His buddy Tim Hilmer (from the Colorado Writing Project) was a big help. At the same time, his group began exchanging directions and process descriptions for preparing and packing gear, recipes, and provisions. These "rehearsals" helped the actual trip go more smoothly.

There were also exchanges of *descriptions* of gear, meals, campsites, and rapids. Campsites, rapids, and possible hikes were *defined*, *compared*, and *classified*. Potential *problems* were discussed and *proactive solutions* proposed. There were also some *cause-and-effect* discussions. What might be the source of most health issues on a long trip? Lack of sanitary measures and failure to take care of wet feet. Solutions? Washing stations before each meal and after "groovering"[1]; daily foot checks and moisturizing.

In short, the group used a tremendous variety and amount of informational and explanatory exchanges to prepare for the trip.

They continued to do so during the trip. Most notable (and exciting) were scouting rapids and sharing various process descriptions for navigating them, with plans A, B, and C in place for each boat, as well as rescue procedures in various scenarios.

These exchanges did the work they were meant to do. The trip went off seamlessly—three weeks of spectacular scenery, major hikes requiring rope systems and rappelling, big whitewater and massive wave trains, eddy lines and swarmy washouts (did we mention the big whitewater?), all without a major flip-over, bad swim, injury, or personal or relational meltdown and with never less than a magnificent meal. Why? In large part because the group knew how to think and communicate with the appropriate thought patterns—in informational/explanatory structures.

Jim and Michael have also found themselves thinking and communicating in such structures recently.

Michael's summer was spent in a much less exciting fashion. As chair of his department, though, he had to compose in the same structures. He exchanged numerous lists of unstaffed courses with his department manager. He wrote summaries of duties to be included in the contracts of new faculty. He detailed the process faculty should use for a common assessment his department does as part of its accreditation work. While the department offices were being cleaned, one of his colleague's throw rugs went missing; he asked her to write a careful description to help him track it down. He had to decide whether to grant transfer credit for a number of incoming students, a decision that requires classification, definition, and comparison. As chair of a faculty search committee he wrote a recommendation to his Dean that

---

1. A slang term for using a portable toilet.

identified problems the new hires could solve and discussed the future effects the hiring would have.

Jim also found himself using various informative/explanatory thought patterns over the summer. He keeps in touch with a group of high school friends who are scattered around the country. The excuse for doing so is mostly to give each other a hard time about their fantasy baseball teams, but often these emails or text messages turn into updates about families, jobs, and relationships.

This summer found Jim's fantasy team in complete meltdown, mostly because six of his players were on the disabled list at one time. In one email exchange with his friends, he listed each player and how they were injured. Then he offered some possible trades (quickly and forcefully denied) in support of which he compared statistics and described how the players could help his friends' teams inch closer to the playoffs. Later, as Jim's team slipped further and further in the standings, he relayed process descriptions detailing how the many injuries were the cause of his team's poor showing. (They fired back that the real cause was Jim's lack of talent in choosing the right players during the draft at the beginning of the season.)

Every year, each two-week scoring period ends with the commissioner of the league, Steve, writing a brief summary of what happened during that scoring period. His summary includes any movement in the standings, and he classifies the outstanding pitchers and the outstanding hitters during that scoring period. During the off-season Jim's friends and fellow fantasy team owners swap emails about any problems and possible solutions facing the league—problems like inactive team owners or the number of players each team can keep on its roster from season to season.

These kinds of texts and exchanges are rooted in a fantasy baseball league and the work of keeping the league operating and healthy, but really they are about keeping the relationships going so that it is easier to be there to celebrate and to console when real-life events require.

What Are the Informative/Explanatory Text Structures?

➤ *Cross-curricular connections*

Every discipline uses these thought patterns extensively, so if we are going to help students think like real readers, writers, historians, scientists, and mathematicians, we need to teach these patterns and text structures in the context of our subject matter. And now we have the added incentive of meeting the CCSS.

The logic behind narrative is primarily time or chronology. The logic behind argument is primarily evidence and reasoning about that evidence. The logic behind informative/explanatory texts is more varied. In fact the CCSS place a clear emphasis on variety: "Informational/explanatory writing includes a wide array of genres, including academic genres such as literary analyses, scientific and historical reports, summaries, and précis writing as well as forms of workplace and functional writing such as instructions, manuals, memos, reports, applications, and résumés."

➤ *CCSS connection*

This book focuses on the following informative/explanatory texts that are cited by the CCSS and, more important, are essential to disciplinary thinking and generative in that they are prerequisite or complementary to understanding and using related text types:

1. *Listing and naming*: placeholding individual elements that are important for a task or situation. (Both patterns seem implied by what the CCSS calls *naming*.)

2. *Summary/précis*: making a point using highly focused, essential key details that relate and form a pattern. (Summary is cited by the CCSS as an explanatory text structure; we see it as expressing necessary and profound disciplinary thinking upon which other kinds of work depend.)

3. *Description*: fleshed out sensory descriptions like sensoriums; reports, scientific reports, and memos; and reviews and critiques, which include judgments. (Descriptions are informational texts according to the CCSS, as are reports and reviews, which we think are primarily descriptive.)

4. *Process description*: steps in a process—recipes, directions, process analyses, and how-to texts. What the CCSS call "sequential" texts belong here if they are not narrative texts to be "lived through" but describe steps in a functional process. (Instructions, directions, and sequential texts are identified as informational/explanatory texts by the CCSS.)

5. *Definition*: extending from short encyclopedic entries to extended definitions. (Definition as specified by the CCSS involves "differentiation," which is cited as very important in disciplinary work.)

6. *Comparison–contrast*: setting two (or more) elements side by side. Rankings involve a series of comparison–contrasts. (The CCSS name comparison an informational text type that also involves "differentiation," something essential in all disciplines.)

7. *Classification*: grouping multiple elements of a specific topical universe. This involves comparing and contrasting group membership (what the CCSS calls "differentiation" is the basis of classification and is essential to disciplinary work.)

8. *Cause–effect*: explaining the relationship between an impetus or set of causes and consequences in events that have already occurred. (Anything predictive seems to us to clearly be an argument. We include this text structure here because the CCSS refer to it as an informational text type.)

9. *Problem–solution*: explaining the nature of a problem and relating the causes of the problem to the solution. (This is always predictive and seems to us to be an argument, but we include this thought pattern here to be consistent with the CCSS).

This list covers the ground suggested by the CCSS but is more than a taxonomy. Rather we see it as a hierarchy, that is, each structure is prerequisite to the next one, as it suggests what students need to know and be able to do prior to being able to use a subsequent thought pattern on the list.

For example, naming and listing key elements or details is prerequisite to putting these together in a summary. Summary is prerequisite to a description that fleshes and fills out the key details in different ways, that is, with sensory details, and by using different organizations (such as the spatial). Describing is prerequisite to defining, since defining requires precisely including and excluding the essential details of test cases—that is, understanding what is essential to a term or idea but also knowing boundaries, being able to make judgments about gray areas, and identifying examples and nonexamples. This is obviously prerequisite to comparing and contrasting different elements, as both will need to be clearly understood and defined prior to being compared. Classifying a larger set of elements depends on comparing and contrasting, even as it goes beyond this to identify the groupings and relationships of *all* elements in a topical universe. Beginning with comparison–contrast and moving through problem–solution structures seems to us to all be about various kinds of groupings of data and all depend on defining, which depends in turn on thick description. Cause–effect and problem–solution are arguments about grouping—about how ideas are related, work together, lead to each other.

Our point: students will have great difficulty summarizing if they cannot first name and list, and they won't be able to compare or classify if they cannot define. Our hierarchy therefore suggests what is prerequisite to reading and composing more complex text types and therefore what we need to teach or at least remind students that they already know and must bring to bear to a new task.

Our discussion of discrete types is not to suggest that they are pure types, because they usually are not. Typically one text type operates as a superstructure that uses a variety of other different text types in service of the overarching text type: "Skilled writers many times use a blend . . . [of] text types to accomplish their purposes" (CCSS Appendix A, 24).

➤ *CCSS reference*

For instance, Jeff likes Seymour Simon's nature books. Simon's book *Whales* is organized by the superstructure of extended definition, since its purpose is to define whales and differentiate whales from other seas creatures. The overall structure is a series of descriptions of different features and parts of the whale's anatomy, habitat, habits, and the like that define whales and differentiate them from other creatures. However, the book starts with a comparison/contrast of whales versus fish. Page 9 is a process description of how whales breathe. Page 10 is a description of the tail. Page 19 and following is a short classification of types of whales. Page 39 is a process description of how the humpback whale feeds. And so on. Though the overall organizing structure is definition, many other structures are used in service of doing the defining.

The variety and combinations of informational/explanatory texts in real-world texts place very real challenges in front of both teachers and students but also provide many powerful rewards for those who master them.

Bottom line: even though different text types share general processes and even though they may be used in combination to achieve particular rhetorical goals, each instance of a specific thought pattern (e.g., comparison) will share very specific conventions and structures. These must be taught and mastered in order for students to be competent with these thought patterns, the text structures that embed them, and the work these can do both in the disciplines and in life.

Leveraging the Promise of the Common Core State Standards

All three of us endorse the CCSS. We think they offer a wonderful opportunity to leverage progressive teaching and bring education in line with what we have known for a long time courtesy of cognitive science, social psychology, and educational research.

The CCSS are not unproblematic. We believe that the focus on college and career readiness is too narrow and agree that the CCSS could include a greater focus on participatory, critical citizenry. But whether the CCSS have such a focus or not, we will explore how we can teach in ways that will prepare our students for college, career, *and* citizenship through the *structured process* of conceptual inquiry. (Please note that we are using *inquiry* as a term of art from cognitive science—as the rigorous apprenticeship into disciplinary thinking—not as student discovery learning, which is how some people conceive of it.) Through inquiry, we can promote and reward the kinds of reading and writing the CCSS foreground in ways that meet not only the college and career readiness standards but also the notion of participating as a critical citizen—of engaging in social action, service, and the like.

Another critique is that the standards were not democratically created with teachers in the lead. Agreed. However, we think the CCSS are respectful of teachers in that they give teachers latitude and decision-making power regarding the use of content and texts, as well as how to craft instruction, design curriculum, assess learning, and collaborate with colleagues. In other words, the story of the CCSS implies respect for teachers and the work of teachers. As current or former National Writing Project directors, all three of us endorse the NWP's notion that expertise about teaching resides with teachers, that teachers must strive for "conscious competence" by doing and coming to understand deeply what we teach students to do, and that teachers are the best teachers of other teachers. We think the CCSS are consistent with these views. The question is whether we, as a profession, will take on the challenge to devise curriculum for our own students and situation, selecting the most compelling content that will provide the context to engage our own students and help them meet the procedural/strategic demands of the CCSS to think with different thought patterns, to make and perform actual knowledge that can be transferred and developed over time.

To be clear, even without the CCSS we would vigorously promote teaching in the way we describe in this book. But teaching in the way we propose helps us all to meet the worthy strategic goals of the CCSS.

Conclusion

In this book, we deal with how to teach various kinds of informational/explanatory thought patterns and text structures in the context of inquiry. In Part 1, we share a heuristic of five kinds of knowledge and five kinds of composing that are necessary to student expertise, and will help teachers explore the structures of informational texts and highlight the importance of instructional specificity. We then follow up with how to make composing (and reading) these kinds of texts matter in the context of inquiry units. In Part 2, we explore the specific processes of teaching the reading and composing of each kind of text structure in ways that we have found compelling and useful to our own students, both in the present moment and in their foreseeable future learning, working, and living.

Thinking About the Structures Behind
Informational and Explanatory Texts

One of our own most challenging moves as teachers is to try to get underneath the stuff we teach, to understand it deeply, to know its purpose, structure, and inner workings, so we can fully grasp why it's important and know how to teach it better. Studying, sticking with focused reflection over time, and coming to deeply understand what we teach typically allows us to believe more deeply in what we are teaching, so we are not just doing what is expected of us but instead what we come to feel called and compelled to do for and with our students.

Achieving this kind of foundational knowledge is a real challenge. Here's one reason: as teachers we've come to realize that there are conventional categories for texts that have lost their original power and meaning because we've lost the connection to why that category evolved in the first place and why and how it is used in the world. This phenomenon seems especially true with regard to informative/explanatory texts.

Throughout our careers we felt we had a good sense of what narrative and argument were. We knew intuitively how these text structures worked, and we understood and valued the work they could do for kids both in our classrooms and out in the world. Not so with informational/explanatory texts. Throughout our careers, expository texts (or what the CCSS call informational/explanatory texts) were simply a category for texts that weren't narrative or argument.

Now, however, we've come to see that there are deep structural similarities among all informational texts that justify this category and allow us to make sense of it. Jerome Bruner has helped us see those similarities through his discussion of paradigmatic thought.

The Greek word *paradeigma* is the root word of *paradigm*; its primary meaning is *pattern, patterning,* or *creative model*. Because of the seminal work of the scientific historian Thomas Kuhn (1962), *paradigm* has come to mean a distinctive thought pattern in a particular discipline or epistemological (knowledge making/problem solving) context. A paradigm, then, is a way that disciplines organize data and analyze and report findings so that the work of that discipline can be systematically accomplished.

In Jerome Bruner's influential book *Actual Minds, Possible Worlds* (1986) he maintains that there are two primary modes of thought: the narrative mode and the paradigmatic mode (12 ff). The most common academic mode is the paradigmatic, which involves logical, scientific, categorical thought that "makes use of procedures to assure verifiable reference and to test for empirical truth" (13). In narrative thinking, the mind engages in sequential, action-oriented, detail-driven thought. In paradigmatic thinking, the mind transcends particularities to achieve systematic, categorical cognition. In the former case, thinking takes the form of stories and gripping drama. In the latter, thinking is structured as propositions linked by logical operators.

Bruner suggests that these logical operators are always based in some way on *categorization*: "To perceive is to categorize, to conceptualize is to categorize, to learn is to form categories, to make decisions is to categorize" (Wikipedia, 8/17/11, Introduction to J. S. Bruner). We've come to see that informative/explanatory texts are, at their heart, different ways to categorize. What this means is that each informational text type requires a different and very particular kind of thought. *That is, each kind of informational text structure embodies a specific way of thinking with and through categories.* In turn, this means that teaching students how to understand, produce, and use informational text structures means that we are teaching them how to think with specific categorical patterning tools. This is something that we explore in detail in each of the practice chapters.

Let's take a look at the different kinds of informative/explanatory texts we introduced in Chapter 1. Lists are a category of names compiled for some shared purpose—items you need to purchase at the grocery store, for example. Descriptions allow us to name and perceive the essential qualities of an object, element, place, or process so that it can be understood, categorized, and generalized from. ("Make sure to buy the gluten-free Bisquick. It's in a smaller box, the box is orange, and it's got a GF label on it.") Definitions are in fact an effort to categorize a term or concept based on its essential elements as well as what it does not comprise. ("The gluten-free label is very important—it means the product doesn't have wheat in it.") Comparisons and classifications are clearly forms of categorization. ("You'll find it in the baking aisle, but not with the other Bisquicks; it's with the organic and natural nonwheat flours.")

Even cause–effect and problem–solution are efforts to link categories such as causes to their resultant categories of effects and categories of problems to categories of potential solutions. ("Gluten has been causing some bowel and digestive problems for me; gluten-free is easier on my stomach and aids my digestion.")

Of course, this deep structural similarity of things being based on categorization doesn't mean that the different kinds of informative/explanatory texts work the same way, so in this chapter we introduce a fuller definition of each kind of informational/explanatory text. (In future chapters, we draw on these definitions when we explore how we teach them.) More specifically, we think about how each of these informational text structures helps people understand and accomplish particular ends—to get important things done for oneself and out in the world.

Naming and Listing

Naming is a powerful intellectual act. Naming gives us power over the named, imbues it with meaning, and allows us both to think about and to use that meaning. On river trips, Jeff and his buddies often name unnamed rapids so that they can remember the qualities of the rapid and refer to it in shorthand. For instance, one nameless rapid where Jeff ran through two holes and had to roll twice was instantly referred to as "Jeff's Jukebox" throughout all stories and comparisons to other rapids later in the trip. (This naming did much more effective work than "remember that rapid around mile 120?")

Once something has been named it can be put into a list. Listing allows us to place hold what we've named into a category of like elements so it can be remembered and used. We find naming and listing prerequisite to all other kinds of informational or explanatory patterning and to all forms of Bruner's notion of categorization.

Summarizing

A summary is a brief focused statement that includes all—but only—essential details of a longer text or data set, along with an organization or a brief statement that expresses how those details are meaningfully related. On the river, kayakers and rafters often have to quickly communicate a summary to one another. For instance, after going down a difficult drop, the first kayaker might need to summarize where to go or not go to the others following. Boaters have a series of signals they give with their paddles to provide such summaries in a very quick, on-the-run fashion.

Describing

A description fleshes out the basic details, gives life and sensory expression to these details, and demonstrates relationships between the details (spatial, chronological, etc.). Descriptions allow us to understand something deeply, including how it is patterned. When describing a rapid, Jeff might talk about the top, middle, and bottom or right versus left approaches. He'll be sure to name and describe major features like tongues, holes, waves, eddy lines, and eddies and how they relate to one another, lead to one another, and the like.

Process Description

Process description allow us to prepare and rehearse a specific activity; to direct and correct our activity while we are doing it; and to consider, reflect on, and plan for the future. The people on Jeff's river trip used process descriptions and analyses before, during, and after every big rapid and before every meal and every camp set up. Before hitting a rapid, everyone had to understand how to navigate the rapid, how to solve problems that might occur, where to pull out to "play safety" for the next boats. While actually in the rapid, you better believe that Jeff was talking his way through it, and if something went wrong he talked his way through a self-correction, reminding himself what holes and waves to avoid. Afterward, there was often much joyous recounting of the processes of what had happened and what had been learned for future rapids.

Definition

A definition explains the meaning and limits of a term or concept. There are two kinds of definitions: short definitions of the sort one might see in a dictionary and extended definitions. We regularly make use of dictionary-style definitions. Think, for example, of teaching someone how to play a new game. You can't learn how to play bridge unless you know the definition of a trump. Extended definitions are very important when exploring conceptual terms in the disciplines, such as *exponent* or *invertebrate* or even *courage* or *hero*. Extended definitions are essential to comparisons and classifications, which categorize and differentiate all the individual examples of a topical universe. On Jeff's Grand Canyon trip, it was essential that the group come to shared definitions of good campsites, rigging procedures, and much more as the trip proceeded. These definitions guided the group in what to look for and do and what not to look for and do in various situations.

Comparison–Contrast

Comparisons and contrasts also help us see similarities despite differences and differences despite similarities, which enhances mutual understanding, allowing people with differences to work toward commonalities or make finely sliced differentiations. Rankings like top-ten lists involve a series of comparison–contrasts.

On Jeff's Grand Canyon trip, many things were compared and contrasted: campsites, hikes, meals, and more. But as usual, the river dominated, and the most common comparisons and contrasts were of rapids. In fact, the Colorado River in the Grand Canyon has its own river rating and ranking system, on a scale of 0–10, that allows various characteristics of rapids—the likelihood of capsizing, the technical nature of navigation, and the consequences of swimming in them—to be compared. Lava Falls, for instance, is a 10—the most difficult rapid on the Colorado. Crystal, equally difficult and perhaps more dangerous if one goes through the first monster hole, is ranked a 9 because there is a sneak route on river right.

Classification

Classifications group multiple elements of a specific topical universe. This obviously involves comparing and contrasting the definitions of group membership. The most famous classification scheme is Linnean, or biological, classification, developed by Carl Linneaus to group life according to physical characteristics and later, under the influence of Darwin, also according to common descent. This kind of classification proceeds from *life*, to *domain*, *kingdom*, *phylum*, *class*, *order*, *family*, *genus*, to the individual example of life, *species*. Classifications proceed from the topical universe (in this case, life) through subordinating categories to the individual example of the topical universe (in this case, species).

Classification has been defined by Mayr and Bock (2002) as "the arrangement of entities in a hierarchical series of nested classes, in which similar or related classes at one hierarchical level are combined comprehensively into more inclusive classes at the next higher level" (169). A *class* is defined as "a collection of similar entities" where the similarity consists of the entities having attributes or traits in common (169). Classification obviously helps us, as researchers and inquirers, see and explain relationships, put things together that go together, and thus locate things, and see the relationships between different data and examples.

Imagine a grocery store or library in which the items were not classified. We'd never be able to find anything. On Jeff's river trip, all gear was classified. Most important, all meals were frozen, classified, and organized in the ice chests in reverse order of how they would be served. Fresh food was classified in its own cooler; nonperishables classified and organized in two dry boxes—all organized and packed in reverse order of when it would be needed. Likewise, gear on the raft was classified into first-aid and rescue, spare parts, kitchen gear, groover gear, and other categories. Even individual gear bags were classified. Jeff had smaller dry bags in his big gear bag for personal toiletries, kayak gear, off-river clothing, warm gear (in case it got cold or if he took a swim in the 47-degree river water), and sleeping/camping gear. Without such a system, packing, unpacking, and finding gear when it was needed would all but have been impossible.

Cause–Effect

Cause–effect structures explain the relationship between an impetus or set of causes and consequences (at least for events that have already occurred—anything predictive clearly seems to be an argument). When we talk about the possible effects of particular actions—like risky behavior—we name the possible implications and this becomes an argument. These implications might just be effects, but they might also become additional problems, and they are worth thinking about when making plans and taking risks.

Causality is considered fundamental to all natural science, especially physics. It is also important to logic and argumentation, much of philosophy, computer science, statistics, and other fields. In everyday life, we all have a fundamental interest in our surroundings and how to shape and control our lives and events in these situations. Cause-and-effect can easily be confused with simple correlations (experiences or events that have occurred in tandem but without causing each other); that's something we will explore in the practice chapter on teaching cause–effect. But if causality can be determined, then not only is understanding achieved but also new ways of being or of solving problems can be found.

On Jeff's raft trip, around day 12, the kayakers' feet all began to hurt. The next day several other boaters' feet were equally painful, red, cracking, peeling. Luckily there were two doctors on the trip who diagnosed *maceration*, or the deterioration and loss of the epidermis due to water immersion and abrasion. Once the cause was connected to the effect, group members took a day off, dried off their feet, moisturized them, and rested them. That helped a lot. For the rest of the trip, they were careful to dry their feet off at lunch and when in camp and keep sand out of their shoes and socks. Understanding the causes of the problem allowed them to address it.

Problem–Solution

Inquiry, the search for understanding, is based on framing a topic as a problem to be solved. When we inquire, we search first to understand the problem and next to find possible solutions to the problem. This is what professionals do from medicine (what is the health problem? how can we solve it?) to education (what is the learning challenge? how can we address it?). Professional practice and knowledge making in any discipline is based on inquiry and therefore on problem–solution. This involves explaining the nature of a problem and relating the causes of the problem to the effects of a solution. Understanding cause–effect contributed to the foot problem–solution on Jeff's trip. Likewise, when some of the fresh produce began to rot, the problem of what to eat at the meal this rotten produce had been designated for had to be solved with available leftovers compatible with that meal. For instance, when the lettuce began to rot, Jeff's daughter Jazzy made a citrus salad with leftover oranges and balsamic vinegar, along with what lettuce could be salvaged.

The Importance of Teaching Thought Patterns

We hope this discussion has made clear why we are so drawn to Bruner and his concept of paradigmatic thought. He makes it clear that the kinds of informational/explanatory texts are *ways of thinking*. Our worry is that these text structures are often interpreted by teachers as *forms* for students merely to fill in instead of as creative and generative patterns of thought. Such a formulaic interpretation and the practices they engender does a disservice to our students because they ignore both the issues of rhetorical stance (the focus on authorial purpose, process, choice, and audience consideration) and the framing writers must address in order to orient readers, as well as the complexity and embeddedness of the structures in practice. In other words, the form becomes more important than the purpose of the text and its creative and contextualized use, particularly in hybridized forms.

The evidence demonstrates that if we want kids to compose, read, and think in these different kinds of paradigms—and therefore be able to do the kind of work these paradigms support in the disciplines and in life—we are going to have to teach students very explicitly how to engage in the specific tasks (or operations) required in the context of the particular knowledge structuring that results in that specific text type.

When we go into schools, we often see posters proclaiming the general processes of writing (Prewrite! Draft! Revise! Proofread!) or the general processes of reading (Activate Background Knowledge! Decode! Ask Questions! Summarize! Monitor Comprehension and Self-Correct!). This stuff is not bad, as far as it goes. These processes are certainly necessary to good writing and reading, and they are certainly employed whenever a writer or reader is successfully doing her work. However, the lists miss the recursiveness of the processes, because the processes interact and do not operate in a linear fashion. Even more important, these processes, though necessary, are not sufficient to help students be able to write particular text structures (Smagorinsky and Smith 1992).

Here's an example. The "fourth-grade reading slump" is a well-documented phenomenon (the term was coined by the researcher Jeanne Chall 1983). In early grades, students generally demonstrate a much greater enthusiasm for reading and a robust sense of self-efficacy as readers (McKenna et al. 1995). But they fall off the cliff at about fourth grade. In our study of the literate lives of boys (Smith and Wilhelm 2002), one informant told us, "I used to be a pretty good reader, but then I just got stupider." When we asked when he got stupider, he replied, "Pretty much right around fourth grade."

Well, certainly this young man did not get stupider. What did happen was that the reading he was asked to do suddenly became markedly more difficult. In early grades he was primarily reading narratives, typically supported by pictures. Narrative, as Hardy (1977) and Schank (1990) argue, is our most natural and primary way of knowing and is dissimilar to any other epistemological form. And this friendly structure is what kids almost exclusively read and write in early grades. Then, around fourth grade, students are asked to read informational text, often in textbooks (the densest source of information known to humanity!), and to make matters worse these structures are often embedded in one another. And since reading is typically conceived of as the capacity to decode, no one helped this young man (and countless other students like him) learn *how* to read and write in ways that embodied the thought patterns and met the demands of these new text structures.

Bottom line: the introduction of informational/explanatory text structures places great demands on students, and they therefore need help meeting the challenges presented by these texts. This is what we help you and your students do throughout this book.

Because the informational/explanatory text types explored in this book are typically complex and significantly different from one another, we'll put off a more thorough discussion of the specific demands of each type until we reach the practical chapter for teaching that type. Instead, we'll turn next to an exploration of the five kinds of knowledge and the five kinds of composing that will inform all our instructional work and apply it to a general model of informational/explanatory text.

Five Kinds of Knowledge

The Foundation of Understanding and Expertise

Fifteen years ago, Michael drove up to Maine with his two (then) young daughters. Jeff had invited him to work with his Maine Writing Project fellows during their invitational summer institute and to enjoy some family time in Maine with Jeff's wife, Peggy, and two similarly aged daughters. On the drive up, there are about two hours along Interstate 95 where nothing can be seen but trees. After about 90 minutes of this, Michael's daughter Catherine blurted out: "Dad, doesn't anybody *live* up here?"

On arrival, Michael related this story and then opined that it was a shame Jeff and his family lived "so far from a city." Jeff demurred, maintaining that Bangor, just five miles down the road, "is a city!" Michael laughed and said that Bangor certainly was *not* a city. Jeff argued that when you entered the town there was a big sign proclaiming, "Welcome to the *city* of Bangor" side by side with a sign proclaiming "Bienvenue a la *ville* de Bangor." "It's a city in two languages and from two different cultural perspectives," Jeff declared.

Michael: Bangor is *not* a city.

Jeff: What are your criteria for a municipality being a city?

Michael: No criteria. One single criterion.

Jeff: Lay it on me.

Michael: You have to be able to go to a great restaurant every week for a whole year and never repeat a restaurant.

There was a pause.

Jeff: According to *that* criterion, Bangor is certainly *not* a city . . . but how many cities would there be in America according to this definition? Three? New York, Chicago, and San Francisco? Your definition is too exclusive.

Michael: Okay, let's add this: you also have to have two major professional sports teams, including one major franchise for football, baseball, or basketball.

Jeff: Okay, that expands it some but Austin has almost 800,000 people and one of the great universities in the world and by your definition it's not a city!

The discussion continued for some time as Michael and Jeff negotiated a definition for *city*. They often recall this discussion with amusement, because it demonstrates their vastly differing perspectives on cities and city life, among other things. But more to the point of this chapter, throughout this lengthy conversation they were using the five kinds of knowledge necessary to all successful reading, writing, meaning construction, and learning of any kind.

Hillocks' Four Kinds of Knowledge

On this same trip to Maine, Michael gave a presentation on the four kinds of knowledge necessary for writing, based on the work of George Hillocks (1986), a greathearted mentor and hero to the three of us. Michael led the group through teaching and learning that emphasized each of the four kinds of knowledge.

➤ *Writing anchor standards 4–9 are all about getting the stuff to write different kinds of texts for different purposes, tasks, and audiences*

The primary and prerequisite kind of knowledge is *procedural knowledge of substance*, what we came to call "knowing how to get the stuff" to write about. This is what Hillocks termed *inquiry*: knowing how to access and generate data. Clearly, to be able to write, one must first have something to write about. To get something to write about, a writer has to know processes for identifying and producing interesting and compelling material. Of course, this kind of knowledge is also necessary for reading, as one can't begin to comprehend unless one knows how to access requisite background and then bring this to bear in decoding and comprehending the text (Wilhelm 2008; Wilhelm, Baker, and Dube 2001). This is the basis of schema theory and is why frontloading, prereading and prewriting activities, are so important.

➤ *Reading anchor standards 5 and 6 and language anchor standard 6*

As we learn how to procure and produce the content to write about, we are necessarily learning to name and understand the concepts we are generating. Hillocks calls this kind of knowledge *declarative knowledge of substance*. In other words, people learn the *what* through the *how*.

This is a central insight: as John Dewey demonstrated in his work at the Chicago Lab School in the 1920s, when you teach students information, or the *what*, they will quickly forget it even if they do well on an information-driven, fill-in-the-blanks test. And they won't have learned any *processes*, the kind of learning foregrounded by the CCSS that transfers to future knowledge production and problem solving. But, as Dewey's student Ralph Tyler showed, if students learn this same content through inquiry—if they learn the procedures for creating knowledge (the *how*)—then the knowledge that is created (the *what*) becomes generative and conceptual and is retained over time. Tyler found that students learning in inquiry environments retained the seminal concepts and processes long after the original learning.

This insight has been corroborated many times over, most recently by test results, disaggregated by type of teaching, from the National Assessment of Educational Progress (NAEP), Trends in Math and Science Survey (TIMSS), and Programme in International Student Achievement (PISA) (see, for example, a review by McTighe, Seif, and Wiggins 2004). These tests are very similar to the Smarter Balanced and PARCC tests that will be used to assess the CCSS.

➤ *CCSS assessment*

Andreas Schleicher, the head of PISA, has often communicated the need for inquiry-oriented forms of instruction that focus on problem solving and procedural knowledge of substance. In recent speeches (e.g., Schleicher 2009), he has demonstrated how the next generation of tests (he focuses on PISA, but the Smarter Balanced and PARCC tests developed to show progress on the CCSS are quite similar to the PISA tests) will require students to know how to use various procedures for generating and shaping content.

The knowledge of how to shape content into conventional and shareable forms is what Hillocks calls *procedural knowledge of form*. This is knowing how to put the most powerful data you have developed into the most powerful forms for reaching your audience. In some contexts, that might be an academic paper using argument of one sort or another, in others a PowerPoint presentation using various informational structures, in others a website that tells stories from different perspectives, and so on.

➤ *Writing anchor standards 1–3 (2 for informative/ explanatory), 4, and 8*

➤ *Writing anchor standard 8 clearly names digital sources, as does reading anchor standard 7.*

Form or structure is one of the most obvious distinctions between argument, narrative, and informational/explanatory texts. The form or superstructure—its overall organizational logic—is what makes an informational text a comparison–contrast or classification or some other type, even if other structures and thought patterns are embedded within this superstructure. In fact, in the real world these text types rarely exist in pure forms; they are almost always embedded in other structures.

As one learns how to shape data—the moves one makes, for instance, to introduce and present a comparison–contrast of different examples or categories—one

➤ *Reading anchor standard 5*

is learning how to produce the structure and conventions of that text type. Simultaneous with learning and enacting procedural knowledge of form, one is learning *declarative knowledge of form.*

Readers, like writers, must use all four kinds of knowledge. To comprehend a text, one must use procedural knowledge of form to re-create the model, pattern, and structures of meaning in one's mind (Wilhelm 2008).

One has mastered declarative knowledge through the procedural when one can say something like, "If I want my readers to attend to the comparisons and contrasts I'm about to make, I need to establish my purpose right up front," or, "A Venn diagram is superior for showing differences *and* similarities; a T-chart is best if you want to focus only on showing differences." Or: "The block method allows you to describe one subject fully, then move on to a parallel description of another. Use this method if you are really privileging or arguing for the second element. Otherwise use the point-by-point method to be more evenhanded."

➤ *Reading standards 3–5, writing standard 4*

The "inquiry square" in Figure 3.1 summarizes the relationships of the four kinds of knowledge (see also Wilhelm, Baker, and Dube 2001 and Wilhelm 2012 for

Figure 3.1 The Inquiry Square: Four Kinds of Knowledge

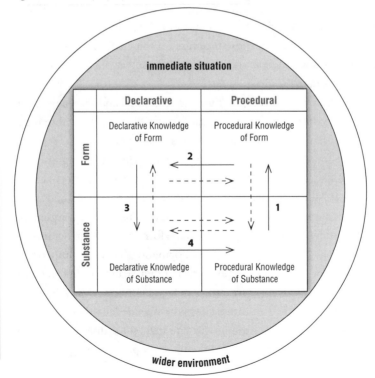

full discussions). This figure reminds us that as we learn how to access and develop content (procedural knowledge of substance), we simultaneously produce and name the content (declarative knowledge of substance). As we learn how to shape and structure the content we've produced (procedural knowledge of form), we simultaneously learn about and name the structures for shaping content (declarative knowledge of form) *and* how the structuring of ideas creates meaning and makes various points (back to declarative knowledge of substance, but on a higher level—no longer about details, but about the larger themes or points; now you know how the material was structured to make a particular point—what Hillocks calls understanding structural generalizations).

The inquiry square also reminds us that the procedural and declarative are learned together, reinforcing and co-producing each other. Here is yet another crucially important instructional principle (forgive our excitement!): as we go through the process of generating and shaping data and mastering procedural and declarative knowledge of substance and form, we are achieving deep, deep understanding of how knowledge is made and structured. We are getting inside the process of making meaning and producing knowledge ourselves. We become a knowing insider, reading like a writer and composing like a reader! This is an emphasis clearly endorsed by the CCSS—there are the same number of reading and writing standards, and the same number of related subcategories.

Karen Miller, a science teacher, had this to say after using the inquiry square to plan instruction: "In science, you are usually just told what to think. The kids do backward science in labs, trying to prove that what the teacher or textbook said is right. It's really all declarative [knowledge of substance]. But when I took the kids through the process [of the kinds of knowledge] and had them generate their own data and then shape this data into different forms and then present these—well, they learned that science is a giant sausage factory. There are different ways to get data and different ways to analyze and understand it. And science is an ongoing argument about data and how to understand it. They also learned that if they can tell a story about the data that accommodates all the data by shaping it in a particular way, *they can do science!* That if they can generate and structure data, *they are a scientist,* and they can contend with other scientists! They don't have to just accept what a 'scientist' says, because all science involves making up explanations for the data you collected and how you structured that data to analyze it. A scientific fact is simply an opinion or social agreement that is generally shared by most scientists about how to interpret available data. As new ways to collect data evolve, as data changes or how data is structured changes, scientific facts change. . . . The inquiry square has democratized

➤ *This is a major thrust of the CCSS— see reading anchor standards 6 and 9.*

➤ *See reading anchor standard 5.*

➤ *CCSS cross-reference*

➤ *Literacy in history/ social studies and science anchor standard 7, any level*

➤ *Literacy in history/ social studies and science writing standard 2, any level*

my science classroom and made science more accessible and exciting to my students! It's been liberating for me and for them!"

Jeff realized that he had spent much of his early career entirely on the declarative side of the chart. For instance, when teaching about the Italian and English sonnet in senior English, he had, via lecture, delivered declarative knowledge of form. ("The English sonnet has the rhyme scheme of abba, cddc, effe, gg and is organized into a twelve-line poem, followed by a *caesura*, or pause, followed by a couplet that provides the point of the sonnet. The Italian sonnet on the other hand. . . .") He then provided insightful exegeses of particular sonnets to provide declarative knowledge of substance. ("Notice how in Sonnet CXXX, Shakespeare makes fun of the courtly and idealized notion of love. In the first line he says 'My mistress eyes are nothing like the sun,' contrasting his lover's eyes with the idealized notion. . . .")

➤ *Writing anchor standard 4*

Jeff also realized that through this kind of teaching his students developed no usable or transferable procedural knowledge. At the end of instruction, they did not have the capacity to generate their own interpretations or write their own sonnets, nor to appreciate the difficulty of writing a sonnet, nor to understand or appreciate why anyone would ever read or write one.

Jeff's students missed out on all the fun and all the power and all that was memorable or transferable because he taught on the declarative side instead of focusing on the procedural and getting to the declarative side through the procedural! It was a revelation!

From Four to Five Kinds of Knowledge

Jeff convened a study group to use the four kinds of knowledge to map out some units. The group quickly added a fifth kind of knowledge, which they thought provided the "foundation" or "surrounding situation" for the other four. They called this fifth kind of knowledge *knowledge of context and purpose* and were delighted to discover that Hillocks (1995) had made a similar addition to his taxonomy.

➤ *Reading and writing anchor standard 10*

As they worked together the study group developed a couple of metaphors that informed and guided their thinking. They began talking about how the five types of knowledge work both like a house and like a cycle. The cycle is depicted in Figure 3.2.

In the house metaphor, knowledge of purpose and context are the foundation—the ground is chosen and prepared, and the ultimate purpose conceived. Obviously you can't get started without a purpose. The purpose (even if it's ultimately changed) gives rise to a plan to fulfill the purpose. (See Figure 3.3.)

Figure 3.2 The Five-Types-of-Knowledge Cycle

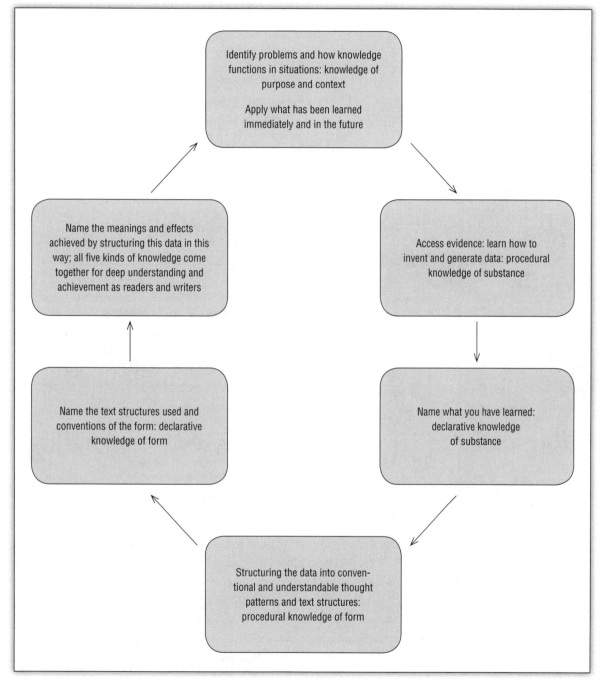

Figure 3.3

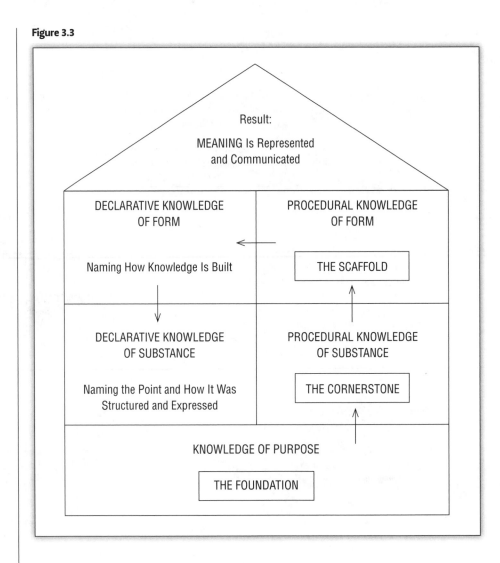

The cornerstone is procedural knowledge of substance—remember, this is what Hillocks calls *inquiry*: knowing how to access and generate and operate on data. Obviously, you need to know how to get and create material to have material, and you need material to build with. You need substance before the substance can be shaped. As you put the cornerstone in place, the knowledge that you create through these procedures creates a matching side of the edifice: declarative knowledge of substance.

Procedural knowledge of form is how you start building the second story of your edifice. You structure the stuff into conventional and communicable forms. As you do this, you learn to name the structures and structuring devices and how they work together to create meaning and make particular points and create specific effects—a major thrust of the CCSS.

➤ *CCSS reference*
➤ *Reading anchor standards 3–6*

Here is a specific example of how the inquiry square heuristic helped Jeff. For many years he had taught fable writing to seventh graders, as required by his curriculum. He did so over the course of a week, and the resulting fables were . . . well, they lacked something. Okay, they were generally really bad—insipid, boring, we might even say heinous examples of the form. Many of the fables featured Jeff's big nose or his nose hair, which Jeff found inappropriate and irritating. Some featured owls driving Maseratis and smoking Cuban cigars, also not appropriate to the substance of fables. They rarely made much of a point, and the morals tended to be tedious, off point, and a paragraph or longer. Having become familiar with the five kinds of knowledge, Jeff realized that fable writing was much more complicated than he thought, and that he had never taught or helped his students to meet the demands of fable writing.

To amend the situation, he first contextualized fable writing within a larger inquiry unit, What Makes and Breaks Relationships? in which reading and writing fables would have a payoff and mean something conceptually as well as procedurally. A favored topic of fables is that of relationships. Think of Aesop's "The Man with Two Wives" or "The Cat Who Loved a Man" paired with a modern fable like "The Blue Shoe" from fablevision.com. Since the culminating composition in the unit was to be an argument, Jeff considered how fable writing would help students compose arguments. Because they would be mining texts for the evidence they would employ in those arguments, Jeff recognized that casting students as inquirers and writers early in the unit would help them recognize how other writers manipulate details in order to make a point—so they could attend to how to do this by using various thought patterns in their own writing. Moreover, if students used a number of texts as a basis for their arguments, they would have to succinctly summarize those texts (more on summary later). Jeff recognized that writing a moral would provide powerful practice in doing just that (see Smith, Wilhelm, and Fredricksen 2012 for many more ideas about how to prepare students to write a literary argument). In short, fable writing could serve the conceptual goals of the unit and lead to the final composition, an argument. (See the completed inquiry square in Figure 3.4.)

➤ *Unit idea*

Then he *actually taught* the students how to identify the purposes fables serve; how to generate and form content; how to provide feedback, revise, and proofread for the kinds of problems that came up; and how to present and justify their fables. And guess what? The fables were all unique, fresh, creative, and fun—and explored how to promote healthy relationships.

Figure 3.4   The Inquiry Square for the Fable Unit

	Declarative	Procedural
Form	Student names the features of the fable, including animals as symbols of particular foibles and their foils, initiating situation, conflict, and consequences, and ends in moral that reflects the trajectory of the fable.	**How to put the substance of the proposed fable in an appropriate form.** What animals could represent the foible and other contrasting values: pig for greed? fox for deceit? ant for husbandry and thrift? What actions and key details could show the consequences of this foible? Initiating event caused by foible—how it escalates—climax—consequences revealing the effect of this foible in this context. Events must be a syllogism leading to a conclusion that can be summarized as a one-sentence moral.
Substance	First: Knowledge of the content of this particular fable. Later: Knowledge of how this content was constructed in this way for these meanings and effects to be expressed.	**How to produce the substance of fables: brainstorming for human qualities that are immoral or irritating.** Choose a major foible that causes problems for self and others. Choose a foible that is correctable. Think about how people with this foible act. Generate foibles and their concomitant actions, alternatives to acting this way, consequences of each way.
Purpose and Context	**Why write or read this kind of text?** **When and why would anyone ever want to write a fable?** **What work does writing and reading fables get done?**	To make fun of human weaknesses. To subtly make fun of particular people's weaknesses without confronting them directly. To show different ways of being in the world that are healthier. To teach lessons about better ways of living—of being in relationships.

Here's Jeff's lesson plan for the unit with the procedural side in mind (with cross-references to Chapters 4 and 5).

Unit: What Makes and Breaks a Relationship?

Unit Phases: frontloading; sharing love songs; reading and writing fables; informational articles about relationships, longer readings like *Romeo and Juliet*

Focus of Fable Phase: knowledge of purpose, substance, *and* procedures of fable writing

Evidence of Student Learning: write a fable; present it at school Fable Fest and Open Learning Fair; include in the presentation slides how your fable compares with traditional fables and why and how your fable was constructed to create certain meanings and effects; submit the fable for inclusion in class anthology.

WEEK 1

Monday	Tuesday	Wednesday	Thursday	Friday
KNOWLEDGE OF PURPOSE AND CONTEXT	**PROCEDURAL KNOWLEDGE OF SUBSTANCE**	**PROCEDURAL KNOWLEDGE OF FORM**	**PROCEDURAL KNOWLEDGE OF FORM**	**BRINGING IT ALL TOGETHER**
Read three fables, one from Aesop, one from Fontaigne, one from Thurber. Brainstorm: How are the fables similar and different? What is a fable? Why do people write and read them? What work do they get done and in what situations?	Where does the content of a fable come from? Given the purposes of fables to identify human weaknesses and find better ways of being in the world, let's brainstorm annoying human traits.	How do we shape the content into the fabulistic form? Close reading and analysis of additional fables. What are the necessary elements of a fable? The necessary structuring and shaping of these elements? How can we shape our fables in this way? Practice identifying animals that reflect human weaknesses and strengths (for our foils). Practice writing initiating situations caused by that foible and how other options would be shown, escalation of the problems caused, climax, and consequences.	Outline your fable—how are all elements of fables and story structure included? What makes a powerful moral? How does your moral reflect exactly the trajectory of the fable through its ending? Read fables without morals, write morals for them, debate the moral with points for tying the moral to the concrete evidence in the fable.	Read and analyze two more fables. Identify criteria for a successful fable and develop rubric. Practice meeting rubric—guided writing of introduction to your fable, rising action, provision of foil, consequences. Practice writing morals.
[Composing to plan— see Chapter 4.]	Now let's identify which of these traits cause problems for others and are correctable. How can these foibles be corrected?			Name the substance and formal features in your draft. (Declarative Knowledge of Substance and Form)
Exit ticket: When and why might writing a fable be useful to you and others?	[Composing to plan— see Chapter 4.]	[Composing to plan and practice—see Chapter 4.]	[Composing to practice—see Chapter 4.]	[Composing to draft— see Chapter 4.]
[Formative assessment: composing to transfer—see Chapter 5.]	Choose a correctable foible as the topic of your fable.			Complete first drafts for Monday.

WEEK 2

Monday	Tuesday	Wednesday	Thursday	Friday
Continue and revise first draft. Study and practice providing useful feedback. Form peer editing groups. Employ major revision strategies: work on additions, deletions, moves, and changes. Model PowerPoint version of fables. [Composing to draft—see Chapter 4.]	Final drafting. Proofread lessons for clarity and transitions. Present minilessons as needed in small groups. Work on PowerPoint versions of the fable. [Composing to finalize—see Chapter 4.]	Final drafting. Model proofreading cues and feedback. Proofread in peer editing groups. Make sure all criteria are met (signed off by two peer editors). [Composing to finalize—see Chapter 4.]	Present final fables aloud at class Fable Fest. Present PowerPoint versions of fables in small groups with visuals and music (slides required that identify the type of fable you composed, why you composed it as you did, and how you constructed the fable to communicate particular meanings and effects). Final feedback and revisions as needed. Post final products to online anthology. [Composing to finalize—Chapter 4.]	Composing to transfer. Process analysis of how you composed your fable and why you did it this way. Reflection on learning about fables, and about love/relationships through fables. Share and submit reflections and process analyses of your fable writing justifying how you met all criteria. [Composing to transfer—see Chapter 4.]

Although this is a condensed example, look at the difference in planning using only the declarative side of the inquiry square:

Unit: The Fable

Evidence of Student Learning: Student-composed fable; quiz

Monday	Tuesday	Wednesday	Thursday	Friday
Overview of general form of fables, then compare form of Aesopian, Fontaignian, and Thurberian fables.	Read and analyze different fables and the themes/morals they communicate.	Read and analyze different fables, and the themes/moral they communicate.	Write a fable of your choice.	Submit your fable; quiz on the form and the content of the fables we've read.

Notice the richer instruction that resulted by using the five-kinds-of-knowledge heuristic to foreground procedural knowledge. Using the five kinds of knowledge helped students achieve deeper understandings and to read fables expertly (which transferred to reading for main idea and much more) and to compose fresh and individual fables.

Through this process students come to understand themselves and other authors as an intelligence behind the text, manipulating and structuring a textual experience for an audience to communicate specific meanings and achieve particular effects. Because of this, students achieve deep understanding of not only a particular text but also textuality in general. And what has been learned and so deeply understood can be transferred and transformed to meet new reading and writing challenges! Eureka of eurekas! Heuristic of heuristics!

➤ *Reading anchor standard 4 and writing anchor standard 4*

Note too how this process can help to meet all the CCSS anchor standards (particularly those focusing on craft and structure, and how these lead to particular meanings and effects) and, more important, how the process constitutes deep knowledge of textuality fundamental to expert composing and reading.

Using the Inquiry Square as a Generative Heuristic for Teaching

Since the study group breakthrough, Jeff has used the five kinds of knowledge to plan every course and unit he has taught, both in schools and at the university. It has informed every unit culminating in any kind of composing assignment and every class in which he teaches how to read or compose a new kind of text. Reading and composing are two sides of the same coin: what the author encodes and structures into a text, the reader needs to notice, decode, and interpret. The five kinds of knowledge also inform how Jeff teaches and supports teachers to think about and transform their instructional practice.

Michael:

The 5 kinds of knowledge creates a lens through which you can see and think about larger segments of time, and how to sequence instructional activities across time in order to achieve student mastery. Across time, I have helped kids master the 5 kinds of knowledge necessary to understanding. This helps me work toward targeted efficiencies; it helps me *plan*.

One of Michael's concerns has always been how much school writing seems so unconnected to what writers do outside school. The five kinds of knowledge have helped him work with teachers to bring school writing more in line with the writing that people do in the world. Comparison–contrast papers are always a big culprit. Why?

The assignment typically starts without a purpose—students begin without any thought of why they should make a comparison. In contrast (ha!), in the world, comparisons and contrast are often made but they're *always* made for a purpose: to explain, for example, that two situations are similar and so what happened in one case can be used to predict what will happen in the other. Or they are made to show that while the situations seem similar they really aren't and so one ought not use the one to predict what will happen in the other. Making either of these points requires writers to identify and explain salient similarities and differences (procedural knowledge

Jim:
For me, the 5 kinds of knowledge is a lens for *assessing* student understanding. It's a way of *paying attention* to what students know and don't know yet. And I know that if students are going to deeply understand and transfer their learning to the new situations, they have to own the 5 kinds of knowledge.

of substance). Not every similarity or difference is equally important. As writers develop criteria for salience, they are learning about the things they are comparing/contrasting (declarative knowledge of substance). When they have gathered at least some of the material, they have to think about how to build the house for their audience. They have to consider, for example, whether to start with the more familiar and move to the less familiar or whether to alternate a discussion of one element of the comparison–contrast with the other or to do them separately. These critically important rhetorical decisions develop procedural knowledge of form, and reflecting on them helps writers develop declarative knowledge of form. In short, the five kinds of knowledge have helped Michael work with preservice and inservice teachers to make their teaching more toolish and readily applicable in the world, and less schoolish.

Jim has used the inquiry square to organize writing units in schools and to frame the methods courses he teaches. The five-kinds-of-knowledge heuristic forced him to change his courses from ones focused on topics to ones focused on practices. Instead of having a week devoted to say, censorship or revision (topics), the courses now focus on doing the kinds of work (the procedures and practices) that are central to any teacher's work—practices like designing instruction, assessing student understanding, and conversing with colleagues. By focusing the courses on *how* teachers work, the preservice teachers who take them are able to get after the *what* of teaching writing or of teaching literature through the *how*. That is, by focusing on the procedural knowledge of teaching, they develop a better sense of how concepts that are central to a teacher's workday relate to one another.

Just this semester Jim's students wrote position statements about what they believe are "significant revision experiences" for writers. This assignment asks preservice teachers to outline a rationale for why and how they would help students revise in the ways that support their growth as writers. The class looked at how different position statements were shaped (procedural knowledge of form: identifying such elements as a clear claim, a range of evidence that includes personal experience and scholarly arguments made by researchers and by teachers, and warrants or reasoning about that data) and identified what content was included and where these ideas came from (declarative and procedural knowledge of substance).

Reflecting on the process of creating the position statements, students typically made connections between concepts like voice in student writing, agency and choice, time to rewrite, and collaboration with or feedback from others. They also remarked on how the difficulty of crafting a statement helped them begin to see how they might explain to others why certain activities they design for their own students reflect their beliefs and values about what constitutes a significant revision experience.

In short, Jim's use of the five kinds of knowledge to plan his course has helped him provide support and experiences that induct and assist his students into thinking like teachers and doing the actual work of teachers instead of just covering material.

Although we all have profited from using the five kinds of knowledge as a thinking tool, we also find that we use them somewhat differently. But we think that that's a good thing. It shows that the heuristic is flexible, as heuristics should be, and can be applied differently by different teachers with different students in unique situations without losing its generative power. The "five kinds" inquiry square is not an algorithm, not a lockstep set of replicable procedures requiring "fidelity," but a flexible, professional set of tools for thinking through and practicing expert teaching—what cognitive scientists call a *heuristic*.

The word *heuristic* comes from the Greek root word *eureka* which means *I discover* (remember Archimedes in his bathtub?). It is defined as "experience-based techniques for problem solving, learning, and discovery" (Wikipedia, retrieved 8/18/2011) or "a generative process that enables a person to discover or learn something for herself" (Merriam-Webster online dictionary, retrieved 8/18/2011). Heuristics, in short, are flexible problem-solving tools based on generative underlying principles. Because they are based on generative principles they can be developed, tweaked, and transformed, and then transferred to new situations. (In a sense, reading anchor standards 1–9 and writing anchor standards 1–9 are a heuristic for accomplishing anchor standard 10 in each area.)

We can also think of a heuristic as a simple, transportable thinking tool that is both declarative (something that can be articulated and shared verbally as a *what*) and procedural (a process of *how* to do something). The five kinds of knowledge have great heuristic value for both teachers *and* for student readers and composers as they work with particular text types and strive to meet and exceed the standards set forth in the CCSS.

The Challenge of Generative Teaching

In contrast to our emphasis on the procedural, reviews of American teaching practices show that teachers tend to purvey information rather than create situations in which processes and heuristics are developed and mastered. Goodlad's 1984 classic study of over a thousand classrooms led him to this conclusion:

> The data from our observation in more than a thousand classrooms support the popular image of a teacher standing or sitting in front of a class imparting knowledge to a group of students.

Jeff:

Formulas and traditional forms of information-transmission teaching do not suffice to prepare students for the challenges in their lives nor to succeed on the next generation of standards and assessments.

The 5 kinds help me to *plan, sequence, assess,* and *monitor* the kinds of knowledge I must help students develop to really understand the reading and composing of particular text types in ways they can transfer to new situations.

The 5 kinds help me see how to teach *strategies in contexts of use.* And the CCSS is entirely about strategies in contexts of use.

Jeff, Michael, and Jim:
The 5 kinds of knowl-
edge is a heuristic for
teaching that helps
students develop
personally powerful
heuristics for getting
work done—now and
in the future. It helps
us and students move
beyond formulas
and algorithms and
toward developing
an ever expanding
and flexible tool kit of
generative principles
and strategies for do-
ing real-world work.

Explaining and lecturing constituted the most frequent teaching activities, according to teachers, students, and our observations. Teachers also spent a substantial amount of time observing students at work or monitoring their seatwork. (105)

What is true of classrooms in general is true of language arts classrooms as well. More recently, Nystrand et al. (1997) observed 451 class periods in 58 eighth-grade language arts classes and 54 ninth-grade English classes. Here's what they found:

When teachers were not lecturing, students were mainly answering questions or engaged in seatwork. Indeed, on average 85% of each class day in both eighth- and ninth-grade classes was devoted to a combination of lecture, question-and-answer recitation, and seatwork. Discussion and small-group work were rare. On average, discussion took 50 seconds per class in eighth grade and less than 15 seconds in Grade 9; small-group work, which occupied about half a minute a day in eighth grade, took a bit more than two minutes a day in Grade 9. (42)

This kind of information transmission will not help students meet the CCSS and, as has long been shown, will not lead to deep understanding, application, or transfer (see, for example, Tharp and Gallimore 1990).

When teachers do move into the realm of the procedural, it seems they teach algorithms instead of heuristics. Algorithms are inflexible, lockstep, one-size-fits-all protocols for performing a task. They are neither generative nor transferable and do not help students understand the deep principles behind a task performance nor the story behind the story of why and how this procedural knowledge was developed and why it works in this particular way. Knowing and being able to use these deep principles is precisely what constitutes understanding according to modern cognitive science (Folk 2004). This is a far cry from what is typically achieved in schools.

Perhaps teachers teach algorithms, or lists of steps for doing something, because they can be presented as information or because it is simpler. But when we do so, we lose all the potential power that comes from true understanding—the power to transform and flexibly use what has been learned in new situations. We've all had experience with students and children who are applying algorithms without understanding.

One of Michael's favorite family stories centers around his daughter Catherine's book report about *The Pigman*, by Paul Zindel. She had included a quote at the beginning to establish that the Pigman was a widower. Michael was puzzled—writers only use quotes when they have to defend a proposition. Every reader agrees that the Pig-man is a widower. Michael asked Catherine why she chose that quote. She looked at him, raised her palms, and said: "My teacher just likes quotes. Look, the rubric says include five quotes! And I did!" Catherine applied an algorithm—inappropriately—because she did not possess a heuristic or have true understanding about how real writers use quotes.

The preservice teachers who enter Jim's classes—often the first classes they have taken in teaching—often want "the list" of activities that will "work." That is, they see teaching as a series of activities with prescribed steps, and they want to collect activity after activity. For them, the algorithm is something like *1. Find activity. 2. Teach activity. 3. Grade activity. 4. Repeat with new activity.* That's a simplified version, of course, but most teachers-to-be have an unconscious desire for a heuristic to think like a teacher. Developing heuristics (like the inquiry square or like considering how to design instruction focused on a specific reading strategy before, during, and after students read a text) becomes our most important work in teacher education courses.

Jeff's daughter Fiona was once studying for an Algebra II test and could not figure out how to do a particular kind of problem. When Jeff asked her when she would ever need to use this kind of problem or "algorithm" in the world, she stared at him like he was an idiot and then hissed: "In school! You would *only use this in school!*"

That's the first sign that heuristic value has not been achieved—the first and prerequisite kind of knowledge, after all, is knowledge of purpose and context. Piles of research from cognitive science show that without a sense of purpose, you cannot learn. Purpose drives our engagement, what we attend to and what we remember (see schema theory research like Anderson et al. 1984 and Bransford and Johnson 1972). Without a purpose, we cannot achieve heuristic value. Likewise, we cannot meet the all-important holy grail of the correspondence concept of expert thinking without a clear sense of purpose.

The Correspondence Concept

So let's review. The five kinds of knowledge are a powerful tool reminding us to teach so that students read and write for real and powerful purposes. The five kinds of knowledge reinforce the importance of engaging students in developing procedural knowledge of substance and form that are transferable to new situations and that will lead them to deep and robust declarative knowledge.

In short, the five kinds of knowledge remind us to teach our students in ways in which they are acting as experts. The *correspondence concept* (Bereiter 2004) is a simple, elegant, and powerful notion from cognitive science that provides additional support for why doing so is so absolutely essential. In cognitive science, inquiry is a process of accessing, building, extending, and using knowledge in ways consistent with how expert practitioners think, know, and perform. If we adopt that perspective, student understanding can only be measured by student progress toward how experts know and use concepts and strategies. As Nickerson (1985) explains: "One understands a concept, principle, process or whatever to the extent that what is in one's head regarding that concept corresponds to what is in the head of an expert in the relevant field" (222).

In the area of literacy, this idea means, put simply, that we should teach the heuristics that real, expert readers and writers use in the contexts in which they develop and use such skills—so what is learned and how it is learned "corresponds" to actual expertise. So, if real readers don't continue to try to read ever more quickly (they don't), we shouldn't teach and stress fluency once students read fluently enough to comprehend. If real writers in English split infinitives (they do), we shouldn't teach students to avoid them. The takeaway: we must apply the "real reader" test and "real composer" test to all our teaching.

Since real readers and real writers use the five kinds of knowledge, they are well worth teaching—the heuristic meets the correspondence concept and will help students be readers and writers in the academy, in the disciplines, and in their lives outside school and work.

➤ CCSS note: The language standards for grammar are expressed as "language progressive skills," but even those are very limited—deemphasizing grammar in favor of using language to create meaning and effect.

CHAPTER 4

Five Kinds of Composing

Making Informational Texts and Making Them Matter

Many readers may be familiar with John Collins' delineation of five kinds of writing (www.collinsed.com/cwp.htm). In our work with students and through our collaboration, we became convinced that there's great value to recognizing and teaching different kinds of composing. We also became convinced that Collins hasn't captured the range of composing students need regular experience with to achieve expertise. We have therefore built our approach to instruction on five very different types of composing.

Composing Versus Writing

First, we want to explain what might seem an innocuous difference. We label ours as five kinds of composing while Collins labels his as five kinds of writing. We think the different labels reveal significant differences in thinking.

Our thinking about the difference between composing and writing has been influenced by our mentor George Hillocks Jr. He challenges the notion that kids learn to write solely by writing, a notion that we find many well-meaning and otherwise progressive teachers endorse. Hillocks' work has convinced us that students can and do learn to write by doing many things that are not writing (hands-on activities, visualizing, debates, group problem-solving activities, small-group discussions), all of which involve talking about content *and* process and all of which represent content *and* process through composing of one sort or another.

➤ Reading anchor standard 7

➤ Speaking and listening anchor standards

Our friend Peter Smagorinsky (see, for example, Smagorinsky 1995, 1997; Smagorinsky, Pettis, and Reed 2004; Smagorinsky, Zoss, and Reed 2006) has also had a powerful influence on us. Peter's work explores the unique and powerful engagement and meaning-making capacities available through composing with visuals, dance and movement, drama, and scale models. Jeff has explored similar themes and also calls into question the privileging of traditional forms of writing in his various books. The CCSS emphasis on multimodal composing is consistent with this challenge. Composing, in the twenty-first century, is about much more than traditional notions of writing.

In *"You Gotta BE the Book"* (2008), Jeff found that readers, whenever they successfully engage and comprehend, are composing meaning in highly visual, dramatic, participatory, and multimodal ways. Every engaged reader of literature he encountered in his research created a story world in her mind, and every reader of informational or paradigmatic texts created an elaborated and highly visual mental model of what was being learned. His informants also often participated in a story world as a character, an unmentioned character, or an agent acting on behalf of a character. Jeff's subsequent work has explored how students can be helped to compose meaning through visualization (Wilhelm 2004/2012), drama and action strategies (Wilhelm and Edmiston 1998; Wilhelm 2002/2012), and various design projects, often using technology (Wilhelm and Friedman 1998; Wilhelm and Novak 2011).

In *Teaching Literacy for Love and Wisdom* (2011) Jeff and Bruce Novak make a strong case for composing through the arts, including digital media, and conceiving of the meaning readers create as artistic compositions. So reading is composing, and again, composing is much more than writing.

Composing is also of different sorts. We've identified five different kinds of composing that we think are crucial: composing to plan, composing to practice, first draft composing, final draft composing, and composing to transfer.

Composing to Plan

The three of us have slightly different takes on the five kinds of composing. Jeff, in particular, thinks that composing to plan is the prerequisite kind of composing and that it necessarily includes articulating the purposes that composing and reading the text type under consideration can fulfill and, further, naming situations and instances in which students have used, could have used, and might use the text type to create meaning and solve problems. Michael, in our book on argument, starts with composing to practice and then moves to composing to plan. Jim does the same in our book on narrative.

Collins focuses first on brainstorming. We find this problematic, because our students often do not have experience with the text type they need to read or write or may not be able to articulate all the purposes. Narrowing composing to plan to brainstorming implies that kids already know what they need to know and this knowledge just has to be activated. This is often decidedly not the case.

For us, composing to plan involves the first two kinds of knowledge: articulating and developing knowledge of purpose and context—which involves decomposing the task at hand—and getting started with procedural knowledge of substance—learning how to both access *and* develop the content that will be required to meet the situated purpose in the composition challenge at hand. Obviously, to compose, we have to understand the task, the purpose of fulfilling it, and the context in which it will be fulfilled. We have to know how to get something to write about—both by mining our own prior experience and by knowing how to generate new material.

Why, for instance, and in what situations is a writer driven to compose a sonnet or fable or comparison–contrast? How does a writer then get the material to compose one? This knowing how to get the stuff is what Hillocks defines as *inquiry*, and we think it is the most important thing we can teach if we want our students to be lifelong learners and problem solvers.

Composing to Practice

The power of practice is indisputable. It's like the old joke: the tourist in Manhattan asks for directions ("How do I get to Carnegie Hall?"), and the helpful local replies, "Practice, practice, practice."

Research into various domains of human expertise make the case that it is practice, not talent, that determines expertise. For most challenging kinds of human endeavors, a minimum of a thousand hours of practice is required for competence, three thousand hours for what might be called mastery, and ten thousand hours to be among the best in the world, as Malcolm Gladwell asserts in *The Tipping Point* (2000).

The neurologist Daniel Levitin reviews various studies regarding practice in *This Is Your Brain on Music* (2007) and concludes:

> Ten thousand hours of practice is required to achieve the level of
> mastery associated with being a world-class expert—in anything.
> In study after study, of composers, basketball players, fiction writers, ice skaters, concert pianists, chess players, master criminals,
> and what have you, this number comes up again and again. Ten

thousand hours is the equivalent to roughly three hours per day, or twenty hours per week, of practice over ten years. Of course, this doesn't address why some people don't seem to get anywhere when they practice, and why some people get more out of their practice sessions than others. But no one has yet found a case in which true world-class expertise was accomplished in less time. It seems that it takes the brain this long to assimilate all that it needs to know to achieve true mastery. (8)

Alfred Binet, the father of the modern IQ test, wrote in his seminal work *Modern Ideas About Children* (1909/1975) that "with practice, training, and above all, proper method, we manage to increase our attention, our memory, our judgment and literally to become more intelligent than we were before" (105).

Likewise, Robert Sternberg (2007), a modern-day guru of intelligence and expertise, affirms that the major factor in expertise is not genetics, "is not some fixed prior ability, but *purposeful engagement*." Or, as Binet asserts, those who are smartest happened to get the right kinds of practice and assistance in the right kinds of purposeful contexts.

In contrast, traditional instruction in both reading and composing seems to be about assigning and evaluating instead of creating supportive environments for practicing, taking risks, and gradually developing expertise *over time* (Tharp and Gallimore 1990; Hillocks et al. 1983).

Even when students do receive instruction, it is often in the form of lectures outlining declarative knowledge of substance or form, not the creation of nurturing environments that require and reward *doing* things (composing particular kinds of texts) and the provision of practice in generating content and shaping it according to the conventions of a genre and discipline. Workshop teaching that uses backward planning and learning targets, which we find to be a progressive alternative to traditional information-transmission teaching, accommodates our model perfectly. However, in practice we have observed that much student-centered instruction, including that using the workshop approach, can be more reactive than proactive in terms of practice and correctives, focusing on responding to and coaching students in relation to an existing or in-progress composition—often of the students' choosing and typically of narrative. Alternatively, we propose proactive preparatory practice related to the kind of composing and text type under consideration, so that material for composing can be generated, procedural knowledge of form can be practiced, and consciously articulated knowledge can be transferred to future composing of this type.

As we have explored elsewhere (Smith and Wilhelm 2006, 2009; Wilhelm 2007), this "practice in miniature" should be extensive and heuristic-oriented and move in at least one if not several of these directions:

- From familiar to less familiar.
- From short to long.
- From oral to written.
- From multimodal to print.
- From concrete to abstract.
- From social to individual.
- From scaffolded to independent.

You'll see how this kind of sequenced practice takes place in the context of conceptual units in the examples throughout this book. The bottom line is that we want students to have plenty of practice articulating and playing out knowledge of context and purpose, building procedural knowledge of form, and (throughout the whole sequence) creating procedural knowledge of substance so that students are generating content they can use in the upcoming composition.

Composing First (and Subsequent) Drafts

Any writer is familiar with writer's block. Pascal expressed it vividly: "Getting started with writing is easy: open a vein and let your lifeblood flow onto the page."

As part of our program of preparing students for success, we want to drive them to the ballpark and give them a ball to throw and plenty of practice knowing how to throw it. Then we are willing to let them go out and field a line drive in a practice game. Just as ballplayers need preparation and practice to achieve a level of expertise that will ensure competent performance, if not victory, students need help preparing to compose and then environmental assistance as they do the composing.

But more than that, the coach has a game plan for the particular challenges facing his players on game day, as well as strategies, cues, and signals for making that game plan a reality. This is the kind of instruction kids need when doing the first draft—they need help getting started and getting into the flow of composing, and they need to know how to address the challenges that will come up.

As you'll see, we provide instructional support in the context of putting together the first draft, as well as support for substantive drafting and revising that involves

➤ *Writing anchor standard 5*

➤ *Speaking and listening anchor standards*

moving, adding, deleting, and transforming what has been composed. Students need help to do this kind of drafting and revising. First and subsequent draft writing is a perfect place to continue directed peer-group response and support, as well as teacher-to-student support.

Composing Final Drafts

➤ *Language anchor standards 1, 2*

➤ *Speaking and listening anchor standards*

Once students are nearing a final draft, they need help polishing and publishing what they have composed. Our final draft composing phase subsumes three of Collins' five kinds of writing: proofreading and editing for focus correction areas (not for all errors but for those that count most and are most correctable in this context; see Smith and Wilhelm 2007), peer response, and publishing/presentation of what has been composed.

As always, we need to make sure that our students get practice and support with proofreading and editing in specific focus areas; that they get practice and assistance knowing how to respond helpfully and substantively to one another's writing; and that they get practice and explicit help publishing and presenting the final draft of their work (or something based on the final draft).

We argue that the focus on correctness should be kept in check until the very final draft of publishable writing. It doesn't make sense to concentrate on this until students have something compelling to say and have practiced saying it. Then and only then will they care to polish their text for the surface-level correctness needed to make the text accessible to a real audience.

Composing to Transfer

➤ *CCSS assessment*

When the final draft, the representation of a student's best thinking to this point, is presented and shared, the instructional sequence is not yet complete. As we've been arguing, if a student is not yet capable of articulating what has been learned and justifying how it was learned (both are required by the reflections on the new CCSS short and long performance task assessments in the Smarter Balanced and PARCC tests) and is not yet able to transfer what has been learned in flexible ways to future tasks, then we would have a hard time supporting the notion that anything substantive has been taught or learned.

Learning, and understanding, as defined by current cognitive science, means that we know the story behind the story of our learning, that this learning is justified according to disciplinary standards, and that we can transfer and use what has been learned in new and dissimilar situations. Research shows that this kind of transfer rarely happens, and only occurs under certain conditions, conditions that we designed the five kinds of composing to meet:

- Deep understanding of the material (declarative and procedural knowledge) to be transferred.
- Plenty of practice applying meaning-making strategies and principles of problem solving to various new situations.
- The capacity to articulate what is understood and how it was developed and to justify what has been learned and how it is represented.
- The capacity to flexibly apply what has been learned to new situations. (See Haskell 2000; Perkins and Salomon 1988; Smith and Wilhelm 2006, 2009.)

Each of the thought patterns and text structures explored in this book requires general processes that work in the same way in each case, but they must also be tweaked for task- and context-specific conditions (for example, all summaries work in the same general way, but a précis or an abstract requires specific additional processes). Students need to know how and why these processes work to be able to transfer what is known to new situations. They need, in other words, deep and reflective understanding.

To reinforce and consolidate these required capacities, we use reflective composing that names what has been learned, how it has been learned, the challenges involved, and how to use what has been learned in projected future situations. Brian Edmiston's research (1990) demonstrates both that this kind of reflection is essential to deep understanding and transfer and that it is the most important and most neglected aspect of literacy instruction.

It's important to emphasize that we use composing to transfer throughout the instructional process from the very start, particularly by using formative assessments. But we always end a unit and follow up on culminating projects by having students reflect on their learning and analyze the process of that learning. This is what we call composing to transfer.

An Aside on Our Teaching Histories

All three of us have spent too many evenings and weekends responding to papers in which we were disappointed. We've come to understand that we should have been disappointed in ourselves and not our students. Why? Because we didn't provide

➤ *The vertical alignment of the CCSS lends itself to this.*

Michael:
The 5 kinds of composing helps guide me to provide the specific activities students need while in the process of meaning making.

Jim:
The 5 kinds of composing is a way to think about student activity—specifically, what activities I need to provide as well as when to help students be successful with particular text structures as readers and as composers.

Jeff:
The 5 kinds of composing help me to see that classrooms need to be places of production instead of consumption: places of conversation, composing, and meaning-making. In consumption, the teacher has control; in production, the students are given control. The 5 kinds of composing shows me how to give my students conscious control and expertise.

Jef, Michael, and Jim:
The 5 kinds of composing is a heuristic for teachers that helps students develop heuristics: for moving beyond lock-step formula to generative and flexible ways of composing and being in the world.

enough opportunity and instruction and practice to guide and support our students toward success.

Because of our five-kinds heuristics (both knowledge and composing), we now have a *much* better idea of how to avoid that disappointment. Jeff, for example, embeds his teaching in inquiry units built around essential questions. In his classes, these units typically take about nine weeks to complete. Students write one major composition each unit, but because of his attention to the five kinds of composing, students are doing more composing than they ever have before. Their little fingers become blistered nubs from so much writing! Every day they compose in a variety of modalities: talking, writing, drawing, debating, doing drama, moving and dancing, talking and writing some more, in ways that develop knowledge of purpose, substance, and form. Every day they plan and practice, plan and practice, plan and practice, practice, practice, and practice some more. Nearly every day there is a formative assessment that constitutes a kind of composing to transfer, and at the end of the unit there is a more extended composing to transfer. Throughout the unit, they enact all five kinds of composing in order to develop all five kinds of knowledge.

Jeff's evenings and weekends are still sometimes spent responding to student work. But because of his attention to the five kinds of knowledge and five kinds of composing, he does much less of this than he used to, and when he does so the evenings are much more pleasant—because his students have spent the requisite time and practice to compose unique and competent pieces filled with voice and creativity. And Jeff has plenty of evidence that this competence transfers to personal writing, writing in other subjects, and writing that students do in future grades and even in college.

These are the goals we have for all our students, and the five kinds of knowledge and composing are the best way we have found for achieving these ends.

CHAPTER 5

The Process and Practical Context of Inquiry

All right. We've laid the theory-and-research groundwork for our instructional process. We think this is important, for as we've argued, effective teaching is informed, wide-awake, and theoretically situated. It's principled and therefore adaptable and transferable. Such teaching has heuristic value.

But now it's time to focus on practical applications! As teachers, we are always eager to get to the practical: we want to know what *to do* to help our students. We'll be exploring many ideas about what we can do to teach specific informational text structures in the chapters to come, but first we want to discuss what we can do to create a context that provides motivation and gives meaning to learning all of those things. That context is inquiry units built around essential questions. (For a full discussion of the power of inquiry, see Wilhelm 2007.)

Once again we turn to George Hillocks. He has argued throughout his career that all forms of reading and composing are in fact forms of inquiry and are best taught and learned in contexts of inquiry. His famous meta-analysis of research on composition (1983), as well as his own research throughout his distinguished career, powerfully shows this to be the case, as has much research before and since (e.g., Newman 1995, 1996; for a current review of research, see Wilhelm 2007).

By inquiry we mean the rigorous induction into disciplinary expertise, into the ways and kinds of knowing exercised in the disciplines. Inquiry is what each discipline does to create knowledge. Inquiry, as we see it and research offers compelling proof, is the most powerful context for all teaching and learning and for all forms of reading and composing.

One of the reasons we love being English teachers is that our discipline creates knowledge about the stuff that matters most in our lives. Teaching English, we have

➤ *The CCSS don't dictate in-structional practices, leaving those up to the profes-sional deci-sion making of teachers.*

➤ *Inquiry nicely matches the social studies/ history, science, and technical subjects literacy standards.*

➤ *Research anchor standard 7 includes the phrase "research projects based on focused questions," terminology that recurs throughout the grade levels until the grade 9–10 and 11–12 standards, which dictate that these inquiries will be "research projects to answer a question (including a self-generated question)." Teacher-generated essential questions meet the goal for research at all grades and are models for student-generated inquiries in the upper grades.*

➤ *Reading standards 7 and 9 for literature grades 11–12 and 8 and 9 for informational texts grades 11–12 explicitly specify American authors and texts.*

➤ *Reading anchor standard 9 (all levels) calls for reading multiple texts on the same theme, and reading standard 7 (all levels) asks students to read texts treating similar ideas in different media—both fit perfectly into an inquiry unit.*

the opportunity to engage students in thinking about the big and enduring questions that are likely to have motivated much of the reading and writing we've done, questions like, *To what do I owe my primary allegiance? What's the best response to injustice? To what extent is the American dream equally accessible to all?* In current parlance, these questions are called *essential questions*.

Of course, progressive teachers in all content areas have long been organizing instruction around real-world problems and issues, and we'll highlight such content-area instruction in our practice chapters.

We've been writing and teaching about building inquiry units around essential and existential questions for some time now (Smith and Wilhelm 2006; Wilhelm 2007; Wilhelm, Wilhelm, and Boas 2009; Wilhelm and Novak 2011), so we're familiar with the kinds of questions teachers typically ask about the process and how to implement it. We'll address those here through some FAQs.

FAQ: What makes a good essential question?

Effective essential questions can accomodate many possible answers and provide a wide variety of opportunities to read and compose. *What is the American dream?* isn't a good question, because in our view there's consensus on the answer. *To what extent is the American dream equally accessible to all?* works much better because of the range of possible answers and how current and compelling such a question can be to students. Plus, to answer this one, students have to first come to an agreement about what constitutes the American dream and then investigate how accessible this dream is to all. (For chapter-length discussions of creating essential questions, see Wilhelm 2007; Wilhelm, Wilhelm, and Boas 2009.)

FAQ: Once you have an essential question, what do you do?

Sometimes the texts or material we teach suggest the question. Sometimes the question comes first. As we plan a new unit, we consider the array of texts, particularly informational texts (creative nonfiction can be highly literary) that speak in meaningful ways to that question. For the question *to what extent is the American dream equally accessible to all?* possibilities include classic literature like *The Great Gatsby*; fiction and nonfiction that chronicles the immigrant experience, both positively and negatively; biographies of any famous person who has risen from modest (or less-than-modest circumstances); and news stories about the Occupy Wall Street movement or the income gap between rich and poor. (We could go on, which suggests that this essential question is generative.)

The next consideration is how to teach students to read and compose different text types in the context of the unit (which is the subject of this book). Here's a general protocol that we call *PPDT* to help you think about how to do so:

- *Purpose and context.* Given your unit, what thought pattern/text structure will be most important? What thought pattern(s) will be both required and rewarded in the context of learning that addresses the inquiry? How and in what situations will this thought pattern/text structure be useful and do work conceptually and procedurally in terms of the inquiry, as well as in terms of students' personal lived experience?

- *Process.* How will you engage the students in planning, practicing, drafting, presenting, and reflecting for transfer, and how will you provide the necessary opportunities for students to reach "conscious competence" for using the thought pattern both now and in the future?

- *Delivery.* How will the culminating project(s) use or integrate this thought pattern/text structure?

- *Transfer.* What purposes will the conceptual and procedural learning students achieve in this unit fulfill in future disciplinary and personal work? How will their learning help them recognize the contexts for future use of the thought pattern? How has the groundwork been laid for transfer and improvement in developing even greater expertise with the thought pattern? How will you help students name and reflect on what they have learned in ways that will foster transfer?

FAQ: How do you plan a culminating composing task?

Together with your students, an important instructional move is to describe the culminating composition and the criteria for it, The description of a culminating composition should include the following elements (Wiggins and McTighe 2005), which we sum up using the acronym GRASPS:

- *Goal(s).* What do we want to understand and be able to do? Why? How do these match the CCSS?

> ➤ *Reading and comparing several texts around single themes also prepares students for the longer and shorter performance tasks on the Smarter Balanced and PARCC tests.*

> ➤ *Writing anchor standard 4*

> ➤ *Writing anchor standard 5*

> ➤ *Writing anchor standards 2 and 4*

> ➤ *New PARCC and Smarter Balanced assessments require that reading and writing skills transfer to new situations.*

> ➤ *Writing anchor standards 4 and 10*

➤ *CCSS writing anchor standard 4 to consider purpose, task, and audience*

- *Role*. What roles will students play: themselves? a character? practitioner in a particular profession or area of expertise (mantle of the expert)? someone else?

- *Audience*. Who is the primary audience for what will be composed? How will the project/composition be shared?

- *Situation*. What circumstances surround the piece (who will read and respond to it throughout the composing process?), the writer (how much time does she have to write it? what resources can she rely on? how long does it need to be?), and the ultimate audience (when and where will they experience the piece? how might they use what they learn?)?

- *Purpose*. What work will this piece of writing do for the writer and for the audience?

- *Standards for success*. What does a strong example of this project look like? What critical standards will be met? (Tie these to the CCSS.)

The general sequences for developing instruction for each kind of composing and each kind of knowledge are recursive. You are not locked in to a specific sequence. The heuristic is flexible and should respond to your students' needs at the time.

Composing to Plan

In this kind of composing students develop knowledge of context and purpose and begin developing procedural knowledge of substance. In other words, they come to understand the purposes and situations in which this knowledge counts and begin generating the material they need to write their own compositions. We generally make use of some of the strategies shown here:

- Brainstorm relevant background (students' past experience with an informational thought pattern, for example).

- Conduct action research. Students monitor how often this thought pattern is used during a day, either by themselves or others.

- Search and find examples of the thought pattern in newspapers, other media, or popular culture.

- Read mentor texts. This typically involves think-alouds or annotations exploring the thought pattern under consideration.

- Rank examples of the final product (from previous students or the Internet). Students begin to compose justifications for their rankings, articulate

➤ *Reading anchor standards 5 and 8*

their own critical standards, and consider what they need to learn to be able to meet these critical standards.

- Summarize purposes and contexts on anchor charts or some other classroom archive or record and consider tentative topic ideas for students' own composition. *Why are these possible topics compelling to me? How do or might they address the inquiry question? Where might I get data? What will be achieved for me and others through this kind of composition?*

- Decompose the task process, and identify what students need to learn to compose the culminating product and meet the critical standards.

Composing to Practice

Students get and shape data by developing procedural knowledge of substance and particularly of form. We typically use some of the following strategies:

- Frontloading that is both conceptual and procedural, that activates and builds background for the task, that motivates and prepares everyone for the inquiry, and that demonstrates the necessity of the particular thought pattern/text structure.

- Practicing and naming techniques for finding, generating, and recording data (visualization, graphic organizers, drama activities, and other forms of multimodal composing).

- Working collaboratively: paired and individual composing with peer group support, revision contests, group edits/write-overs.

- Practicing and naming "crux moves" necessary to attain conceptual understanding and use the thought pattern/text structure. (This is essential in developing "conscious competence.")

- Shaping and patterning thinking through various kinds of composing.

- Practicing and naming linguistic markers (introductions, transitions, language conventions) that help shape thinking and data into this thought pattern/text structure.

We typically begin with data closer to home for students—more connected to their experience—and perhaps not as directly related to the final compositions. But we quickly move on to getting and shaping data that *is* on point. We also move from concrete to more abstract experiences (using oral activities, visualization, drama, and other multimodal forms of composing before doing straight text); from group work

➤ *Planning and practicing always interact synergistically to help the composer generate material and shape it—and to learn transferable strategies for generating and structuring thought patterns.*

➤ *Reading anchor standards 5 and 8; speaking and listening anchor standards 1 and 6; writing anchor standard 6*

➤ *Speaking and listening anchor standard 1*

➤ *The anchor stan-
dards, which are few
in number and apply
to all levels and in all
disciplines, encourage
and support practice
over time in different
contexts.*

to more individual work; from shorter to longer activities; from low-risk activities to high-stakes final drafting and evaluation according to critical standards. In any case it's important to give students *plenty of practice*! Put things together that go together: the more you can combine practice of form with the substance of the curriculum and current inquiry, the better. (We call this a *twofer*. We love going for twofers, threefers, and fourfers!)

Composing to Draft

Students put all five kinds of knowledge together as they start to flesh out a draft of the text structure. This involves deep revisions of substance and form. We try to do the following:

- Continue to articulate and formalize critical standards to use as a guide for drafting. Help students get started (e.g., create good introductions and outlines, decompose the task).
- Train peer responders to apply criteria. The deep understanding of the thought pattern achieved during practice greatly enhances peer editing. It is also helpful to provide protocols for response and ask students to practice responding to model papers.

➤ *Writing anchor
standard 5*

- Let students practice revision strategies like moving, deleting, changing, and adding data to the text structure to enhance coherence and global meaning.
- Remind students to consider creating multimodal exhibits to the composition or a multimodal version of it.

Composing the Final Draft

Students polish the composition and correct surface irregularities. During this phase students:

➤ *Language stan-
dards 1, 2, and 6*

- Practice and integrate grammatical structures and vocabulary that will increase coherence of the text for the audience.
- Proofread and correct typical problems or "target areas" at the sentence level.
- Pay attention to transitions, navigational devices, and multimodal reinforcement.

Composing for Transfer

Composing for transfer takes place throughout the unit by way of formative assessments in which students demonstrate, articulate, justify, and reflect on what they are learning. At the end of the composing process, it's important to help students reflect on what has been learned and how to carry it forward—when and how they will use what was learned about this thought pattern/text structure in the future. We use the following techniques to promote transfer:

➤ *This reflection is a key component of PARCC and Smarter Balanced short and long performance-based assessments.*

- Conducting daily formative assessments within planning, practice, and drafting activities.
- Writing reflectively on what has been learned—what was successful, obstacles encountered, how obstacles were negotiated, what needs to be done differently next time.
- Reflecting on the process of learning, the importance of what was learned, future applications for the learning, etc., through writing, think-alouds, drama, and art.
- Imaginatively rehearsing future problem solving and living.
- Analyzing the learning process—*how* learning occurred.

Reflection prompts include:

- What did you learn that you expected? that you did not expect? conceptually? procedurally? socially?
- How did you learn it? What worked? What did not help or interfered with learning?
- What were some successes of your learning? How do you know?
- What were some obstacles and how did you experience and overcome them?
- When do you anticipate using what you have learned?
- What will you do differently the next time you engage in such a task?

FAQ: You guys are always going on about teaching in a meaningful context of use. Why is that so important?

The last forty-plus years of cognitive science research demonstrates that all deep learning occurs in a context which supports—actually, co-produces—that learning and in which all understanding is deepened by being applied in real situations. (See Brown, Collins, and Duguid 1989 for an excellent review of the seminal research on this topic.) In other words, we can't really come to understand and use what we have learned unless it is learned in a meaningful situation like inquiry, which creates a situation analogous to that in which experts in the field learn. This is why we like drama so much—drama-in-education strategies create an immediate and compelling simulated context that students can immediately connect to real life.

An example of situated memory is the "doorway effect" (Oz and Roizen 2012; Schulz 2010): you walk into a room and can't remember why you came in. Here's why. If you had walked across the same room, you would not have forgotten your reason for moving—you are in the same context, and that context supports learning and memory. But go through a doorway, and your memory is hardwired to be wiped clean; it auto-purges the information you needed in the old room to be prepared for the demands of a new context. The same is true of our students: without a meaningful context for learning they lose motivation, they can't activate meaningful schema necessary to the learning, they won't see applications, and they have no reason to remember what they have learned.

FAQ: How do you find time to provide all this instruction and practice and still cover the curriculum? How do you deal with the issue of time?

We do it by integrating content and process—by putting things together that go together, by integrating the teaching of conceptual and procedural knowledge that is complementary and mutually enhancing and reinforcing.

Remember the fable sequence in Chapter 3? We were able to combine fable reading and writing with conceptual learning about relationships. And we were able to do this teaching in the direct service of further conceptual and procedural learning directed toward composing arguments. We saved lots of time through twofers and threefers—teaching things together in ways that had multiple payoffs in the unit. The time we saved was spent on practice that led to deep understanding. You'll see many more examples of how to do this kind of combining in future chapters.

Many of the schools we've taught in divide genres into separate units, divorce reading from composing, and isolate grammar from writing. This kind of separation

➤ *The Common Core standards are separated into those for reading, writing, speaking and listening, and language, but integration is implied (and explicitly addressed on page 4 of the introduction under the heading "An Integrated Model of Literacy").*

doesn't make sense to us. Whenever we learn anything, solve any problem, whenever we engage in inquiry, we learn in a purposeful and meaningful situation and we use all the literature, texts, materials, and processes that pertain to that inquiry. We read a variety of literary texts, including poetry, explanatory / informative texts, arguments, multimodal texts, and popular culture texts that help us think through the content of the unit. (It's why we situated fable reading and writing within the context of a wider inquiry into relationships.)

As we work within our curriculum, we have our students practice composing using the thought patterns and text structures that the focus of the inquiry requires and rewards.

For example, a unit framed by the question *what is a good relationship?* implies that students will practice defining a good relationship and that their culminating projects will involve composing extended definitions of elements of a good relationship. The question also suggests that we should read love songs, love fables, love poetry, *Romeo and Juliet*, informational articles on relationships like those found in *Psychology Today,* along with extended definitions of various kinds of relationships (those on the Planned Parenthood website, for example). A unit framed by the question *what makes the greatest leader?* implies that students will be comparing and contrasting. *What are our civil rights and how can we best protect them?* suggests a problem–solution structure.

➤ *Unit ideas*

We no longer do genre units but include in every unit whatever genres help us with our inquiry. Likewise, we study grammatical conventions that help us write the kinds of text structures we are composing in the context of that composing. Things that go together are best taught and learned together.

If we need or are required to teach a particular text structure, we can revise our essential question to require and reward that text structure. "What makes and breaks relationships?" requires an argument of judgment. But this essential question can be revised to "What makes a good relationship?" if we want students to write an extended definition, or to "What kinds of good relationships are there?" if we are writing classifications, or "What can society do to promote good relationships?" if we need to compose an argument of policy. And so on.

As far as timing, we often design units to fit the typical nine-week grading period. This accommodates the extended practice kids need "mining" texts for ideas and generating and shaping those ideas. We typically spend seven weeks on frontloading, reading, planning, and practicing; the final two weeks are devoted to drafting and finalizing compositions and culminating projects. (This can be adjusted for other time periods; just allot enough time for kids to immerse themselves in the content and provide enough practice getting and forming the stuff to compose!)

Since kids need stuff to write about, it makes no sense to separate content units from composing and grammar. This is in line with the research on situated cognition (see Brown, Collins, and Duguid 1989) and how contexts (like inquiry) and time spent practicing (composing to plan and composing to practice) co-produce understanding. (You'll see examples of how all this works in each of the following chapters.)

This may not be how your curriculum currently works, but the process is the same even in shorter units. We meet all the standards and cover all the content of our curriculum by reorganizing our instruction into integrated inquiry units. We are less rushed, and our students learn more deeply—and do better on high-stakes tests (see Chapter 2).

Here's a final point: the CCSS offer a huge opportunity to reconceive curriculum. Since the focus of the CCSS is on procedures, and the content for leveraging these procedures is largely left up to districts and teachers, there is a tremendous opportunity to adopt inquiry instruction that integrates the kinds of knowledge that go together. We hope that all teachers will grab this opportunity with both hands. It's an unprecedented opportunity to exercise our professional expertise and decision-making power.

FAQ: How do you deal with issues of grading? You recommend spending so much time practicing. What do you enter in your grade book? Parents expect to see daily grades!

We provide kids with a "PPD" every day: a *purpose* for the day's lesson that is connected to the inquiry and leads them toward and prepares them for the culminating project; the *process* we will undertake during the activity; and a *deliverable*. During every activity, we want students to produce something tangible that demonstrates effort and their current level of understanding. Sometimes this deliverable is produced in groups, but when it is, everyone has to identify his or her contribution. As we go through a unit, more and more work is individual, though students are always able to confer with their peers. The deliverables always provide a quickly accessible formative assessment that makes student learning visible and informs our teacherly thinking about what kind of practice and support is needed next.

Through the first seven weeks of a unit, the kids are planning and practicing. If they put in an honest effort and produce the deliverable, we give them ten "effort" points each day, entered on our electronic grade sheets (which parents can view). These points are not based in any way on expertise or even growth.

Here's why: first, we think there is an ethical problem with evaluating what you have not yet taught. We don't think it is fair to apply critical standards until we have, over time, helped students meet those standards. We tell our students that we will spend seven or eight weeks being their coach, then one or two weeks being the referee—seven or eight weeks being their advocate, then one or two weeks being their judge.

Here's another reason: we like the metaphor of coaching for teaching. All three of us have been coaches of various athletic teams and other extracurricular activities in the arts or student government. Coaches don't start off day one with a high-stakes test like a competition. They spend the first sessions learning players' strengths and weaknesses, then planning how to exploit strengths and address weaknesses through weeks of . . . you guessed it: practice! Then they monitor a controlled scrimmage, then a game-conditions scrimmage—moving the players ever closer to the high-stakes test of an actual game or meet. They do whatever is necessary to help the players be successful—win or lose—in game situations.

Yet another reason: according to motivational attribution theory (see Dweck 2006) students are more likely to develop a growth mindset and willingness to work through problems over time if they attribute success to effort. The more they attribute success to talent or aptitude, the less motivated they will be and the less willing to spend time practicing and working through the challenges necessary to growth and learning. Providing grades for effort until students have had the support necessary to be successful is highly motivating and cultivates the growth mindset. In our own studies (Smith and Wilhelm 2002, 2006) we found that boys privileged competence above all else. They were willing to undertake very complex challenges like those required by the CCSS and the required assessments *if* they felt the teacher would provide the necessary assistance and support, reward effort, and provide/celebrate visible signs of their developing competence along the way.

➤ *CCSS assessments*

There's one final concern. Our time and energy are limited, and we have to decide how to best spend these valuable commodities. George Hillocks' research has convinced us that we get a lot more payoff in terms of student learning when we spend time on planning versus evaluation. He has also shown that we need to evaluate in ways *in which* and at times *when* that feedback can be used immediately—in revision and for transfer. Therefore, we prefer to base in-process effort grades throughout on formative assessments. We perform summative assessments only at the ends of units on culminating projects and according to published and negotiated critical standards.

And we always allow students to revise using our feedback. We hold students accountable but only after we have helped them master what we are assessing.

We tell our students that if they put in the effort and practice, we are confident they will develop the capacities to complete the culminating projects successfully. If students screw up and don't receive their effort points for a day, we often have them write a proposal or appeal letter (more writing!) and then allow them to make up the work. We want them to do the work, after all, and we want them to get the necessary practice, so we put the responsibility on them. We tell them we will help them in any way we can. We have some extra time to do this because we are not grading stacks of papers. We can quickly peruse formative assessments between classes and during lunch. We are pretty full-on during the day but take less work and grading home.

Remember, even though there is only one major composition assignment per quarter, our kids are writing more than they ever wrote before—and all this writing helps them develop and place hold content for their culminating compositions and practice shaping that content into a conventional thought pattern/text structure as required by the discipline. When it comes time to sit down and draft, they are practically done: they have all the stuff and plenty of practice shaping the stuff. Assignment completion on our major writing assignments, even for struggling students, is always (or very nearly) 100 percent. That was far from the case when we gave more assignments and provided less assistance to our students.

FAQ: What are good culminating projects?

First off, it is vitally important that all culminating projects fit real-world purposes and are addressed to real-world audiences.

One of our culminating projects as English teachers is always a composition (individual, although our students always work with peer revisers and editors). But we believe every teacher needs to be a teacher of literacy and should include reading and composing in all units, particularly since the CCSS standards for literacy in the disciplines make the same case and require more literacy activities. We've worked with content-area teachers for many years, and we've not found a single unit in any subject, including shop or physical education, that can't be framed as inquiry and enhanced with reading and composing activities.

➤ *For example, see history/social studies, science, and technical subjects writing standard 2.*

➤ *Writing anchor standard 6*

We also like to include group multimedia projects in all our units. Most of the work on these multimedia compositions, be they digital compositions using video, hypermedia, the Internet, drama, visual arts, dance, or other arts, is done during the last two weeks of a unit. However, we introduce the students to the kind of composing they will be doing in the first few days of the unit: we show them models and have them rank them, we articulate criteria together, and then we assist them throughout the unit to develop and practice the thinking tools they will need to develop and shape the material for their final products. This makes sense given the demands placed on students in regards to twenty-first-century literacies and the CCSS standards for composing processes, collaboration, speaking and listening, and multimodal composing.

➤ *CCSS connection*

We are moving more and more toward multimodal social action and service projects in our own teaching, since this requires that what we learned together with students be applied to the real world. For example, during our relationship unit a group of boys took a forum drama around to the district elementary schools as part of an antibullying project.

Another consideration: when students both write a piece *and* create a multimedia composition, the students get to use the thought patterns and content they have studied at least twice at the end of the unit. They get to demonstrate their learning through actual accomplishment and a resounding proof of purchase! The learning is reinforced and consolidated as they work individually on their final papers and together on multimedia compositions. And students very much want to share and view others' multimodal projects providing another authentic audience for the works.

Again, you might have to tweak our model for use in your own classroom, but this way of doing things has worked very well for us.

FAQ: How do you train and use peer responders? My students are useless at helping one another improve their compositions.

We have found that students who acquire all five kinds of knowledge through the five kinds of composing develop deep understanding of not only the content of their composing but also the process and form of their writing. This gives them the skills to be a helpful peer responder and editor for one another as a real audience, someone who can give substantive advice about what to keep, move, change, add, or delete.

We have also found that our students break away from formulaic writing as a result of their deep understanding of the composing process and are better able to reflect on their composing process and self-assess the products of their writing.

Nevertheless, it's important to provide protocols for helping students respond to one another. One of our protocols is PQP—*praise*, then ask *questions* about the content and form, then offer suggestions for *polishing* and revising. Another one we like is *keep, move, change, add, delete*. We ask peer revisers to make one suggestion for something to keep, with a justification, then provide five suggestions for moving, changing, adding, or deleting something along with an explanation why this would strengthen the writing. The writer decides what advice to take but must justify in writing any advice she rejects. Structures like these (and others in this book) help students both provide substantive advice and deeply consider that advice (see Smith and Wilhelm 2007 for more on this).

We also help students practice how to be good group members, how to phrase advice, and how to set and monitor standards for good sharing. This is outside the purview of this book, but this kind of work helps students meet CCSS standards for collaboration, speaking, listening, and much else. Jeff devotes a section of *Engaging Readers and Writers with Inquiry* (2007) to these processes.

FAQ: What about timing? It seems you spend the great majority of time on planning and practicing.

Absolutely right. In any domain, people develop the five kinds of knowledge primarily through composing to plan and composing to practice, so that's where we put our emphasis. Certainly, learning continues through drafting and finalizing, and deep understanding continues to be consolidated and integrated. But most learning occurs through practice, as shown in the seminal research of Ericsson (Ericsson and Lehmann 1996), the researcher who first made the case that competence requires one thousand hours, mastery three thousand hours, and expertise requires ten thousand hours of assisted and focused practice. That research also indicates that you can create new habits of mind through consistent daily practice over the course of just six or seven weeks—the amount of time we like to dedicate to planning and practicing in any unit.

Think about it this way. Jeff is a marathon Nordic skier. Last year he competed in the World Masters and U.S. Nationals ski marathon championships. He skied about two thousand kilometers during the season. Eighteen hundred of them were racked up in training, much of it work on technique. He also did core exercises, lifted weights, and stretched throughout the season. He had engaged in dry-land training and biking since the previous May. It's safe to say that by the time Jeff won his bronze medal in the U.S. Nationals, 98 percent of his time had been spent on planning and practicing.

Or consider writing this book. The three of us individually are drawing on any-where from twenty to over thirty years of teaching experience. Jeff has been actively planning to write this particular book for twenty-three years and has been collecting materials during all that time. What you are reading is the result of years of both formal and informal research and the practical endeavor of trying things out in the classroom. Even with fifteen drafts, the actual writing was less than 2 percent of the process.

And consider any presentation you might have given. The bulk of your time was no doubt spent planning, practicing, and bringing forward (transferring) your prior knowledge and experience. That's why we emphasize planning and practicing and transferring—it's where most of the learning gets done. It's the preparation for suc-cess. And we'd rather *proactively prepare our students for success* (in fact, that's what we call teaching) than spend our time reacting to student failure and frustration. Without the planning and practice and transfer, an exceptional final product can't be achieved and used as a springboard for future success.

FAQ: What about sequencing? Do you follow a particular sequence of activities?

The processes of learning and composing are highly recursive. We teach via a *struc-tured process,* but the structure is highly flexible. We rely on what we learn from our students about their progress to make decisions about how long to spend on a par-ticular concept or teaching move. But we always start with composing to plan and composing to practice (particularly through frontloading) and spend most of our time on planning and practicing. But during that time, students are also trying out and drafting ideas and techniques they will use in their first drafts. We use compos-ing to transfer every day, both through dedicated formative assessments and through the actual work we are doing (which is always part of the process of practicing gen-erating and forming material to be used in the drafting and finalizing). During the drafting and finalizing stages, we are still instructing—that is, planning and practic-ing. We are teaching what is appropriate at that point in the process (proofreading for grammatical correctness, for example). It doesn't make sense to do that kind of work until students have a draft they are proud of and want to share with an audi-ence. If at any time during the drafting or finalizing stage we notice students are still struggling with one of the crux moves or concepts necessary to their culminating project, we go back to practicing.

FAQ: Okay, I like what I'm hearing. Still this looks different from what students, parents, and even colleagues are used to seeing in classrooms—how do you deal with that?

Our advice is to be proactive versus reactive. In other words, let students and parents and colleagues know what you are doing before you do it, through a parent newsletter, a class website, parent nights, whatever method works for you.

Another great idea is to get at least one colleague or teaching partner to work with you. Research on teaching teams shows that pairs or small groups of teachers working together seem to be the most innovative and the best able to sustain innovation (see Arnold 1997, for example). It's like having a running buddy. We are much more likely to get up for our workout if there is someone else who shares our commitment.

➤ *CCSS assessment*

Use the CCSS as a lever. Show up front how you are working to meet the CCSS in ways that make sense according to the CCSS; prepare students for the Smarter Balanced or PARCC assessment (bringing up assessments and sharing test items often captures people's attention); and help them meet the demands of the world and the workplace.

Also use student engagement as a lever. Use the research presented here and elsewhere about human motivation, cognition, and understanding to justify your approach. Share student work at learning nights and in other ways. The quality of the work we get from our students using this process is our most convincing evidence that the process works.

Invite others to join you. If you have like-minded colleagues, or are part of a PLC, a collaborative inquiry group, or a network of teachers like that provided by the National Writing Project, form a group to explore ways of improving instruction and/or meeting the CCSS. We've typically found that you can form a coalition of the willing, with the blessing of administrators, if you don't ask that everybody in the school be on board. Many schools have been transformed by a small group of teachers modeling how to meet the common goals of the school in a more engaging way. Others are much more willing to follow once you've blazed the trail. Teacher research groups can likewise document and share success, modeling teacher professionalism in providing ever more effective instruction.

CHAPTER 6

Naming and Listing

Prerequisites for Problem Solving and Performing the Possible

Jeff is a namer. We've already mentioned how he names rapids in the rivers he runs. He names his cars. His first car was named Ophelia (an apt name, because she broke down and broke Jeff's heart). His last car, used extensively for outdoor trips, was The Viking Mobile. He gives his students nicknames—this year Melissa, for example, so flexible and upbeat, is Mellifluous. His daughter Jasmine has numerous nicknames, each a unique story. At a recent cross-country meet Jasmine competed in, a neighboring fan asked Jeff how many kids he had in the race. Jeff had to laugh—he had only one, but he was cheering for her with six different names.

Jeff also makes lists. Every weekend he makes a day-by-day list of what he must get done during the coming week. Every morning, he revises that list into a daily list that he carries around to keep him on track. He also has a bucket list that he keeps in his calendar, along with a short list of what he would most like to experience or achieve in the short term. He's the family organizer, the keeper of grocery lists and equipment lists and to-do lists for the house. He keeps lists to get things done.

Jim also is a namer and a keeper of lists. His notebook includes lists of books he wants to read, papers he needs to read and respond to, possible future projects, quotes or observations from the day, a running list of song titles and artists he wants to include on his annual CD swap with friends in November, and of course, whatever he needs to get done that day. Over the years, these lists have moved from lists of general topics to lists of really small and concrete action steps he can take. For example, instead of *write Chapter 3*, his list includes *write a summary sentence for the chapter*; *write the promise paragraph to readers*; *write the list of references*; *rework the section on characters*; and so on. For Jim, listing and naming are ways he copes with feeling overwhelmed.

Naming helps him see what to do; listing gets it out of his head so he's not paralyzed with inaction.

Michael does the food shopping for his family, and lists are essential if he has any hope of getting everything his family needs. In fact, he's taken to writing them on eight-by-eleven-inch sheets of paper to reduce the likelihood he'll leave them somewhere in the grocery store. And over the years he's made them more and more specific as his memory becomes less and less reliable. *Stuff for the cookout* has given way to *Italian sausage, all-beef franks*, and so on. Lists are also essential in his professional life. He characteristically thinks through how an article or a chapter will proceed and doesn't begin writing it until it's ready to hatch. But while he's doing that thinking, he captures it with a list. Otherwise he'd lose the sense of the whole. He has a whiteboard in his office that contains two lists: what he needs to do in the coming month and the items that should appear on the next department agenda.

Naming and listing fulfill many purposes: in fact, we think they require a kind of thinking necessary for all other informational/explanatory texts. Cognitive science agrees: listing is a first step in knowledge activation and generation, moves us toward problem solving, and always involves naming (Damasio 2010).

Why Naming and Listing Matters

➤ *Standard 2a for reading and composing informative/ explanatory texts at each grade level*

Naming and listing are hugely important in education. Research in activity theory (see Halverson 2002, for example), an increasingly important theoretical framework, has identified any number of distinct purposes for naming: conceiving, remembering, making accessible, bringing into existence, making real, place holding an idea for tweaking/revising/honing/sharpening, reconceiving or reframing concepts and processes, manipulating ideas and combinations of ideas, communicating, thinking through, categorizing, seeking and establishing patterns, defining, comparing, classifying, making meaning, solving problems, theorizing.

Here's just one illustration. Research on learning strategies (see, for example, http://nichcy.org/research/ee/learning-strategies) indicates that when students name the strategies they are developing and using, the strategies are more available to them and more likely to be used and transferred to future situations.

Likewise, the CCSS use similar language to name the processes important to meeting both the reading and writing standards. This is a smart move, because teachers are able to name and share what they are teaching and students are able to name what they are learning in the same terms. For instance, across grade levels and situations, the CCSS use *claim*, *evidence*, and *reasoning* to talk about argument and *task*, *purpose*, and *audience* to discuss rhetorical stance. They also name specific strategies for effective writing, both generally and for specific text structures. This consistent naming gives power and focus to our instruction and assessment and helps our students achieve conscious competence.

Other disciplines also place a huge emphasis on naming. The persistence and historical continuity of linking naming with power are unmistakable:

> A common concept in history is that knowing the name of some-
> thing or someone gives one power over that thing or person. This
> concept occurs in many different forms, in numerous cultures—in
> ancient and primitive tribes, as well as in Islamic, Jewish, Egyptian,
> Vedic, Hindu, and Christian traditions. (Graham 2009)

Graham also points out that in Genesis, God names before he creates: "God said 'Let there be light, and there was light.'" Naming is the necessary prerequisite to creation. Naming in fact helps things come into being. God gave man the right to name the animals and stewardship over them. The right to name gives a right to power.

The mathematician Alexander Grothendieck put a heavy emphasis on naming as a way to gain cognitive power over concepts, processes, and objects as a prerequisite to understanding. Graham cites a contemporary of Grothendieck's who wrote: "Grothendieck had a flair for choosing striking, evocative names for new concepts; indeed, he saw the act of naming mathematical objects as an integral part of their discovery, as a way to grasp them even before they have been entirely understood."

The neurobiologist Dan Siegel (2007) makes a similar point: what happens neurologically in naming is different from what happens in storytelling and other forms of organizing experience, in both process and result. Brain scans of subjects who had induced emotional distress (by remembering a loss in their life, for example) revealed that the right brain became overstimulated, flooded with emotion, and often overwhelmed. However, when the distressed person named the emotional state (a left-brain function), the entire brain calmed down, and additional behavioral and emotional options became available. As Siegel puts it, "You have to name it to tame it." (He emphasizes that the naming has to come from a mindful state of observing the phenomenon at hand.)

For both teachers and learners naming confers *descriptive power* that helps us make sense of the world; *rhetorical power* that helps us communicate, confer, and make meaning together about the world; and *inferential power* to see new connections,

> ➤ *Though naming as a strategy is not explicitly foregrounded in the CCSS, it is implied in many places—reading standard 5 for grades 9–10 and reading standard 6 for grades 11–12, for example.*

make new meaning, deepen understanding, and see possibility beyond what is explicitly and directly known. Through this process we develop and exercise applications of both *personal power* and *disciplinary power*. It's clear that naming is prerequisite to the mastery of all thought patterns and text structures.

How We Name Things

➤ *See the three tiers of vocabulary in Appendix A of the CCSS.*

In order to name something, we use two different processes. On the one hand, we use preexisting names for the concepts. On the other hand, as we create new understandings and new knowledge, we create and assign new names to new insights and discoveries. We do this by (1) inventing a name or (2) modifying an existing name by using simile, metaphor, onomatopoeia, rhymes, or alliteration; by developing acronyms and abbreviations; by combining preexisting names; or by using known prefixes and suffixes.

In this book, for instance, we use George Hillocks' names for the first four kinds of knowledge and then use existing words to name the essential fifth kind of knowledge we discovered: knowledge of purpose and context. We likewise use existing words to name the five kinds of composing. Naming them helps us understand and test them and reject or refine a name if necessary. Monitoring our own composing and discussing what we've learned about what happens when we and our students compose also leads to naming.

Sometimes we rename ideas for our students to make these ideas more accessible. Though we generally use the "term of art" from the disciplines as the names for things (to meet the correspondence concept most closely), sometimes these terms are difficult for our students and stand in the way of understanding. For example, Michael and Jeff (Smith and Wilhelm 2007) suggest creating more readily accessible names for some grammatical terms. When Jeff realized that his students did not understand what an adverbial conjunction was and how it worked, he began calling it a *logical linker*, which was more helpful to them. Michael and his ninth graders made lists of *promise words*—subordinating conjunctions and relative pronouns that promise a two-part (instead of a complex) sentence. On some occasions, Jeff uses neologisms to teach, such as *twofer* or *threefer* to describe details that convey multiple kinds of information. Michael and his preservice teacher education students call themselves *Englishers* to remind themselves that the seventh through twelfth graders with whom they are working might have a different attitude toward their subject. Likewise, when Jim is working with student teachers, who are often worried about classroom management, they use the term *magnet students* for the one or two students in each class to whom the other students are attracted—the students whose leadership they can enlist to support the health of the classroom community.

How We Use Lists as Intellectual Work

Once we have named something, we often put it into a list. A list may seem a rudimentary text structure, but George Hillocks (1995) explains that it is one of four basic text structures, that it does important intellectual work, and that it can elicit "any of the basic affective responses" (119): the empathic (in which the reader enters and lives through the world of the text), the opus-oriented (in which the text focuses the reader's attention on discovering relationships among its parts for expressing deep insights), the detached/logical (in which the reader's attention is focused on the step-by-step relationship of presented information), and the involved (in which the reader's attention is focused on the values and emotions engendered by the text).

Hillocks isn't alone in being convinced of the power of lists. Take a look at this exchange between the magazine editors of *Der Spiegel* (2009) and world-renowned textual scholar Umberto Eco:

> **Der Spiegel:** Mr. Eco, you are considered one of the world's great scholars, and now you are opening an exhibition at the Louvre, one of the world's most important museums. The subjects of your exhibition sound a little commonplace, though: the essential nature of lists, poets who list things in their works and painters who accumulate things in their paintings. Why did you choose these subjects?

> **Umberto Eco:** The list is the origin of culture. It's part of the history of art and literature. What does culture want? To make infinity comprehensible. It also wants to create order—not always, but often. And how, as a human being, does one face infinity? How does one attempt to grasp the incomprehensible? Through lists, through catalogs, through collections in museums and through encyclopedias and dictionaries. There is an allure to enumerating how many women Don Giovanni slept with: it was 2,063, at least according to Mozart's librettist, Lorenzo da Ponte. We also have completely practical lists—the shopping list, the will, the menu—that are also cultural achievements in their own right. (www.spiegel.de/international/zeitgeist/0,1518,659577,00.html)

Moving away from the high-brow we find equally strong endorsements for the power of listing. Here's what the story / opinion-sharing website Squidoo has to say:

> As odd as it may seem, there is power in putting your tasks or goals on paper. Now it's real. You can see it. You're committed. That little voice in your head will begin to nudge you in the right direction. *Putting a goal in writing* helps refine your focus and propels you forward with intent.
>
> Once you can hold that piece of paper in your hand, it brings visibility to the tasks / chores / goals and you'll increase the likelihood that you will get the job done, whatever that may be. (www .squidoo.com)

In short, naming and listing are hugely important both in school and out. As a consequence, they are well worth teaching.

Model Unit: What Do We Need to Survive and Thrive in Middle School?

➤ *Unit ideas*

The question stem *what do we need to survive and thrive?* can easily be adapted for use in all content areas: *what do we need to survive and thrive . . . on a camping trip, in outer space, in algebra class, in the future (in a career, for example), in case of a terrorist attack, as a sustainable planet, while living in another culture, on a trip to Italy?*

This unit on surviving and thriving in middle school requires and rewards naming and listing. The phrasing of the essential question also suggests a culminating project—to develop a guidebook for new middle schoolers and their parents, as well as an introductory video on navigating middle school. Both include checklists: what you need to know about your locker, about getting around the school, about your schedule, what to do if you are bullied, etc.

Composing to Plan: Knowledge of Purpose and Context

➤ *For more information about the five types of composing/ knowledge, see Chapters 3 and 4.*

Because one of our major instructional principles is to use student experience as a bridge to new challenges, we begin by asking students to share their own nicknames or those of others they know. We then ask them what that nickname indicates in terms of personality traits, feelings, comparisons, implications, evaluations, and the like. As an example, Jeff shares that his middle school nickname, Nerf, came about because his head of long, curly hair looked like a nerf ball (and also implied a certain flexibility and lovability, or so he likes to think).

After sharing nicknames and what can be inferred from them, students discuss what nicknames are most interesting, informative, and memorable. From here, we ask students to invent a favored nickname for themselves, for a favorite popular culture figure, a potential band, a wrestler, or a product like a new cell phone. This activity tunes students in to names in literary texts. Peter Rabinowitz (1998) identifies names as well as initials as a "rule of notice"—authors typically choose them to imply deeper meanings.

Next the students brainstorm criteria for a good name: it is accurate, it makes what is named easier to remember and more understandable, it captures some kind of essence, it gets after the right feeling, it is memorable, and so on.

We then move on to lists, asking the kids to think of times in their lives when they have made lists. As they share their ideas, we share ours, and ask the students to keep adding to their list of when they use or might use lists. Jeff typically shares that his family has a grocery list on their kitchen counter. Any time a family member wants an item from the grocery store or notices that the family is getting short on some necessity, he or she puts that item on the list. When Jeff asks his students what the purpose of this list might be, answers vary from *keeping track of what you need* to *making sure you don't forget things and have to go back to the store* to *helping the person going to the store know what to buy*, all functional purposes students can relate to. We might call these functions *keeping track* and *place holding* and argue that they help us remember in ways that promote efficiency and save time.

Jeff also shares the "basic five" kayaker's list. Every kayaker, before leaving home, makes sure she has her (1) boat, (2) PFD (lifejacket), (3) paddle (or *blade*), (4) helmet, and (5) skirt. If she forgets one of these, she will not be kayaking but rather become the shuttle bunny, carrying other people's kayaks and transporting her friends to the put-in and from the take-out. This list also helps promote efficiency. Jeff also makes the point that on a river or backpacking trip, food and gear lists become more complicated, high-stakes, and important. There's no opportunity to run to the store for something that is missing.

The lists are the starting point for using what's on them in other kinds of text structures. For instance, Jeff always reorganizes the family grocery list to match the aisles in the grocery store before he heads off. This makes doing the shopping much easier. Likewise, gear lists are divided up among rafts (or packs or backpacks, depending on the kind of trip)—one raft is the kitchen boat, another the groover barge, etc. Once again, we see how text types are all about functionality—what kind of work

➤ *Lesson ideas: Brainstorming and monitoring life experiences*

➤ *Crux moves*

needs to get done—and embeddedness. Text structures often lead to or are nested in one another.

We next ask students to find and analyze the writing they and their family members do, focusing on how lists figure into each kind of writing. We combine the lists the next day and brainstorm the purposes of each type of writing, as well as consider how listing is implicated. This kind of ethnographic research makes students' own lives and literacies worthy of study and connects their lives to the inquiry and learning at hand.

Sometimes, Jeff's grocery list will include an item like "green clover-looking thing for guacamole." It takes some discussion to figure out that what is meant is *cilantro*. The description, though amusing, is not going to be helpful to the grocery shopper. What's needed is a name that matches the name used by the grocery store.

Composing to Plan: Procedural Knowledge of Substance

➤ *Lesson idea: Making and monitoring lists*

In the next activity, we give students some contexts in which people might make lists and ask, *when might such a list be useful? what kinds of items might go on the list?* Some possible contexts are:

Celebration/holiday presents to buy

Expenses of owning/operating a cell phone (bicycle, car, apartment)

Repairs to be done around the house

Packing for school (music or athletic practice, vacation)

Requirements for the perfect boyfriend/girlfriend (date, meal, school, home, surviving middle school)

Materials needed to build a fence (write a guidebook or complete a video guide for surviving middle school)

Bucket list for the summer (school year/life)

Once students have completed the activity on their own, they compare and add to their lists in pairs. *Were there items or ideas that were hard to name? How did they go about trying to find or assign names to things?*

As we debrief, we compose for procedural knowledge of substance by listing procedural strategies for generating lists: search your memory, use your imagination, rehearse a process and consider what you need at each step, use a brainstorming technique, work with someone else, attend to surroundings, and so on.

We also classify the kinds of lists we've identified according to various kinds of logic or patterns of thought, which leads students toward procedural knowledge of form. One of Jeff's classes recently came up with:

Unorganized (simple) lists

Paired lists—for different kinds of items at two separate grocery stores, for example, a food co-op or a farmer's market and the local national chain

Matching lists—a list of people to get holiday gifts for and a list of possible gifts for each person, for example

Reference/compiled lists: dictionaries, telephone lists, lists of team members

Ranked lists: by importance, chronology, size, intensity, the order in which something will be found (items in the grocery store, for example) or experienced, the likelihood of possible outcomes

Play lists (which might be sequenced by personal preference)

Top-ten lists in order of preference or importance and influence

Scrapbooks: a collection of items in chronological or some other significant order

The important thing is for students to understand that lists always occur in a problem-solving situation and are made for a particular purpose. Depending on the purpose of the list and the possible relationships of the items listed, the order of the list might be significant—an idea explored below in composing to practice.

➤ *Crux moves*

Composing to Practice: Generating Lists

Once students understand the importance and contexts of naming and listing and have started thinking about how to do so, we give them plenty of practice generating lists. The following group techniques can be used to get started with any thought pattern/text structure, as long as students have some prior experience with and knowledge of that pattern.

➤ *Lesson ideas*

➤ *Speaking and listening standard 1 for each grade level specifies working in groups.*

- *Popping corn.* Students throw out ideas to the group. For example, to develop knowledge of purpose and context, students could respond to *when do we need to name things? what are the purposes of naming? what would be a good name for* X? Usually, a scribe records the ideas on the board or anchor chart, which can be studied and refined later.

- *Stretching.* Students name a specific number of ideas (40, 77, 100). They can work individually, then in pairs, then in larger groups, as needed to come up with the requisite number. Qualitative research encompasses a similar idea called the *forced memo.* Every now and then, the researcher reads through data and forces herself to write about the data, to name what it means to her, what connections she might see, etc. It is akin to the next two techniques in that it accesses unconscious processes and attempts to overcome conscious resistance. Knowledge retrieval, knowledge creation, and creativity can often be enhanced by accessing the unconscious.

- *Focused meditating* (Latin for paying single-minded attention). Students take three or more deep breaths, relax, then try to block out all other thoughts except the topic of the brainstorm. If the mind strays, as it will, they refocus on the topic as soon as they realize they are straying. After a specific amount of time, they write down whatever has come to mind.

- *Freewriting.* Students let their thoughts flow without worrying about spelling or grammar or punctuation. The goal is to free their mind. Typically the teacher sets a goal—*write for five minutes* or *fill three pages*, for example. Then they just write. If they have nothing to say, they still keep their pencil or pen moving on the paper (or their fingers moving on the keyboard), even if just to write *I don't know what to say about how to name X* or *I can't think of what I might need to survive middle school* or *I can't think of anything X suggests to me.* Eventually, the ideas come.

- *Brainwriting* (pass-around or gallery walk). Students work in a group, but each one first thinks and writes individually. Within a time limit (three minutes, for example) they write down a specified number of ideas on their own sheet of paper. Papers are then passed to the next person in the row or circle. Students read the ideas passed to them and use them to trigger new ideas to add to the sheet. After this has been done a number of times, students, as a group, discuss, refine, and combine the ideas on the sheets. In the gallery walk version, students list and post their ideas on chart paper, and members of the class then walk around, spending at least one minute at each chart adding at least one idea. Several studies (Diehl and Strobe 1987 and 1991, for example) have found that people who first brainstorm in isolation before sharing with the group consistently generate more and better ideas than those who brainstorm as a group from the beginning. They don't limit their ideas initially and do cross-pollinate one another's ideas during the sharing that follows. Ideas are first recorded immediately and privately. Everyone has a clear purpose and an equal deliverable. Then all ideas are valued and responded to. Students who do not like to speak in front of the group are not hampered.

■ *Rolestorming.* Brainstorming during which students imagine themselves to be someone else with an interest in the topic (what would they name this thing if they were someone else? what would they list about surviving middle school if they were a parent? teacher? partner? best friend? opponent? someone from a different culture?) or they take on the *mantle of the expert* (Wilhelm 2002/2012).

■ *Thinking metaphorically* (ideas adapted from http://celestinechua.com/blog/25-brainstorming-techniques/). Brainstorming names using similes or metaphors. Students complete a model sentence: _____ is/was/are/were like _____. In the first blank they put a description, phrase, or idea they are trying to name or explore. Then they try to come up with as many answers as possible for the second blank, writing them down as they do. After they have produced a list of options, they look over their ideas. What kinds of ideas come forward? What patterns or associations do they find? How could an idea be distilled into a single-word name or short phrase?

■ *Drawing.* Students draw the essence of an idea and then use the drawing to brainstorm names. Conversely, they can illustrate a term or concept without words (Wilhelm 2004/2012).

■ *Making analogies* (ideas adapted from http://celestinechua.com/blog/25-brainstorming-techniques/). Students put an idea or goal alongside similar ideas or goals in different areas/contexts and identify parallel themes/solutions. For example, if they are trying to name a piece of art or artistic technique, they look at titles and techniques from music, gaming, dance, etc. Are there any commonalities? What worked for each of the others that they can adopt or adapt in some way?

■ *Triggertalking/triggerwriting.* Taking the best ideas generated by another brainstorming techniques and using them as triggers for more ideas.

This is quite a list. We use only those techniques that we think will help our students develop procedural knowledge of substance in the context of the unit. For example, if naming and listing are easy, as in this unit on what is needed to survive middle school, we complicate and enrich things with rolestorming, putting the kids in the position of parents or teachers. When we read a piece written for teachers

➤ *Writing anchor standard 8 and speaking and listening anchor standards 2, 4, and 6 deal with multiple perspectives and multimodality.*

➤ *Seeing patterns and thinking multimodally is implied in all the reading and writing standards at all levels.*

about the transition to middle school, we brainstorm related terminology that would be friendly and useful to students.

Composing to Practice: Developing Vocabulary

Naming is obviously aligned with developing vocabulary. Research (Graves 2009) clearly demonstrates that having kids memorize definitions does not develop vocabulary, because students are not generating their own understanding and using it in context. In other words, they are not composing to plan. Graves argues that vocabulary development is fostered by four actions. The first is wide reading. In inquiry, students read widely around a central issue, and relevant terms are repeated and co-produce an understanding of other related terms. The second is being taught individual words *in context* and immediately using them in reading and composing. Third is developing strategies like how to use context to discern meaning. Fourth is having word consciousness—understanding how words are made (Greek and Latin roots, prefixes and suffixes, etc.).

Composing to Practice: Organizing Lists/Procedural Knowledge of Form

It's also important to help students understand that lists can be organized in a meaningful order and thus become *significant*. For example, Jeff's list of chores for the weekend is a simple (unorganized) list unless the completion of one chore is necessary to complete other chores, in which case the list would have a meaningful chronological and hierarchical order.

Comparing lists and reorganizing them to be significant is a great way to introduce students to the notion of patterning and give them practice noticing patterns. This develops procedural knowledge of the list form and prepares them for work with more complex text structures. The order in the lists below is significant and meaningful:

Bothered	Comfortable	Water
Irritated	Well-off	Food
Angered	Affluent	Shelter
Outraged	Superrich	Affection

In the first list, the adjectives go from least to most angry. There is a progression of intensity. There is a logic of superordination and subordination. If the items were rearranged, the implicit meaning and usefulness of the list would be changed. The second list goes from less to more rich; the third list moves through Maslow's hierarchy

➤ *Reading anchor standard 10, language anchor standard 3*

➤ *Language standards 4a and d at any grade level*

➤ *Language standards 4 and 5*

➤ *Language standard 4b at any grade level*

➤ *Lesson ideas*

of human needs from what is most to lesser importance to immediate survival. Understanding the pattern gives more power to the list and allows the reader to anticipate what might come next or what might be added to the list and where it would be placed. Adding items to existing lists is another great exercise for students that involves procedural knowledge of substance and form.

A great follow-up is to provide lists with an element that does not quite fit, and then ask students to make other such lists. For example in a unit on teen health, Jeff provides this list:

Banana

Apple

Snickers

Rice cracker

Students quickly identify that the list is about healthy snacks (or complex carbohydrates, if they're really paying attention!) and that Snickers (filled with simple sugars) is the outlier. They then make and circulate other food- and health-related lists with an outlier. Groups identify the topic of the list, identify the outlier, add to the list, and reorganize it into a significant list if they can.

Composing to Practice: Survival Simulations

Three free simulations available at http://wilderdom.com/games/descriptions/ SurvivalScenarios.html prompt students to create significant lists related to survival. They also let students develop, name, and reflect on skills in group interacting, speaking, and listening that we use throughout the school year.

NASA Exercise: Survival on the Moon

The first simulation has been developed by NASA for use by teachers. Obviously there are many science connections here.

Scenario

You are a member of a space crew originally scheduled to rendezvous with a mother ship on the lighted surface of the moon. However, mechanical difficulties have forced your ship to land at a spot some 200 miles from the rendezvous point. During reentry and landing, much of the equipment aboard has been damaged. Since survival depends on reaching the mother ship, the most critical items available must be chosen for the 200-mile trip. Below are the fifteen items left intact and undamaged after landing. Rank them in terms of their importance for your crew in allowing you to reach the rendezvous point. Place the number 1 to the right of the most important item, the number 2 to the right of the second most important, and so on through number 15 for the least important.

Students work alone, and then in groups who must reach consensus, so they end up with two sets of rankings.

Your Ranking NASA Ranking

_____ Box of matches _____

_____ Food concentrate _____

_____ Fifty feet of nylon rope _____

_____ Parachute silk _____

_____ Portable heating unit _____

_____ Two .45-caliber pistols _____

_____ One case of dehydrated milk _____

_____ Two 100-pound tanks of oxygen _____

_____ Stellar map _____

_____ Self-inflating life raft _____

_____ Magnetic compass _____

_____ Twenty liters of water _____

_____ Signal flares _____

_____ First-aid kit, including injection needle _____

_____ Solar-powered FM receiver–transmitter _____

Answers

Item Ranking and NASA's Reasoning
After students have completed their rankings, the answers are shared and compared to the individual and group responses.

Box of matches, 15 (virtually worthless—there's no oxygen on the moon to sustain combustion)

Food concentrate, 4 (efficient means of supplying energy requirements)

Fifty feet of nylon rope, 6 (useful in scaling cliffs, making repairs, and tying materials together)

Parachute silk, 8 (protection from the sun's rays)

Portable heating unit, 13 (not needed, since you're on the lit side of the moon)

Two .45-caliber pistols, 11 (possible means of self-propulsion in low gravity)

One case of dehydrated milk, 12 (bulkier duplication of food concentrate)

Two 100-pound tanks of oxygen, 1 (most pressing survival need; weight is not a factor since gravity is one-sixth of the Earth's—each tank would weigh only about 17 pounds on the moon)

Stellar map, 3 (primary means of navigation—star patterns appear essentially identical on the moon as on Earth)

Self-inflating life raft, 9 (CO_2 bottle in military raft may be used for propulsion)

Magnetic compass, 14 (the magnetic field on the moon is not polarized, so it's worthless for navigation)

Twenty litres of water, 2 (needed to replace liquid lost on the light side of the moon from perspiration)

Signal flares, 10 (can be used to signal distress when the mother ship is in sight)

First-aid kit, including injection needle, 7 (needles connected to vials of vitamins, medicines, etc., fit special aperture in NASA space suit)

Solar-powered FM receiver–transmitter, 5 (for communication with mother ship, but FM requires line-of-sight transmission and can only be used over short ranges)

Scoring

To the left of each item, mark the number of points your score differs from the NASA ranking, then add up the points. Disregard plus or minus differences. The lower the total, the better your score.

0–25 excellent

26–32 good

33–45 average

46–55 fair

56–70 poor (suggests use of Earth-bound logic)

71–112 very poor (you're one of the casualties of the space program!)

We follow this activity by having small groups of students complete a desert survival simulation, a nuclear holocaust survival simulation (ranking people and skills in relation to their importance to the survival of humanity), and a more complex winter survival simulation (all available online). We allow lots of time for students to reflect on and consolidate what they have learned using these debriefing questions:

- How were decisions made?
- Who influenced the decisions and how?
- How could better decisions have been made?
- Did people listen to one another? If not, why not?
- What roles did group members adopt? How were these roles similar and different?
- How were disagreement and conflict managed?
- What kinds of behavior helped or hindered the group? What were the costs and benefits of this behavior in terms of group dynamics and survival?
- How did people feel about the decisions?

    How satisfied were you with the final decisions? (Each student rates his/her satisfaction out of 10, then each group determines a group average. The groups compare/discuss their satisfaction level with other groups.)

- What have you learned about the functioning of successful or unsuccessful groups?
- How would you do the activity differently if you were asked to do it again?
- What situations at work/home/school do you think are similar to this exercise?
- What are the criteria for creating a significant list? (Possible ways of judging: definitely needed, maybe needed, not needed; absolutely necessary, helpful, luxury item or not useful. Crux moves: Do you have everything that is needed? Can you justify your rankings with criteria related to the situation? If you have included luxuries, can you justify doing so?)

Composing Rough and Final Drafts

After practicing with the listing activities previously noted, we prompt students to create lists related to the context of our *what do we need to survive and thrive in middle school?* inquiry. Here are some possible prompts, along with lists students have created:

➤ For more information on why the five types of composing and the five types of knowledge are essential to planning for maximum student learning, see Chapters 3 and 4.

Who might help us understand what is necessary to surviving in middle school? (Middle schoolers, teachers, counselors, parents, psychologists, researchers)

Who might use our lists? (Middle schoolers, parents, middle school teachers, middle school counselors, elementary school teachers, elementary guidance counselors)

What do students need to know and be able to do to survive the first few days of middle school? (How lockers work, how class changes work, how to navigate the halls, how the lunch room works, how the guidance office works, how team teaching and home room works, how the bus schedule works, how physical education works, how advising groups work)

These names and lists lead directly to planning and creating the guidebooks and introductory videos. Doing so reinforces composing to plan and knowledge of purpose and context while simultaneously generating procedural knowledge of substance leading to declarative knowledge of substance. As students rearrange the lists by order of importance or when the challenges and needs will be encountered, they use procedural knowledge of form to develop declarative knowledge of form.

Because naming and listing are relatively simple and familiar actions, students do a lot of drafting and revising in short order. They can publish their lists on chart paper displayed around the classroom, and use these lists as the grist and raw material for maps, webs, graphic organizers, and other texts that help them understand additional patterns and compose more sophisticated text structures.

During drafting, it's important to apply the critical standards the class has developed while composing to plan and composing to practice. Students typically stipulate that names must be accurate and must help readers understand and remember and that lists must be comprehensive and organized/patterned to be as explanatory and usable as possible. We ask students to use these criteria (and revise them as necessary) as they draft lists together and then individually.

Before final revision, publishing, and archiving, we show our lists and videos to a focus group of fifth graders from the neighboring elementary school and their parents and teachers, since they are the audience for our work.

➤ *Writing anchor standard 4*

Developing Classroom Culture

For units taught early in the year, we name and list guidelines for peer responders: what would a good peer response group sound like, look like, feel like? We use these lists to articulate standards and processes for helping each other, like the PQP (or PQS) protocol: begin by saying what you like (*praise*), things you wonder about the

➤ *Lesson idea*

content, form, and process of composing (*questions*), and your suggestions for improving the names or lists (*polish/suggestions*). We also introduce students to stems for asking helpful questions (*tell me more about why X is on the list? why did you put X before Y?*) and making respectful suggestions (*I wonder what would happen if . . .*). (For more stems and suggestions, see Wilhelm 2007.)

Composing to Transfer: Meanings and Effects of Naming and Listing

The CCSS require that students attend to and understand the meanings and effects of various kinds of text structures, so we make sure our students develop this kind of knowledge as they work with names and lists.

Throughout all of our units, we use daily formative assessments so that students can name and celebrate what they understand and we can name what they know and what they could do next if we provide the right instructional support. The work students do each day gives us all feedback on our progress.

➤ *Lesson idea*

Another specific formative assessment we use a lot in this unit is "muddy/marvy" (Wilhelm, Wilhelm, and Boas 2009). In this technique, students use one sticky note to record a new insight they've gained, whether about naming, listing, or the topic of the inquiry. (They can also note how they came to reach this insight or say why it's important.) On a second sticky note, they write down one question or concern they have about their understanding or about their progress toward the culminating project. These notes are posted on charts labeled *Muddy* and *Marvy*. We read through these de facto "lists" noting patterns of understanding and misunderstanding.

➤ *Lesson idea*

We conclude the unit with some fairly simple reflective composing using the past–present–future protocol:

- Past: What did I learn about naming, listing, and/or understanding the transition to middle school? How did I help others throughout the unit?
- Present: At this moment, what do I find most important about the unit? In what other ways can we use naming and listing and be of service to others right now? How can I name myself and others, as well as ideas, in ways that will be positive for me and those around me?
- Future: How do I anticipate naming and listing will help me in the future in school and in my life? In what other ways might we provide service to other people through lists, names, guides, and videos? How could the unit be improved for next year's students?

This kind of composing to transfer helps students consolidate what they have learned and consider its value and future use. Teachers can also benefit, by soliciting feedback to inform future instruction.

We conclude the unit by looking at some poems and songs that use naming and listing—for example, "My Favorite Things" (perhaps the John Coltrane's version!) and "The Great Lover," by Rupert Brooke, and looking at the kinds of responses this organization technique elicits.

➤ *Lesson idea*

Conclusion

Hillocks (1995) argues that a basic text structure must have the capacity to support the four kinds of response we describe at the beginning of this chapter. He makes the case for "significant" lists this way:

> Certainly, lists have an informational function, eliciting a *detached response*. I would not have my grocery list any other way. Can lists generate any other response? Poets and songwriters know they can, and they use lists to generate *empathic responses*. A case in point is the song "My Favorite Things" from *The Sound of Music*. According to Elliott (1960), one of the earliest forms of satire was the list of curses or invective used to drive scapegoats from communities during the ritual of ablution. Such lists of invective occur in various domestic and even international disputes, when one party threatens another with a list of scurrilous names. The intended effect of the list is to frighten the recipient in a very direct way (the *involved response*). The abuse leads one to expect, directly or indirectly, bodily harm or worse. Finally, the satiric technique of presenting a list in which one item contrasts with all the others, thereby undercutting its implication (*zeugma*), demands the *opus-oriented response*. A famous example occurs in Pope's "The Rape of the Lock" in the description of Belinda's dressing table:

> > Here files of pins extend their shining rows,
> > Puffs, powers, patches, Bibles, billet-doux.

> Placing Bibles in this list strongly implies that Belinda ranks her religion along with the other accouterments of appearance. (118–19)

Here, Hillocks is going after what we discussed in Chapter 3: deep understanding of how the content is structured in particular and nameable ways (procedural and declarative knowledge of form) in order to make particular points and achieve particular effects (procedural and declarative knowledge of substance at the local and global, surface and deep levels, a major thrust of CCSS standards for reading and writing). This constitutes deep understanding of the text at hand as well as how the text structure itself works and can work in general. Promoting such understanding with lists lays the groundwork for doing the same with the more complex text structures to come.

Our major point is this: listing and naming are important text structures in themselves and are basic prerequisites to all the other text-structures considered to be informational/explanatory, so kids had better learn how to generate and use these thought patterns in the wide-awake ways Hillocks delineates. Names and lists are also a fantastic way to introduce the five kinds of knowledge and five kinds of composing.

CHAPTER 7

Getting to the Point

The Process and Promise of Summary

Sometimes you have to get to the gist and get there quickly. Sometimes it's not just efficient but absolutely necessary to get right to the heart of the matter. When Jeff is kayaking down a blind drop, signals from the kayaker in front summarize what is absolutely necessary to know about danger spots—nothing more and nothing less is communicated. The signals provide the tersest possible summary of what needs to be known.

Sometimes at school Jeff needs to find out or convey something about a student or situation to his team teaching partner. He might have two minutes between classes to communicate or absorb what needs to be known. He and his partner better be super summarizers or things can go awry!

Jeff's daughter Jasmine didn't understand the concept of summary for quite some time. When she was little, Jeff would come home from work and in the bustle to get dinner ready and read to the girls before bedtime, ask his wife, "So what did you do today?" Jeff's wife, Peggy, would cut to the events Jeff couldn't already assume: "We went to the library and playgroup." Jazzy would stamp her feet. "*No!* First we got up and had raisin bran and apple juice for breakfast. Then we cleaned up and got dressed. Then. . . ." It has remained a family joke, although Jazzy long ago learned the advantages of getting to the point through summary.

Similarly, Michael and Karen have learned not to ask their daughters Catherine and Rachel about movies the girls have seen recently, especially if Michael and Karen have any interest in seeing the movies. Catherine details every turn of the plot and Rachel, who has an uncanny memory for dialogue, chimes in with many of the lines. On the other hand, they've experienced years of frustration after asking that classic

➤ *Summarizing is explicitly mentioned in reading anchor standard 2; implied in writing standard 2b, levels 6–12; and necessary to meeting several other standards.*

81

parent question, "What's happening at school?" Hard to believe that two young women who can talk so long about a movie can be so abrupt when asked to talk about school! In both cases, all Michael and Karen want is a summary—but they get either too much information or too little.

The art of abstracting key content from one or many information sources has always been an essential part of disciplinary learning in social studies, science, math, and many other domains. You can't pursue a discipline unless you carry a summary of the basic facts and principles for specific situations forward through your problem solving.

> ➤ *History/social studies and science and technical writing standard 2b, any grade level, and reading anchor standard 2*

There are also many business applications for summaries. Michael's wife Karen often mentions how PowerPoint presentations are key to working with her purchasing group. Efficient meetings require just the right amount of information. Too much or too little isn't useful. Jim likewise finds that summaries provided at faculty meetings, particularly regarding ever changing school policies, are essential for keeping him in the loop.

Summary is also an integral part of navigating our everyday lives in this age of information glut. We keep abreast of world affairs by listening to news bites or reading Internet summaries. We base investment decisions on economic and stock market updates and the patterns we discern in these summaries. We often go to movies after reading brief descriptions and reviews like those on the Rotten Tomatoes website. By using good summaries and knowing how to summarize ourselves, we make more effective decisions in less time.

Summary Summarized! Why Summary Matters

Summary is a basic cognitive skill and a general process of reading and composing, meaning that all successful readers and composers necessarily bring forward the gist of a text every time they successfully read or compose (see Wilhelm, Baker, and Dube 2001; Wilhelm 2012). The summary thought pattern is the basis of other forms such as the abstract, précis, synopsis, recap, compendium, digest, sketch, character sketch, résumé, memo, lab report, review, executive summary, and various forms of microwriting. Equally important, summary is employed in some capacity in virtually every kind of writing. Think of a novelist providing a quick account of the developments that got the characters to where they are in the story or a teacher writing a lesson plan for a substitute or a grant writer discussing related research. Closer to home, try to think of any of your own writing in which you didn't do some summarizing.

Although all forms of summary share many essential characteristics, different kinds of summaries in different contexts written for different purposes vary in important ways. When the three of us write an abstract of research we've done, we have to articulate our research questions, the theoretical background for our work, the methods we employed, and our most important findings. When Michael wrote a research newsletter, though, he focused only on findings and implications. The conventions differ with the kind of summary and how it's used for particular purposes in specific situations. This chapter deals with the general processes of summarization in relation to the five kinds of knowledge and composing, but slight tweaks are necessary to develop the task- and text-specific processes required by the purpose, context, and structure of the text being summarized, be it a character sketch, a résumé, a review, or something else.

How Do We Summarize?

Jacqueline Berke (2007), in her classic composition text *Twenty Questions for the Writer*, asserts that summary is briefly and accurately recounting the main points in a larger body of information and that the problem the summarizer faces is "how to strip it bare of details and implications; how to condense and communicate its core meaning" (129). She maintains that this is a highly creative and intellectually profound task, and researchers into the process would agree (see, for example, Van Dijk et al. 1977 and Brown and Day 1983). Berke argues that "there is no greater challenge to the intellect and no more accurate test of understanding than the ability to filter an idea through your mind and restate it briefly *in your own words*. Indeed, to read and study efficiently; to do research; to take satisfactory notes; to write papers, critiques, and examinations; to grasp an idea and hold it in the mind, to carry it forward to the next required task—all require the ability to 'boil down' materials to manageable scope and see their basic purpose, their main points, and the relations of these points to one another" (129). Berke summarizes the basic process of all summarization this way: "Capture the purpose and topic, the key details, and the pattern expressed by the relationships between those details to communicate the key idea(s)."

➤ *Reading anchor standard 5*

Notice how Berke highlights knowledge of purpose, substance, and form.

Brown and Day (1983) focus explicitly on just how one accomplishes this process. Based on their seminal research and that of Van Dijk et al. (1977), they identify six macro-rules for summary—the crux moves students must master to compose summaries and therefore the ones we focus on in composing to practice.

The first two macro-rules involve *deletion*: summarizers must discard both trivial and redundant information. The next two rules involve *substitution*, of a superordinate

➤ *Crux moves*

term for a list (called a *generalization rule*) and a superordinate action for a list of actions—(called an *integration rule*; this was the young Jazzy's problem—she did not integrate actions that fell under a larger category like "we ate breakfast"). The final two rules involve pure *summary*. First, the summarizer takes a meaningful section of text, like a paragraph or related paragraphs, and then finds an encompassing topic sentence or key detail statement if there is one; if not, the summarizer invents one.

➤ *Reading anchor standard 7*

Producing a summary of a number of texts and data sources is even more challenging than summarizing a single source. This task requires applying all of Brown and Day's macro-rules to the various texts and patterns of meaning (like points of comparison and contrast) to be summarized. This kind of summary is essential in this modern world teeming with rapidly expanding and available sources of information. "Automatic technological summary," or ATS—searching and summarizing data electronically—is a challenge currently being taken on by computational researchers.

Of course, as Paolo Friere and other critical theorists remind us, we must also learn to read and summarize our experience and the world in an effort to reframe and remake that world into one of more possibility. Summarization, in all its forms, is a profound and basic cognitive tool.

Model Unit: What Do We Need to Know to Be Informed Voters?

We teach any kind of text structure in the context of immediate use, and we use inquiry-oriented structured process to develop and reward the requisite knowledge and expertise over time, so that deep understanding and transfer is achieved. This model unit is based on the essential question *what do we need to know to be informed voters?* Students explore what people need to learn about to be informed voters in an upcoming election, an inquiry that rewards reading and composing summaries and also fosters civic engagement. We've done any number of variations: what do we need to know to be an informed citizen, team member, basketball fan, reader of statistics, environmental steward. All of them get kids to summarize.

Composing to Plan: Developing Knowledge of Context and Purpose

➤ *See Chapter 3.*

➤ *Lesson idea*

When we introduce summarization to a class for the first time, we spend a few minutes exploring real-world contexts and purposes of summarization using a technique we call *real-life seek and find*, in which students reflect on when and how they use summaries in their own life. Immersed as they are in the summaries of signs, facial expressions, text messages, and tweets, they usually get us off to a good start. They suggest many contexts in which they must summarize with their friends and family—discussing schoolwork or making social plans in the hallway between classes; agreeing on strategies while playing games; etc. Though the contexts and therefore the purposes vary, purposes generally have to do with the following ideas:

- Understanding necessary information or the point of something.
- Quickly communicating the gist to someone else.
- Learning what to do at the point of need.
- Getting familiar with and retaining crucial information.
- Saving time.
- Turning information into a usable form—into knowledge.
- Managing large quantities of information more easily.
- Carrying forward overarching meanings or themes.
- Finding a point of entry into something complex.
- Separating important and overarching ideas from less important and supporting details (superordination verses subordination).
- Gathering, place holding, and organizing information when doing projects, completing tasks, composing papers, and creating performances

We keep an anchor chart on the wall to which we add purposes and contexts for summarizing as they come up—both in students' lives and in the context of the unit work. This anchor chart reminds students to keep thinking about contexts and purposes of summarization.

Summaries are crucial whenever we characterize something or explore disagreements—actions all inquiry units require. In our units we often have students summarize the scenes, episodes, articles, and primary documents they encounter during the inquiry. Any text or group of texts we read as we pursue an inquiry require place holding major ideas in a series of summaries, communicating these summaries, and continuing to hone and improve the summaries and use them to improve our understanding.

Once students are introduced to this unit inquiry, they begin developing procedural knowledge of substance to generate data for their culminating project: composing a voter's guide (distributed in the community, as well as online) that includes permanent information about voting and being an informed citizen, and information specific to current election.

Students need to know up front how summaries will be important to pursuing the inquiry and producing the culminating projects. It's also important that students make their own spontaneous use of summaries for their own purposes and name how and why they use the summarization strategies.

➤ Lesson ideas

We begin by asking students to find and bring in various manuals and guides: car manuals, video game manuals, guides to vacation planning, and the like. We study these in small groups and identify the specific and general purposes of the guides and the shared elements of all manuals and guides. We then search the Internet to find examples of voter's guides and identify the specific elements of voter's guides.

Then the students research the upcoming election (interviewing local political reporters, contacting local legislators, reading newspaper and online articles) and prepare general lists of perennial topics and topics specific to this election (candidates and their positions, referendum topics and their implications). We then decompose the task by dividing up the topics and planning how we will find further information, validate it, and present it in our voter's guide, which will comprise these elements:

- *Introduction.* "This Foothills Area Voter's Guide has been compiled by students in Boise, Idaho, dedicated to the ideal that all people should have access to nonpartisan information about the why, how, and what of voting and other forms of civic involvement. Some sections are presented in the six languages represented in our class. It is a quick guide to federal, state, and local elected offices, propositions, referendums, initiatives, political parties, and voting issues."

- *Permanent information.*
  Idaho political parties, histories, positions.
  Job description, responsibilities, and terms of each office.
  How to register to vote.
  Voting stations.
  Absentee ballots.
  Informational websites.
  Who currently represents us?
  How to discuss issues with others.
  How to join political interest groups.
  Glossary.

- *Specific information for this election.*

    Date of the election.

    Profiles and platforms for major candidates:

    > Federal: President, senator, representative.

    > State: Governor, lieutenant governor, secretary of state, state superintendent, legislators, judges.

    > Local: Mayor, city council.

    Referendum descriptions: what's at stake, pro/con positions, citizen groups supporting each position.

Composing to Practice: Developing Knowledge of Form and Substance

Because summarizing is both crucial and complex, students need a great deal of practice. We gradually release responsibility to our students by modeling (I do it for you), mentoring (I do it with you in small groups, you do it with me and each other in small groups, you do it with each other), and monitoring (you do it alone). For students to develop expertise, we must model summarizing repeatedly with different kinds of text structures and content within the context of the inquiry unit and mentor students over time, giving them ample assistance and the time and opportunity to practice, practice, practice.

We've already mentioned that summaries entail first getting to the main idea and then expressing it concisely. This is an essential element of reading comprehension: when students can summarize what they've read, they have proven their comprehension. Reading to "mine texts" (Greene 1991) for information is also a major move for composers, and a major way we exercise procedural knowledge of substance.

In his book on think-alouds (Wilhelm 2012, 128ff.), Jeff fully articulates a heuristic useful in helping students "read" for the main idea, self-monitor for correctness, and then use what they have learned to compose a summary. The heuristic (see Figure 7.1) encompasses the macro-rules for summarizing, rules that if followed entail practice in all the crux moves of summarization. A short version is captured by the acronym TDPP: cite the Topic (which might be articulated or need to be surmised), the key Details, how the details were Patterned, and the Point made about the topic by those patterned details. However, different kinds of summaries work in different ways. For example, a useful frame for summarizing narrative is

> ➤ *These devices cover the basic elements of informational, narrative, and argument text as described by the CCSS.*

➤ *All anchor reading standards, especially 1–3, 5; writing standards 5, 8, 9*

Knowledge of Purpose

➤ *History/ social studies and science and technical writing standard 2b, any grade level; reading anchor standard 2*

Procedural Knowledge of Substance and Form

Figure 7.1   Reading for the Main Idea

I.   Identify the topic (or general subject) of the piece.

To find clues:

a)   Look at the title.

b)   Look at the first and last paragraph: the topic is often named and always implied.

c)   Ask yourself, what is discussed through the whole selection? What general subject spreads across the whole text?

d)   Look at captions, pictures, words in bold, headings, and so forth. What do all of these have in common? What do they all have something to do with?

e)   Remind yourself: the topic must connect to all the major details and events from the selection. Caution: not every detail has something to do with the topic. The topic is the common element or connection among the major details.

f)   What do all the major details have in common?

Check yourself. It's not a true topic if:

a)   It's too general or too big (the topic statement suggests or could include many ideas not stated in the text).

b)   It's off the mark, totally missing the point.

c)   It only captures one detail, rather than all the key details.

d)   It captures only some of the details—for example, maybe you didn't think about the ending or the climax or a shift or major change of some kind.

Questions to ask yourself:

a)   Does the topic I've identified give an accurate picture of what the whole selection is about?

b)   Was I as specific as possible in accommodating all the key details?

c)   After naming the topic, can I now fairly specifically picture in my mind what happened or was communicated in the text? Can I picture something radically different that also fits my topic statement? If so, how can I revise my topic statement to correct this problem?

II. Identify the key details/events and the pattern and trajectory they work together to create.

Pay attention to the rules of notice. Authors often plant important ideas in:

a)   Details that reflect or refer to the title.

b)   Details at the beginning of the text or front and center of the picture.

c)   Details at the end.

d)   Surprises, revelations, anytime your expectations are not met.

e)   Repetition, especially repeated details, terms, or ideas.

f)   Attention given to a detail (a long explanation or description, for example).

g)   Subheads, boldface type, italics.

h)   Single-sentence paragraphs.

i)   Changes in character, tone, mood, setting; plot twists.

j)   A question near the beginning or the end.

The overall text is organized into a particular kind of narrative (chronological order), argument (logical presentation of reasoning), or informational/explanatory text (paradigmatic organization). This structure patterns the text in flexible yet predictable ways. This superstructure is usually revealed near the beginning and then throughout the text by the use of transitions and transitional devices that show how ideas are related to one another. (Remember, other structures may be embedded in this superstructure.)

Figure 7.1 *Continued*

Check yourself. It's not a key detail if:

a) It's interesting, but it doesn't develop the topic/lead to the central focus or point of the text.

b) It reminds me of something personally important; however, if removed from the piece, the work would not lose any significant meaning or impact.

c) There are no transitions to other ideas or expression of relationship from this idea to another one.

Questions to ask yourself:

a) Are all the details related to the topic?

b) How do the key details relate to one another?

c) What kind of overall text structure is patterning the details?

d) What pattern do the details make when they are added together?

e) What point does this overall patterning of ideas add up to and imply?

f) What can I extrapolate or interpolate from the pattern?

III. Identify the main idea (the theme or point the author makes about the topic).

a) The statement of main idea that I identify must make a point about the topic and cover the whole selection.

b) Is the main idea directly stated? If not, it must be inferred from the pattern and relationship of the key details.

c) Which details help me decide on the main idea? Why are these details important?

d) The main idea considers how the details relate to one another or lead to one another. (What caused or correlated or led or compared to what?)

e) The main idea must consider the ending and how the details, characters, setting, perspectives, events, and their interactions led to this conclusion.

Check yourself. It's not the main idea if:

a) It is so literal and specific it doesn't allow me to apply the main idea to my own life.

b) It is too general; it's more like a topic statement than a main idea or point.

c) It is true but misses the point of this text. It wasn't what the author was saying about the topic through this combination of these details.

d) It misses the point.

e) It only fits one detail, event, or part of the story, not the coherent whole.

f) It does not incorporate all the details, but only a few.

g) It doesn't fit the ending or final situation.

Questions to ask yourself:

a) What point do the key details repeat and add up to when taken together?

b) Is the main idea or point a statement about the topic?

c) Is it something useful that can help me think or act in the world?

Also consider:

a) Do I agree with the statement as applied as a generalization to life and the world?

c) Will I use this idea to undertake action in the world or to think about the world? Why or why not?

(from Wilhelm 2012)

Declarative Knowledge of Substance and Form

Declarative Knowledge of Substance at Deep Level: How the details (substance) were structured and organized (form) to express a point (deep substance).

➤ *Lesson ideas*

SWBS, or Somebody Wanted . . . But . . . So, which captures the characters, initiating situation, complications, and consequences. Arguments, on the other hand, can be summarized using the CDR heuristic, or Claim, Data, Reasoning (see Smith, Wilhelm, and Fredricksen 2012 for more on the structure of arguments).

Once we've introduced students to summarizing "the word," we move on to summarizing "the world" (Friere's terms), using a variety of activities.

One–minute life summary. Recently, there was a worldwide contest to become the caretaker of a Great Barrier Reef island off the coast of Australia. The single criterion for employment was having led an interesting life. The job application was a video-taped one-minute life summary. Students find and watch examples of these online, rank them based on what was included and excluded, and then film their own. (Later in the inquiry they create videos in roles as candidates, historical figures, or authors they encounter. A video can also be used to summarize a referendum or different positions on a referendum.) We've also done a poem or picture-book variation called What's Most Important About Me.

➤ *Fits within the CCSS emphasis on multimodality*

Summing it up. Students imagine they are placing a classified ad or sending a telegram, where every letter or word they use has a set price. For instance, each word costs ten cents and they have a $2 limit. (Amounts can be adjusted depending on the text and student facility with summarizing.) We often set up a learning station with a folder of articles related to the inquiry. Students practice creating summaries of short texts whenever they have free time. This technique is great for helping students eliminate trivial or redundant material. (Adapted from TeacherVision: www.teachervision .fen.com/skill-builder/reading-comprehension/48785.html#ixzz1WcxaP2Sk.)

Ideas can also be collapsed in imagined "news tickers," tweets, and Facebook updates related to the unit inquiry, perhaps as an author or a character—Obama tweeting about the importance of his health care proposals and their potential effect on the economy, for example. (See Wilhelm 2002/2012 for other ideas about summarizing in role.)

Framing. As students prepare to put together their voter's guide summaries, they have to consider what text structures to use. Should they summarize the positions of candidates separately, or compare and contrast competing candidates' views in the same summary? Should they use problem–solution to explain a water safety referendum? pros–cons? define *water safety* and explain how the referendum would (or would not) achieve it? Once they decide, they prepare a skeleton outline on which to build a paragraph-length summary using that structure.

Figure 7.2 Sentence Frames

Use transition words and overall structural cues to choose the frame that correlates with the structure of the paragraph. Then plug the most appropriate keywords into the frame so it reads as a comprehensible sentence.

If the main structure of the text is description–definition, use the frame "A _____ is a kind of _____ that _____ ."

If the main structure of the text is compare–contrast, use the frame "X and Y are similar in that they both _____ , but X _____ , while Y _____ ."

If the main structure of the text is a sequence, use the frame "_____ begins with _____ , continues with _____ and ends with _____ ."

If the main structure of the text is cause–effect, use the frame "_____ happens because _____ and _____ (and _____) in the context of _____ ."

If the main structure of the text is problem–solution, use the frame "_____ wanted _____ but _____ so _____ ."

(Adapted from eHow: www.ehow.com/how_4579583_summarize-passage-onesentence-summary-frames.html#ixzz1WiPKpge5)

Framing is another form of scaffolding. The "frame" forces students to write within the structure and helps them internalize particular moves and transitions they can use more flexibly and creatively later. It guarantees a level of safety and relative success. It is particularly helpful for struggling students. Here's how it works. Students read a text closely and circle a maximum of ten key concept and transitional words that reveal meaning and structure. Once they know the structure, they summarize using the appropriate sentence frame in Figure 7.2.

ShrinkLits. The book *ShrinkLits* (Sagoff 1970) hilariously summarizes canonical literature into very short poems. The book begins with a poetic summary of the *Elements of Style*, by Strunk and White, to demonstrate why texts should be shrunk to the minimal length:

"Omit needless words!"
said Strunk to White.

"You're right!"
said White.

"That's nice
Advice.
But Strunk,
You're drunk
With words!
Two-thirds
Of those
You chose
For that
Fiat
Would fill
The bill!"

. . .

Students enjoy writing shrinklit versions of political platforms and debates or of books about political issues and intrigue (Joan Bauer's YA novel *Hope Was Here* or *Election*, by Tom Perrota, for example).

Movie clubs. Students form weekend movie clubs and watch classic movies related to elections: *All the President's Men, The Manchurian Candidate, Dave, The Adjustment Bureau, The American President, Mr. Smith Goes to Washington, All the King's Men, Choose Connor Strand*, and even *Napoleon Dynamite* (Vote for Pedro!). If they summarize the movies, they earn extra credit as they are extending their learning both about elections and about summary.

Collapsing lists. A quick technique to develop the substitution strategy (Brown and Day 1983) is to collapse long lists of details into general categories. (This is also a move toward definition, compare/contrast, and classification.) Most magazines, as well as the feature section of newspapers, are filled with lists and articles including lists: Best Summer Reads, Ten Top Autumn Hikes, Reasons to Be Thankful, Hottest New Video Games, etc., etc. Cut off the headline or just provide the list to students and ask them to come up with the headline or general topic. Or make up a list: *brushing teeth/mouthwash/putting on pajamas/saying goodnight to parents* could be collapsed into *getting ready for bed*.

Headlines and captions. This is also good for the substitution strategy. Take articles from the newspaper and cut off the headlines. Students practice writing headlines for stories or match the severed headlines to the "headless" stories. Or separate photos and graphics from their captions and have students match them or write their own captions. (In this unit, we use articles, photos and political cartoons related to the upcoming election. A twofer!)

Slogans. Students enjoy writing slogans for particular candidates or referendums. First have them research and rank various political slogans and come up with criteria: drill the candidate's or referendum's name, use strong words, use poetic words and devices (rhymes, alliteration, assonance, onomotopoeia), catchy, direct and not trumped up, smooth, easily repeatable. Then have them create slogans summarizing the substance of various positions.

Bumper stickers. Students compose bumper stickers that summarize a platform or position.

Talking points. In the role of campaign managers, students create talking points for public meetings on various issues.

Jigsaws. Jigsaws help students learn complicated material by dividing the task into manageable chunks. The technique can be used in any content area. Present the topic to be learned and divide students into small groups. Each student in a group is responsible for reading and summarizing the information relative to a different subtopic, presenting her summary to the group, and justifying the information's importance. Each student's summary is a piece of the jigsaw puzzle, necessary for the complete picture. Each student becomes a teacher, and the workload is divided and conquered. Jigsaws help students decide how to produce their guide and decide which section should go first, next, etc.

Multimodal summaries. Summaries can be composed and presented as dramatic or visual tableaux, with or without words or captions. Examples are a character summarizing events before a Congressional committee, a newscaster reporting on a campaign debate, visual timelines, posters, flowcharts, songs, parodies, MTV videos (see Wilhelm 2002/2012, 2004/2012). It's important that students reflect on how these frames reflect general principles of summarizing and understanding; they need to think heuristically, not algorithmically. Have them articulate general purposes, principles, and moves for summarizing and capture them on an anchor chart.

> ➤ *Fits within the CCSS emphasis on multimodality*

Composing to Draft: Putting It All Together

When it's time to draft the voter's guide summaries on particular candidates or issues, most of the work is already done. Students have accessed and generated material to write about and repeatedly practiced shaping it. Figure 7.3 reviews the summary

Figure 7.3   Research Review on Summarization

- Summarization is very complex and requires repeated practice.
- As a study strategy, summarization promotes deep processing.
- As students link their prior knowledge and personal experiences to main ideas in text, they enhance comprehension and retention.
- Summarizing is a skill at which most adults must be proficient to be successful in work and in life.
- Summarizing allows both students and teachers to monitor comprehension.
- Understanding context, purpose, and general discourse patterns/text structures determines case-specific inclusion and deletion rules: in this specific case, what is significant and therefore put into a summary. (This foregrounds the importance of knowing purpose and context and understanding text structure as prerequisites for writing summaries.)
- Understanding text properties and thought patterns enhances summarization.
- Conversely, summarizing helps students understand the explicit and implicit organizational structures of texts, data, experiences, and lessons.
- Summarizing effectively includes making logical and categorical connections among the details, which leads to the expression of an overall impression or point.
- Understanding patterns among details helps us see the parts as an integrated whole and thus remember the information.
- Summarizing is improved by direct instruction regarding cues that help us notice what information is important, how the text is structured, and the inferences that are implied.
- Summarizing throughout a longer text, data set, or experience is ongoing, gradual, and cumulative (good readers are always summarizing and bringing meaning forward).
- Summarizing and reviewing are processes that integrate and reinforce the learning of major points.

(Brophy and Good 1986; Brown and Day 1983; Kintsch and Van Dijk 1978; Van Dijk 1977, 1979, 1980; Van Dijk et al. 1977; Van Dijk and Kintsch 1983)

essentials we need to keep in mind as we help students with their drafts. (Sharing it with colleagues, particularly from other disciplines, prompts them to think about the usefulness of summarization in their subject area.)

As students work on their first drafts, we show them the following techniques for shaping the draft.

Chunking. Chunking makes a writing task less daunting by decomposing it into steps and sections. Students choose one section of the outline, issue tree, or branch diagram they have composed (see Chapter 11 on classification for complete descriptions of these techniques for naming and dividing ideas into categories) and write that chunk. Then they choose another section. Eventually the sections are stitched together with transitions. This unit is a perfect place to introduce chunking, because various students summarize various ideas (chunks), which are then put together into a guide. In any unit, we can help students see that a prompt or task requires different elements and chunks and they need to decide which ones they want to do first, second, etc.

As professional writers, this is how we work. Jeff wrote all the introductions to the chapters of this book first, then the conclusions, then the descriptions of each text type. Chunking—working on one element at a time—made the task more manageable and allowed him to see his progress. He could also immediately apply what he learned about writing introductions when he wrote the next introduction.

Circles and cross outs. When reading over their notes/drafts, students circle the main details they want to include in their summary and cross out those that should be excluded (at the same time citing their reasons and thus articulating principles and a heuristic for inclusion and exclusion). They highlight transitions and explain what they indicate about text structure, thereby revealing the categorical or logical connections between details. They double-circle repeated words or ideas and, if the summary is still too long, cross out previously circled details (which helps them generalize and integrate).

Structured controversy and forums. Once sections of the voter's guide have been drafted, groups share the positions of their candidate or the positions of one side of a referendum issue. Other groups listen to and summarize the positions/arguments, thus revealing whether the important points are clearly portrayed and understood. Students also rehearse and share their draft summaries by videotaping and getting feedback on a newscast about the key issues facing voters .

➤ *Multimodal literacy, technology, and speaking and listening standards*

Keep, move, change, add, delete. We've used this technique for years (see Smith and Wilhelm 2007) to help students with peer revision. It promotes specific and helpful peer feedback and is particularly useful with summarization. Peer advisors begin with justified praise—a "keep" suggestion and explanation. Then they provide four more suggestions (specific and explained) for adding, deleting, changing, or moving material that will help the summary more closely mirror the text structure of the original or more accurately convey its point. Students must accept or reject each piece of advice they are given and explain why; this ensures that they carefully consider the advice they are given.

Multiple versions/debates. Students compose several variations of a summary and have their peer advisers rank them. Or each member of a group revises a summary, and the group then compares the revisions with the original, discussing the pros and cons of each. (The writer is thus able to explore options, but how the summary will be worded is still up to him or her.)

Composing to Share and Publish the Final Draft

At this point students should have acquired a deep declarative knowledge of summarizing and of the texts they've summarized: of both substance and form at the global (entire text) and local (sentence) level—they should be able to describe how the overall text is structured to convey meaning and how particular words, phrases, and sentences work toward this end. In this unit, students also need to justify how their contribution fits the overall voter's guide and how it will promote informed voting.

This is the time for language study and surface corrections. Particular text structures reward particular kinds of sentence construction—for example, listing typically requires knowing how to use commas to denote ideas in a series or how to use a colon to introduce a series broken out into a list. These techniques are also useful for conveying related ideas succinctly in a summary.

Teaching students how to proofread (Smith and Wilhelm 2007) is also rewarding during this phase. What to proofread for is determined by the overall text structure and the kinds of sentences likely to be found there. For instance, because students writing lists and summaries often use run-on sentences or fragments, this is good time to teach them to proofread for such errors (see Smith and Wilhelm 2007 for specifics on proofreading for fragments and run-ons).

Another common problem in student summaries is the implied or ambiguous pronoun. The implied error usually occurs when the antecedent of the pronoun is not expressed but must be inferred from the general meaning of the sentence or summary. A common manifestation is using *it*, *which*, *this*, *that*, or *these* to refer to an entire preceding phrase or clause rather than to a definite noun. Our students love to make this mistake! Truth be told, it's a problem many adult writers suffer from—*we* know what we're referring to and it's hard to imagine an audience who might not. Implied references can be corrected by summing up the idea of the preceding phrase or clause with a specific noun or by rewriting the sentence to omit the pronoun or to give it a clear antecedent. Here are some examples:

Weak use of *it*: Obama campaigned all week in Ohio and enjoyed it very much.

Better (omit pronoun): Obama campaigned all week in Ohio and enjoyed *this experience in the Buckeye state* very much.

Weak use of *which/that*: Romney was in a state of shock from all the attack ads, *which* was obvious from the vacant expression in his eyes.

Better (provide an antecedent): Romney was in a state of shock from all the attack ads, *a condition that* was obvious from the vacant expression in his eyes.

Also clear: That Romney was in a state of shock from the attack ads was evident from the vacant expression in his eyes.

Weak use of *this*: Herman Cain developed a consuming passion for wielding influence. *This* brought about his downfall.

Better: Herman Cain developed a consuming passion and penchant for wielding influence. *This iniquitous propensity* brought about his downfall.

An ambiguous reference (sometimes called a *double reference*) is a pronoun for which there are two possible antecedents. The result is a lack of coherence and clarity. An ambiguous pronoun can be avoided or corrected in several ways: restate the antecedent; use a synonym for the antecedent; or rewrite the sentence to clarify. We ask students to find such errors, create different ways of fixing them, and rank the fixes, as modeled below:

Ambiguous: Jeff asked Barak Obama to invite *his wife* to the political rally. (Is it Jeff's wife or Obama's wife that Jeff wants to be asked?)

Better: Jeff asked Barak Obama to invite Michelle Obama to the political rally.

Best: Barak Obama and his wife were invited to the political rally by Jeff.

Ambiguous: Obama told Jeff that he was a political guru of genius.

Better: Obama told Jeff that Jeff was a political guru of genius.

Best: Obama considered Jeff a political guru of genius and told Jeff so in front of a national television audience.

Proofreading cue: Look for *it, which, this, that,* and *these* and ask whether the pronoun refers to a preceding phrase or clause, or if it could refer to more than one definite noun. If so, fix it!

The previous activity helps students proofread for these problems (oops, I mean *pronoun reference problems!*) in their own and others' papers. The help of peer editors is particularly important here, because pronoun reference problems occur primarily because the author knows what she is referring to even though the reference may not be clear to the reader.

Composing to Transfer: Getting After Principles of Understanding and Use

As we've said, the five kinds of composing often overlap. Many of the composing to practice activities above are also a kind of composing to transfer—*if* students reflect on general principles of summarizing particular text types (how the macro-rules help us know what to include, collapse and exclude, for example) as they relate to purpose, context, and text structure.

Composing to transfer requires students to articulate heuristics—the general purposes, principles, and moves related to summarizing and situations in which to use summarizing in the future, both in and outside school. Heuristics are transferable.

Any composing that constitutes a formative assessment is also composing to transfer. Any time students produce or evaluate a summary, we have a formative assessment of what they have mastered and still need to work on. We use the three formal formative assessments below throughout the unit; they're all twofers, since they also require summarizing.

One-sentence summaries. On a sticky note, students explain an idea or concept from a reading, presentation, small-group discussion, video, etc. The summary can be subjective or objective. On the reverse side, they cite a principle or justification for something they included or excluded. (The summary could be a small-group consensus.)

3–2–1. Students cite the three most important things they learned (about the topic, or about summarizing), two things that were surprising or interesting, and one question they still have.

Concentric circles/changed thinking diagram. A concentric circle chart helps students articulate declarative knowledge they are consolidating, whether about

Figure 7.4

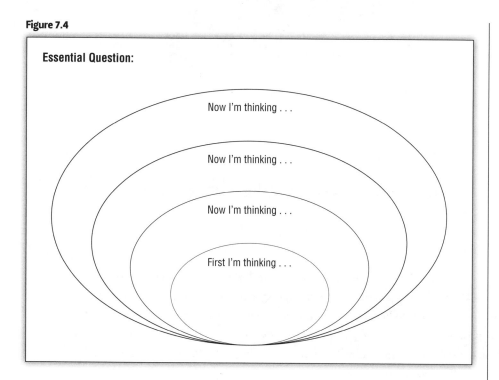

Essential Question:

Now I'm thinking . . .

Now I'm thinking . . .

Now I'm thinking . . .

First I'm thinking . . .

substance or form. After the first week or section of a unit, students fill in the center circle. After the second week (or other natural segment), students fill in the next circle, showing how they have learned something new or have a more nuanced understanding of concepts or processes. They fill in another circle at the end of each of the remaining segments of the unit. At the end of the unit, students have a visible sign of their progress (see Figure 7.4).

Conclusion

The text structures we explore throughout this book form a hierarchy, with one text structure, like naming and listing, being prerequisite to another, like summary. You may have noticed how naming and listing thought patterns both implicitly and explicitly inform the reading and composing of summaries. Summaries, which capture key details, are the foundation for developing the specificity that is the essence of description and process description, our next thought pattern and text structure. So on to Chapter 8!

Getting Oriented and Directed

Description and Process Description/Explanation

Our lives are filled with descriptions. Just today, Jeff's daughter Jazzy called to describe an artwork she is creating and her process of registering for classes and moving into her dorm. His daughter Fiona, a singer-songwriter, emailed him a process description of composing a new song. His friend Frank Dehoney described some heirloom winter beets he is sending Jeff, along with directions for planting and cultivating them.

Michael and his administrative assistant Gwen Miller regularly exchange cooking stories. Their post-Thanksgiving discussion was full of descriptions, both of how their new dishes tasted and how they went about making them. Michael's wife Karen has a birthday coming up. She wants a purse and provided a very precise description so that Michael wouldn't mess up when he bought one.

Jim just had a bookcase delivered to his office. Because the bookcase did not include the hardware for installing the shelves, he had to provide a very precise description of it so that the English department's administrative assistant would know what hardware to order. After the hardware arrived Jim had to listen to a very detailed process description of how to install it.

Description is also featured in the many blogs Jim reads. Today at lunch, for instance, bleedcubbieblue.com, a blog for Chicago Cubs fans, included a description of the Cubs' projected payroll for next season, a description of the qualities and skills the Cubs' general manager is looking for in a new assistant manager, and potential free agents. In another blog, this one on cooking (extrapoundcake.com), Jim read descriptions of a sweet potato risotto ("a skillet full of sautéed sweet potatoes, onion and ginger mixed with soft Arborio rice, dry Riesling wine and a few big dollops of rich mascarpone cheese topped with toasted walnuts for a little crunch") and Riesling wine ("sweet wine that might remind you of pears or apricots").

Why Descriptions and Process Descriptions Matter

Descriptions and process descriptions not only fill our daily lives but also are essential to knowledge making and understanding in all disciplines. Description, as generally construed, is a text that accurately renders the resonant properties of things. Discourse theorists point out that a description can be either objective (concrete and factual) or subjective (personal and involving opinions and feelings). The type an author creates is based on her purpose and the kind of response she wants from an audience.

Descriptions are more sensory and elaborated than lists and summaries. They go beyond the key details to provide some sense of how those details have been experienced. John Updike's oft-anthologized essay "Central Park" is a great example of transforming what could have been a mere list of sensations into a fully realized description of what he experienced on his walk through Central Park on the first warm day after winter.

Berke's *Twenty Questions for the Writer* (2007) highlights description as a basic text in that six of her twenty questions arguably lead to a form of description: how can *X* be described? what kind of person is *X* (character sketch)? what is my memory of *X*? what are the facts about *X* (descriptive factual report)? what is the present status of *X* (descriptive status report)? what is my personal response to *X* (description, but if the process of arriving at this interpretation is described, this would become an explanation or process description)? Four additional questions lead to some form of process descriptions: how did *X* happen? how is *X* made or done? how should *X* be made or done? how should *X* be interpreted? (The last two, depending, could also be viewed as arguments about a process.)

Description is central not only to work in English language arts but also to work across disciplines. *Descriptive science* is considered the basic science category; it includes science "whose emphasis lies in accurate repeatable descriptions such as: X causes A in circumstances B" (Wikipedia, retrieved 9/6/2011). David A. Grimaldi and Michael S. Engel (2007) suggest that descriptive sciences are basic and prerequisite to all understanding, problem solving, design, and other forms of making knowledge. "Descriptive" can be applied to "the array of classical -ologies and -omies: anatomy, archaeology, astronomy, embryology, morphology, paleontology, taxonomy, botany, cartography, stratigraphy, and the various disciplines of zoology, to name a few" (646).

Grimaldi and Engel further maintain that all knowledge in science, math, history, the arts, and the social sciences is based and built on descriptive knowledge. Along these same lines, the oceanographer Daniela Pace (2010) argues that applied science depends on prediction and that prediction depends on description. In other words, scientists can only extrapolate and design interventions and solutions based on thick descriptions. We describe, then we come to understand the relationships in the data, then we can infer the meaning of patterns, which in turn allows us to interpolate and extrapolate data points. The theories that then develop are what allow us to propose, design, and implement solutions.

Declarative knowledge (a term we use often, also known in cognitive science as *descriptive knowledge* or *propositional knowledge*) is knowledge that is, by its very nature, expressed in declarative sentences or indicative propositions. This quality distinguishes descriptive knowledge from what is commonly known as "know-how," or strategic or procedural knowledge (the knowledge of how, and especially how best, to perform some task; describing this performance is the domain of process description).

Description, the first thought pattern we explore in this chapter, is used to relay declarative knowledge so it can be grasped; process description, the second thought pattern featured here, is used to convey procedural knowledge in an explanatory fashion so the procedure can be understood and replicated.

Model Unit: What Is the Best Possible School?

Jeff's daughter Jasmine participated in this unit as a third grader; her teacher that year was part of Jeff's inquiry-across-the-curriculum project. The essential question for this unit is *what is the best possible school?* This question foregrounds description. The major subquestion—*how can we become the best possible school?*—obviously rewards process description. Separate research groups explore how to improve the cafeteria, how to improve the playground, how to improve traffic patterns inside and outside the school, how to improve the library, and how to improve extracurricular offerings. Each group writes many descriptions of a best school, of their school, and of processes for improving the school in a particular arena.

You can see here that scientific understanding is based on the 5 kinds of knowledge.

➤ *Reading anchor standards 1–3*

Composing to Plan Description

We typically employ two primary strategies to help students understand why the text structure we are teaching is important: (1) casting them as ethnographic researchers who examine how they use the text structure in their own lives and (2) creating an instructional context that rewards and requires the use of that structure. Therefore, we begin this unit by asking students to monitor their conversations and communications for a day and log every time they describe something or hear something described, both in and outside school, along with the context and purpose of the description. Then we make sure the unit rewards description.

➤ *Lesson idea*

➤ *Writing anchor standards 1–4*

    Description, of course, is part of any inquiry. Units like *what is a hero? what is right action? what is courage?* foreground definition but also require students to read and write a lot of descriptions. Units like *who was the most influential American? who was our greatest leader? what is the best movie of all time? what is the most innovative musical group?* foreground comparison–contrast but also require description. Sometimes, however, a unit particularly rewards description (*how does place inform behavior? how does culture shape our identity?*) or features a culminating project that involves lots of description (comparing descriptions of the culture of one's school to that of Maycomb County as portrayed in *To Kill a Mockingbird*).

➤ *Writing anchor standards 2 and 7–9*

Composing to Practice Description

Once students have a clear sense of purpose and context, they can begin planning their particular descriptive piece. First we use models to establish criteria for effective descriptions.

    We show students, in small groups, four or five pieces of descriptive writing that have been written by previous students, found online, or composed by us. The examples differ in various ways, but all are successful to some degree. In other words, ranking them is not easy and requires debate and the naming the principles of effective description. Students rank the quality of the examples from best to worst, first on their own, then as a group. Even more important, they explain why they ranked them in this way. What, specifically, makes the best one the best? Why is the second best pretty good, but not quite so good as the best one? In doing this, students articulate and describe critical standards, which are displayed on a class anchor chart to guide their own descriptive writing. (Articulating and using critical standards is an essential and oft neglected area of learning.)

➤ *Lesson idea*

➤ *Lesson idea*

We prompt students in this process by asking them to point out specific techniques and vocabulary the author employs to make his or her writing pack a powerful punch. What "power moves" and "power words" help the reader infer and paint a vivid picture in her mind?

➤ *Language anchor standard 3*

Then we ask them, individually or in small groups, to revise the poorer writing to make it more closely adhere to the critical standards they have articulated. They can cross out the weak moves and boring, inert words ("wimpy moves/words") and replace them with "power" moves and words that show instead of tell. For example: *The river water was _____.* (This could also be turned into a simile [move] using a vivid power-packed adjective and noun [words]: *The river water was as _____ as the _____.*)

➤ *Lesson idea*

Students should now be able to use these criteria to plan how to get and shape the stuff they will need to write their own description, decompose the task, and create a schedule for executing it.

Mentor texts can help students identify other techniques and moves they might want to develop and use in their own descriptions, which can be added to our anchor charts. Good mentor texts for description are *Dr. Dog*, by Babette Cole, and *Let's Do Nothing*, by Tony Fucile. Kids can also do an Internet or library "search and find" for powerful descriptions.

➤ *Grades 6–12 writing standard 4*

Next, we help students meet the articulated criteria. The heart of composing description is expressing evocative specificity from a particular perspective. To do so students must be able to use these crux moves: (1) closely observe and record observations, (2) "see" in a new way, perceiving what is observed with fresh eyes, and (3) clearly convey their perspective and fresh way of seeing in a way that creates an overall experience and impression for a reader.

The poet John Ciardi maintained that whatever is looked at carefully becomes worthy of being looked at carefully. How can we help kids *really* see things? How can we help them take off the blinders and notice what they typically do not? One way is to ask students to identify and briefly describe in their journal five things in the classroom they think no one else will notice. They then compare their entries, with applause and appreciation or maybe a prize for each item no one else has recorded or for descriptions that meet our class criteria.

➤ *Grades 6–12 writing standard 7*

A description enables readers to see, experience, and understand what is described; it triggers an informed and complete human response. The writer of a description must provide enough—but only enough—details for readers to infer the whole. She also has to do more than render those details accurately. The Canadian West Coast artist Emily Carr puts in nicely: "We may copy something as faithfully as a camera but unless we bring to our picture something additional—something creative—something of ourselves—our picture does not live" (1972, 11).

One way to help students bring something personal and creative to their descriptions is through guided visualization (see Wilhelm 2004/2012). Ask them to close their eyes and visualize themselves standing in a particular landscape, starting with something familiar like the school's football field or cafeteria (although you can quickly move to places much farther from home like a desert, Antarctica, or a rainforest). Prompt students to look around and notice what's above them, at their feet, behind them, on all sides. What's moving? What is in the background? What colors do they see? What small things and large things do they see? What do they hear, smell, feel, taste? What mood are they in and what emotions do they feel? The more details you solicit, the better the heuristic students will build for the kinds of things to notice and include in a description.

➤ *Lesson idea*

Now, ask students to write a description of the place they have imagined. Remind them to meet the criteria for effective descriptions they have articulated. Coach them to add power-packed moves and words to their descriptions and eliminate boring moves and inert wimpy words. Have them share their descriptions as a class and then add more "magic" or "power" moves and words and eliminate inert ones.

➤ *Language standards 3 and 5*

Another activity that focuses students on sensory experience is the "enjoyment game," which Jeff and his friend, the poet Paul Corrigan, invented on hikes and canoe trips when Jeff's daughters were younger. One person describes something she or he is enjoying seeing, feeling, touching, hearing, or tasting, and everyone else, in turn, adds to the description. A variation is to describe something in the physical surroundings. Everyone, in turn, adds to this description until all the details are captured.

➤ *Lesson idea*

George Hillocks' observing and writing activities (1995) are also great for enhancing observation and description. For example, Hillocks has students try to describe one seashell in a pile of similar seashells well enough that the rest of the class could identify that specific shell.

➤ *Lesson idea*

We also use showing-versus-telling exercises. A favorite is to rewrite the school lunch menu so the offerings sound fabulously delicious, then rewrite the same menu so no one would want to eat anything on it.

➤ *Lesson idea*

Once students have practiced using effective details, they need to explore different patterns of organization: spatial (places or objects), parts of a whole (places or objects, subjects and segments), chronological (situations or events, experiences, memories), super/subordination (order of importance). Students can first read short descriptions using various patterns and decide why the author chose that particular pattern, then describe something themselves and justify their pattern choice.

➤ *Lesson idea*

An exercise that helps students infer organizational and structural devices is to have them reorder a short, well-constructed text in which the order of the sentences has been jumbled and identify the textual cues that helped them do so. Here's an example:

> Reorder the following sentences into the most coherent description. Identify the organizational structure of the paragraph by noting how each sentence is linked to other sentences.
>
> _____ 1. The kitchen flows into the living area of hardwood floors and modern and colorful Danish furniture.
>
> _____ 2. Continue counterclockwise through the music room, and you will find yourself in a kitchen with blue marmoleum floors and energy-efficient appliances.
>
> _____ 3. Here, a full set of floor-to-ceiling windows allows you to sit of an evening and enjoy the views of the mountain beyond the deck.
>
> _____ 4. The grand piano and harpsichord dominate the room.
>
> _____ 5. When you enter the house through the front door, you will see a music room immediately on your right.

The original paragraph read:

> When you enter the house through the front door, you will see a music room immediately on your right. The grand piano and harpsichord dominate the room. Continue counterclockwise through the music room, and you will find yourself in a kitchen with blue linoleum floors and energy-efficient appliances. The kitchen flows into the living area of hardwood floors and modern and colorful Danish furniture. Here, a full set of floor-to-ceiling windows allows you to sit of an evening and enjoy the views of the mountain beyond the deck.

The organizational structure is spatial: the reader is directed through space. We identify the first sentence by the words _enter_ and _front door_. _Grand piano_ and _harpsichord_ are semantic connections to _music room_, so that sentence must be next. Then we are guided to visualize walking through the music room to the kitchen. The kitchen "flows into the living area," which is described. Since this is the only room with furniture, it must be where you would "sit of an evening" in the final sentence.

Sometimes a number of orders make sense, but each order will have a different effect, and how this effect was constructed can then be explored. Often we have students circle and draw arrows between words and phrases that connect one sentence to another. As we do this, we create anchor charts of transitions for spatial or object description: *above, across, across from, also, before, below, beyond, further, here, in the distance, nearby, next to, over, overhead, on my left/right, opposite to, to the left/right,* etc.

➤ *Lesson idea*

➤ *Grades 6–12 language standard 3*

Composing to plan and composing to practice focus on specific kinds of description. For a *character sketch*—a descriptive blend of physical characteristics, actions, interactions, values (substance)—the central issue is usually to make an overall impression or point about the character and to establish a persona. Students can practice composing a character sketch of a stranger or taking the point of view or perspective of a character in a book describing another character or person. Students need to create a sense of personhood based on a few well-selected, representative details that a reader can use to "figure forth" (make inferences). (Boswell recommended capturing a character by letting the reader see him live [form].)

Students can also practice identifying the quality most essential to their personhood, the single quality that sums them up. Mary McCarthy calls this quality "the key that turns the lock" (cited in Berke 2007, 67). What are the most "showing" or "salient" (as J. D. Salinger called them) details about a person, from which we can infer much else? (See Smith and Wilhelm 2009 for more ideas on writing character sketches in ways that will help readers develop strategies to infer character.)

➤ *Lesson idea*

➤ *Crux moves*

A *factual report* is a description that disseminates established, agreed-on information. There is no thesis and no authorial persona or voice. Such a report is generally assigned by someone up the chain of command who has a need to know something quickly and concisely. Fact selection is key, as is sharing agreed-on facts versus opinions. The author chooses what and how to present the facts that will fulfill a particular purpose for a particular audience.

Memory descriptions are typically of places, events, or people. Recounting a memorable meal is a great exercise in sensory description, although the setting and other characters may also enter in.

➤ *Grades 6–12 writing standard 10*

Composing Draft Descriptions

Drafting requires addressing global issues of structure: what structure (spatial, sequential, etc.) will assist the reader best? Anchor charts of transitions can be very helpful. What's most important is that students use the criteria they developed while composing to plan and composing to practice to guide them. We challenge students to start with criteria regarding substance and limit themselves to four or five overall criteria. If they use more, they lose focus and we need to spread the help we give them too thinly.

➤ *Lesson idea*

A class of ninth graders proposed the following criteria, which cover the essential elements of description:

➤ *Grades 6–12 writing standard 2a–2f*

- The composition evokes and sustains a powerful overall impression and effect and leaves the reader with a strong mental image or model.
- Specific, concrete details and sensory words are used effectively throughout.
- An appropriate ordering of the details is skillfully used (spatial, sequential, etc.).
- Appropriate transitional words and phrases are used throughout the writing to keep relationships among elements and ideas clear.
- Sentences that include several details correctly use commas (and maybe even semicolons and colons!) for items in a series.

Students need to articulate and apply their own critical standards, both as composers of their own work and readers of the work of others. If we want students to get good at something, they need the practice and opportunity to master those skills. Nothing supersedes the importance of being able to set and apply powerful critical standards.

The students in the third-grade class in which this best-possible-school unit was used came up with these criteria:

➤ *Corresponds with the CCSS emphasis on purpose, authorial choice, and audience consideration*

Make sure that you, the author of fantastic description:

Use specific words and sense words that paint a picture and give a feeling to the reader.

Use the right words to link ideas together so the reader can follow the description.

Make a strong overall point to the reader.

Composing Final Drafts of Descriptions

➤ *Lesson idea*

Here students consider adding, deleting, or moving specific descriptive words and phrases. We often create lists of banned "wimpy words" (noun: *thing*; adjectives: *good, bad*; verbs: *said, went*; etc.) or moves and brainstorm "power words" or moves to replace these boring old standbys. These recommended words and moves are posted around the room as reminders. Students can find "devastating descriptions" in the books they are reading and display these descriptions on the bulletin board or on anchor charts, identifying the words and moves that make these descriptions sing.

Getting feedback is important when finalizing a draft. Our students share their descriptive essays with the peers in their learning group and also with an adult (a mentor or a parent). Students ask their reviewers whether the descriptions make it easy to imagine what is being described. Asking students to review the criteria checklist with the reviewers in advance and attach it to their paper ensures that the student authors, peer editors, and adult reviewers are on the same page.

➤ *Grades 6–12 writing standards 4–6*

Composing to Transfer Knowledge of Description

The basic forms of composing to transfer are formative assessments, reflective journals, process/task analyses (see below), anchor charts, and anything else that brings to articulated consciousness the processes and principles that inform planning, collecting data for, forming/drafting, revising, and sharing a particular text structure. In composing to transfer knowledge of description, students articulate the general purposes, principles, and moves of composing description and name the situations in which description can be used in the future, both in school and at home.

We suggest using a variety of formative assessments throughout the unit, as well as creating and displaying an anchor chart of rules of notice. What is it you have to notice about an object, place, person, or situation/event to accurately describe and understand it? What do you have to notice when you read a description? What can you infer from these details and moves? *Fresh Takes on Teaching the Literary Elements* (Smith and Wilhelm 2009) includes a thorough list of what might be on such a chart for people (character, page 52) and places (setting, page 96). For character, it's important to include such things as first impressions and how these impressions are created: groups belonged to, actions, language, beliefs, passions and interests, appearance, how others relate to and compare with this character. Surprising behavior needs to be especially attended to, as well as the reasons for this behavior/change in character.

Students can also find a very descriptive photograph or painting and write a short reflective piece identifying the aspects of good description the photo or painting conveys.

➤ *Lesson idea*

Drama activities (particularly the mantle of the expert strategy) also help students reflect on the principles and aspects of description. The students in this unit became members of a blue ribbon panel tasked with ranking descriptions of a great school, classroom, or playground on the basis of stated criteria.

➤ *Lesson idea*

Process Descriptions/Explanations

Process descriptions add the element of logical, often causal, connections among the details of a description so that someone else can reimagine or replicate the process being described. Specific examples include most explanations; directions; recipes; how-tos; think-alouds; and process analyses.

The emphasis in this text pattern is on clarity, particularly in expressing relationships between elements and steps. The writer must imagine a reader who is trying to follow the directions or thought process—to "perform" or "enact" the words in some way. Therefore, the words must be accessible, and expression and transitions must be clear and show the relationship of one detail to another. Enough—but not too much—information must be provided, so focus is retained and distracting details are omitted. The writer must go step by step, conveying the order of the procedure with words that lead to replication in thought or in deed.

Process descriptions are the basis of history; of methodology in math and science; and of many other subjects. Process descriptions are also important in fine arts, in practical arts like cooking, in sports and other performance-based activities, in the social sciences, and in theoretical sciences like economics. An implicit (and, often, explicit) cause-and-effect relationship is the basis for the common expression *those who do not understand history are doomed to repeat it*. If you don't understand how things work—in literacy, math, science, history, or indeed any discipline—the relationship of complex causes and their various effects, then you will not be able to predict and exercise any measure of control over these processes.

Process analysis, in which you not only describe your own process of doing something retrospectively but also explain the connection between steps and why things work the way they do, is absolutely necessary to understanding, according to current cognitive science. Understanding is "knowing the story behind the story," knowing *how* things work and consciously understanding the principles behind *why* things work the way they do. This distinguishes knowing "information" from possessing and using what can be called "knowledge." For example, a cook may know the steps of a recipe and be able to follow them; the chef understands how and why of the chemical reactions between ingredients. The chef can therefore adapt recipes, be creative, and invent. The chef possesses deep understanding that allows innovation and transfer. The chef has "conscious competence" that the cook does not yet possess.

The chef, or any expert, enacts the 5 kinds of knowledge through the 5 kinds of composing.

Model Unit: How Can We Make the Best Possible School?

Any essential question beginning with *how* or *what is the process for* leads to process descriptions. *How can we create the best musical performance/art exhibit/sconce? What determines who wins a basketball game? How can we determine chemical unknowns? How can I become the person I want to be? How can we predict the future of the economy? What would be the best process for reducing the budget? How can we best protect and promote civil rights?* It's hard to imagine any unit that can't be reframed to include at least a subquestion that requires and rewards highly purposeful and compelling process descriptions. The model unit at the beginning of this chapter can be tweaked from *what makes the best possible school?* to *how can we make the best possible school?* A subquestion for one of the groups becomes *how can we make the best and safest possible playground?*

Composing to Plan Process Descriptions

Effective instruction begins with frontloading context and purpose. Students need to access relevant background from their own experience and then develop strategies that will allow them to access data outside their experience.

> ➤ *For more informa-tion on the importance of the five types of knowledge, see Chapter 3.*

Students can think back to times they needed to explain a process to someone or explain why or how something happened as it did. For example, athletes often explain certain plays or sequences to one another after a game (or as they watch the game tapes), trying to figure out how and why some event played out as it did.

> ➤ *Lesson idea*

Search-and-identify activities in which students peruse a newspaper or Internet news site looking for process analyses are also effective. In today's *Idaho Statesman* (which we like to call *The Statesperson*), for example, the top local news story is how to protect historic houses in Boise. One of the top news stories is an analysis of how to cut the budget deficit. Leafing through other sections, one finds several recipes; a process analysis of particular plays and drives from the BSU football team's victory over the University of Toledo; a process description of how to prepare for a fall fishing trip in the mountains, along with directions to specific remote fishing spots; and the steps in wrapping up your summer garden and preparing your winter garden. Health columns describe how to solve back problems with posture and weight lifting and how to prepare for ski season with certain exercises. Even the advice columnist describes how to deal with a pregnant teen.

➤ *Lesson idea*

It's an easy matter to take this list and brainstorm the purposes of process descriptions and the situations in which they are not just useful but essential. We often ask students to note all the process descriptions/explanations they provide or hear during a day, and the lists are usually quite impressive. From here it is easy to brainstorm purposes and situations that can reward process descriptions throughout a unit and lead to a culminating project.

Composing to Practice Process Descriptions

➤ *For more information on the importance of the five types of knowledge, see Chapter 3.*

➤ *Crux move*

Composing to practice encompasses continuing to develop procedural knowledge of substance and giving great attention to developing procedural knowledge of form. Here's the heart of the matter for process descriptions, explanations, and directions: *you absolutely have to imagine and accommodate the reader.* This text structure is designed to help a reader understand and/or do something. This purpose must be emphasized in every step and every kind of composing in creating a process description. For that reason, it is important to provide students with real audiences and purposeful activities with immediate function and feedback.

➤ *Fits with the multi-modal aspects of the CCSS*

➤ *Mentor texts*

Mentor texts that include process descriptions are great models. David Macauley's *The Way Things Work* and his more recent *The Way We Work* provide many excellent examples of process descriptions that include amazing visuals. Students can jigsaw-read and share different parts of the text, noticing and naming some of the devices Macauley uses to describe processes. Students can discuss how the visuals and text complement each other and promote further understanding. Other good mentor texts include *Why I Sneeze, Shiver, Hiccup and Yawn*, by Melvin Berger; *Mr. Putter & Tabby Bake the Cake*, by Cynthia Rylant; and *Born Yesterday: Diary of a Young Journalist*, by James Solheim.

➤ *Lesson idea*

Writing in the style of a mentor text is always a powerful opportunity to notice, name, and apply process description tools. Boise State Writing Project fellow Anna Daley uses a technique called Author Says/Author Does to focus her students on noticing and naming (see Figures 8.1 and 8.2). In the Author Says portion students recount or summarize the main points—the declarative knowledge of substance. Author Does focuses students on procedural knowledge of form: how is the author structuring and conveying this substance through her construction of the text? What signposts, cues, and navigational structures are being provided to guide the reader to the major details and point of the text?

➤ *Lesson idea*

A lesson on following *only* the directions is also effective. Bring in bread, jam, butter, peanut butter, and a knife, and lay everything out on a table. Have students write directions for making a peanut-butter-and-jelly-sandwich. Then have a student read her directions while you follow them to the letter. For example, if the directions

Figure 8.1 Author Says/Does Analysis Instructions

As one close reading strategy, annotate your article noting what the author is *saying* in addition to what the author is *doing*.

To do this, first read through the article and draw a box around sections of text that you believe work together. For example, you might think that the first three paragraphs of a text work together to hook a reader's interest and that the next two paragraphs work together for some other purpose.

Then, next to each "chunk" of text, annotate your *says/does* analysis. Summarize what the author is *saying* in this chunk of text. Easy, right?

Then, describe *how* the author is saying it. In other words, what is the author *doing*? What shape, form, or construction is the author using to say what she is saying?

Here are some words and phrases that describe what the language of a particular text or portion of it might do:

describes	evaluates	provides history	elaborates
narrates	cites	categorizes	develops
lists	exemplifies	predicts	deepens
itemizes	offers a hypothesis	reasons	contrasts
explains	supports	traces	emphasizes
compares	introduces	provides an example	
illustrates	claims/states a proposition	synthesizes	

Source: Adapted from AP Lang and Comp materials by Anna Daley

Figure 8.2 Excerpt of an Author Says/Does Analysis of Joseph Conrad's *Lord Jim*

SAYS/DOES ANALYSIS		
Paragraph	**Says**	**Does**
1	The main character is compelled to continue his life at sea despite the paradoxically boring, alluring, and threatening nature of such an existence.	. . . establishes the primary setting and dominant tones of the passage and characterizes the main character.
2	As he recovers from an injury, Jim oscillates between apathy and the despairing confrontation of life's transience.	. . . explores Jim's reaction to an event in relation to broader themes.
3	Jim's injury requires that the ship leave him behind at port.	. . . indicates the transition to another setting.
4	The hospital at which Jim stays and consorts with fellow patients is tranquil and removed from the dangers of the sea.	. . . introduces new setting and contrasts it with the previous one.
5	Jim encounters passionate, reckless sailors who dream of achievement, as well as those whose only contentment in life lies in the pursuit of comfort.	. . . juxtaposes two disparate groups of characters as an exploration of man's motivations.

say to take two pieces of bread without first specifying opening the bag, try to grab the slices through the bag without unwrapping it. This will lead to a lot of laughter, but makes the point that directions must be very precise, orderly, clear, explicit, and contextual. We cannot assume prior knowledge unless the audience is known to be knowledgeable. Discuss what is unclear or assumed in the student's directions, and list the kinds of problems encountered and how to solve them. Then student pairs can write directions for each other about how to do simple tasks like making paper airplanes. Partners must explicitly follow the directions and only the directions, which provides immediate feedback about the clarity of the directions. A variation it to have students give directions to places in the school and then follow them to the letter, monitoring what makes directions clear, confusing, just wrong, or unfollowable!

Another popular activity is to show students a picture of a Rube Goldberg machine and ask them to describe how it works. (*Examples can be found on* www .rubegoldberg.com/.) These are great fun, since the Goldberg machines often resemble playground equipment. Students could also design their own Rube Goldberg machine to solve a problem (looking ahead to problem–solution) or critique the Rube Goldberg machine with an accompanying process description. The point of a Rube Goldberg machine is to make simple processes complicated, so it is a negative example of a process description. Students can explore how processes are made more complicated by the machine, and how process descriptions make things simple and clear.

Having students describe a process using a flowchart that combines text and visuals is also a valuable activity. Figure 8.3 is an example from a math class that brainstormed solving an algebra problem and then came up with a flowchart summarizing the process.

Sunday cartoons (Dilbert is particularly good in this regard) often implicitly describe a process and can be used as the basis for a process description of what has happened. We often ask students to describe what has happened in George Booth's famous cartoon "IP GISSA GUL." (Many versions can be found online; http://busiek .com/site/ipgissagul.php is one site.)

Another great practice technique is to model process descriptions by thinking aloud, calling attention to specific textual, navigational, and grammatical/lexical features (see Wilhelm 2012). For example, lab reports have a specific form and tone. Recipes are directive, using imperatives, with many sentences starting with verbs. Students create anchor charts describing the features of the various process descriptions we think through aloud. They then refer to these charts when they read or compose in the particular form. Also, we do one think-aloud *for* students and another *with* students. Then they can think through that kind of process description *by themselves*, and we have gradually released responsibility.

➤ *Lesson idea*
In these activities, students develop procedural knowledge of substance and form while developing critical standards.

➤ *Multimodal standards, reading anchor standard 7, writing anchor standard 8*

➤ *Lesson idea*

➤ *Lesson idea*

Figure 8.3 Flow Chart Describing Problem–Solving Processes

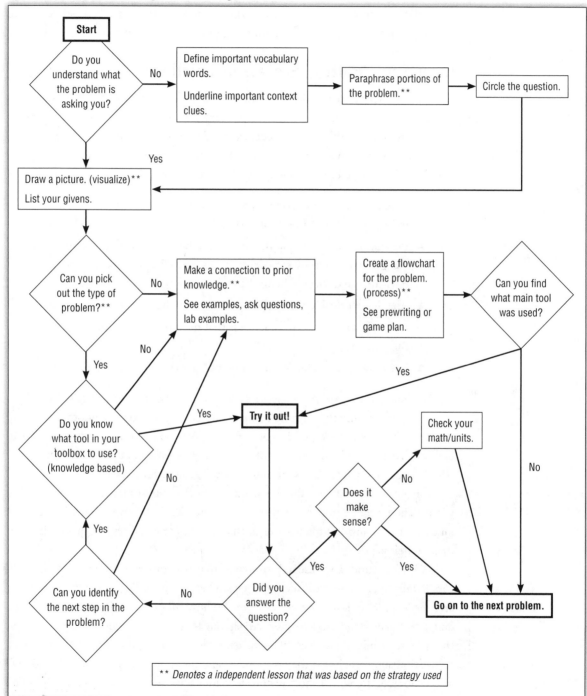

Source: Created by Stephen Zownorega and Blair Covino

It is important for students to articulate purposes, processes, principles, tools, and pitfalls for composing process descriptions in ways that have heuristic value for guiding their future reading and composing of process description.

Composing Drafts of Process Descriptions

Composing to practice activities should result in the articulation of critical standards in response sheets, criteria checklists, primary trait sheets, etc. Students use these tools to give one another useful feedback and develop declarative knowledge of substance and form at more global levels. The general criteria for process description below can be tweaked for specific kinds of process descriptions:

- Orient the reader! Introduce an overview of the process you are describing and why, the contexts of use, and so on.
- Provide a clear road map that navigates the reader through the process, using discrete step-by-step descriptions, as well as visuals, graphics, and navigational devices if helpful.
- Anticipate possible missteps and how to monitor and correct them.
- Define unfamiliar terms and tools that must be understood to follow the process.
- Use only "need to know" information! Get rid of "nice to know" info!

➤ Lesson idea

Modeling your own response to a student process description based on these or similar criteria and then asking students to help you respond to another will help them use the criteria to respond to one another. We also use a technique called *roundtable* or *charette*, in which student volunteers display their paper on the whiteboard, read it aloud, and get feedback from their small group or the class.

➤ Speaking and listening standards

All our students peer edit the work of three other students in their learning group. The teacher's rule is: see three before me! Students have to have three peers (and a parent or an adult mentor) agree that they have met all criteria before they can turn in their paper.

➤ Writing anchor standard 5

We have found, and research supports, that students can be excellent peer editors *if the process of peer editing a specific kind of text according to specific criteria has been modeled, if students have been mentored in peer editing with the required processes,* and *if they understand and have practiced meeting the criteria.* It's very helpful to assign the peer responders a deliverable—for example, requiring that they offer one *keep* suggestion about each text they respond to and then four *change, move, delete,* or *add* suggestions, along with a short justification for each. Peer editors can also underline crux moves on drafts and insert carets where crux moves could be inserted. (See the instructions in Figure 8.4.)

➤ *Lesson idea*

Composing Final Drafts of Process Descriptions

Final drafts should exhibit all five kinds of knowledge, including procedural knowledge of form at the global and local level. Final drafting includes smoothing the language and making surface proofreading corrections. Students should pay specific attention to sentence specificity and connections between elements. For example, they may need an inductive lesson on how colons show how an impetus or catalyst leads to new results. *Pull the trigger: the bullet will then explode from the gun and pierce the balloon, exploding it, and then embedding itself in the target beyond.* Or: *Mix the yeast into the batter: wait until the mixture rises to the top of your mixing bowl.* Students work together to induce how the convention of the colon works in this case, and then generate their own examples for use in their own process descriptions. (For more on inductive language lessons, see Smith and Wilhelm 2007.)

➤ *For more information on the importance of the five kinds of knowledge for planning and student learning, see Chapter 3.*

➤ *Lesson idea*

Composing to Transfer Knowledge of Process Description

Think-alouds are powerful tools for naming what one does *as* one is reading and writing, so they encourage transfer. Process analyses do too. A process analysis is *retrospective*. It's a reflection, after the fact (though soon after!), on the process of reading, composing, or solving any problem or navigating any kind of text. The process analysis describes how you went about completing the task, what decisions were made and

Figure 8.4   How to Mark a Draft

- Draw a straight line (_____) under words or images or transitions that strike you as effective for re-creating a process or that accomplish a crux move of process description. These words or phrases might include strong verbs, specific details, memorable phrases, clear and strong transitions, and striking images.

- Draw a wavy line (~~~~) under words or images or transitions that are weak or unconvincing. Put these lines under words the writer repeats too often and ideas that seem vague, flat, or unnecessary.

- Put brackets [ ] around sentences or groups of sentences that you think should be combined.

- Put parentheses ( ) around sentences that could be clarified.

- Circle overuse of the passive voice (*was written*, for example).

why, what obstacles were encountered and met, and what options were considered and discarded or could be used in the future.

As a teacher research and reflection activity, we often ask the pre- and inservice teachers with whom we work to compose process analyses of inquiry lessons, classroom activity, peer coaching, or the use of teacher research methods to help them reflect on teaching and learning processes and consider how this reflection can inform future teaching and learning episodes. We also use process analyses regularly with our elementary and high school students—from which we often learn more about their thinking and expertise than we do from the actual compositions or performances!

A process analysis answers these questions:

What did you do, in what order?

Why did you do what you did in that order?

What worked? Why did it work?

What did not seem to work? Why not? What did you do in response?

How did you feel at various points in the process?

What options did you have that you did not pursue?

What could or will you do differently the next time you have this task or are faced by similar challenges?

To what degree were you successful? How do you know?

How can you be even more successful next time?

> *CCSS assessments*

Analyzing one's process is important for all students and all teachers but particularly for novices: there is great value in naming what you do well, what other options exist and when you might play out and pursue them, etc. Both the short and long performance tasks on the next generation of assessments, including the two CCSS assessments, Smarter Balanced and PARCC, require students to write a process analysis (called a *reflection*) on how they solved the provided problem. Process analysis leads to conscious competence and to transfer. (For a chapter-length discussion of process analysis, see Wilhelm 2012.)

Conclusion

Descriptions are ubiquitous in and of themselves and central to the work of most disciplines. They are also central to the reading and composing of other informative text types. It is to one of these text types, definition, to which we now turn.

Divining and Defining

What's the Big Definition?

In our work as educators, we often have to define terms, concepts, processes, standards, even theories. For instance, Jeff has devoted himself as both a researcher and a practitioner to promoting literacy in contexts of inquiry. But *inquiry* is a term people construe in different ways—even in research literature. So unless Jeff is sure his definition is shared, he has to begin by making his definition of inquiry clear: based on work in cognitive science, *inquiry is the rigorous apprenticeship of learners into the processes of expert reading, composing, and working in specific disciplines.*

Living life, Jeff has to define things every day. Recently, Peggy asked Jeff to reserve a "nice hotel" for their anniversary. He immediately asked her to define *nice hotel.* He knew he was likely to misunderstand and perhaps get into some anniversary trouble! Next, his training partner Willie told him to do two "hard workouts" on his anniversary trip. "Define *hard workout,*" Jeff said, "level 3, 4, or 5? Endurance or cardio?" Athletes classify workouts in various ways and *hard* is a cover term that could include many different kinds of strenuous workouts. Jeff wanted to be sure what Willie meant, which meant Willie had to define the class of "hard workout" precisely.

As is true at every university, each year Michael and his colleagues have to assess tenures and promotions. Their discussions are rife with definitions. What exactly is a high-quality article or journal? What is excellent teaching? Before judgments can be made, reviewers have to define the criteria.

And think about how many definitions are involved in parenting. Michael has discovered that *don't stay out too late* means something very different to his daughters than it does to him and his wife Karen.

Jim likewise is faced with daily defining. For instance, today he met with the fellow members of a hiring committee to debrief their telephone interviews with six candidates for a faculty position. The committee needed to determine not only who is a *strong* candidate but also who seemed to be the *best* candidates to bring to campus for in-person interviews. The committee members asked one another, "How does the candidate complement our existing faculty? What new expertise would the candidate bring to our faculty? How would he or she help us stretch?" Highly contextualized questions like these helped the committee reach specific and situated definitions of *strong* and *best* and decide which candidates met those definitions.

Our Informational/Explanatory Text Continuum

Clearly, defining depends on robust descriptions and deep understanding of a concept or phenomenon. We put definition next on the continuum of informational text types because it depends and draws heavily on thick description and we think it is prerequisite to comparing and contrasting. Comparisons and contrasts always involve defining the criteria one employs in making them. For example, all of us have been both secondary and university teachers. If we were comparing and contrasting our teaching jobs, we might talk about which job has been more rewarding or more difficult or more social or more stressful. To do so we'd have to agree on what those terms mean. Moreover, many, maybe most, comparisons and contrasts lead to some kind of summative judgment. Which of two movies or restaurants or pitchers or paintings is better? You can't know unless you've defined what *better* means.

Defining *Definition*

We are concerned in this chapter with two types of definition: the short or encyclopedic/dictionary definition, and extended definition, which obviously requires more thought and figures prominently in the disciplines.

Regarding the dictionary definition, the Purdue University Online Writing Lab (OWL) says:

> A formal definition is based upon a concise, logical pattern that
> includes as much information as it can within a minimum amount
> of space. The primary reason to include definitions in your writing

is to avoid misunderstanding with your audience. A formal definition consists of three parts.

1. The term (word, phrase, or concept) to be defined.
2. The class of object or concept to which the term belongs.
3. The differentiating characteristics that distinguish it from all
   others of its class.

For example:

- Water (*term*) is a liquid (*class*) made up of molecules of
  hydrogen and oxygen in the ratio of 2 to 1 (*differentiating
  characteristics*).
- Comic books (*term*) are sequential and narrative publica-
  tions (*class*) consisting of illustrations, captions, dialogue
  balloons, and often focus on super-powered heroes (*differentiating characteristics*).
- Astronomy (*term*) is a branch of scientific study (*class*) primarily concerned with celestial objects inside and outside of
  the earth's atmosphere (*differentiating characteristics*).
  (http://owl.english.purdue.edu/owl/resource/622/01/)

The OWL examples are a good introduction to "dictionary" definitions, and the
easy-to-follow formula is the basis of extended definition. We prefer to present examples of definitions to students and have them induce the formula.

The online *New World Rhetorical Dictionary* defines *extended definition* as a writing
strategy that describes the finely detailed nature of a concrete or abstract subject.
"Extended definition is a kind of essay . . . expanding [a definition's] scope by considering the subject in more finely layered terms and considering larger issues related to
the subject" (for example, the different ways varied groups of people might define
a term like *freedom*, the limits placed on freedom in particular situations, examples/
counterexamples, borderline test cases, etc.).

In a seminal study on teaching extended definition, Hillocks identifies the following strategies for defining: "1) to circumscribe (identify) the concept generally, 2)
to compare examples in order to generate criteria which discriminate between the
target concept (to be defined) and related but essentially different concepts, and 3) to
generate examples which clarify the distinctions" (Hillocks et al. 1983, 276).

In this and other studies, Hillocks found that having students *collaboratively think
through problems that require employing necessary strategies to expert task completion* led

➤ *Writing standard 7,
all grade levels*

➤ *Lesson idea*

to significantly higher engagement, enjoyment, learning, and performance than presenting text structure information in a lecture or working from models without analyzing those models to determine criteria of substance and form.

Both short and extended definitions are situation dependent. Words and concepts can mean different things to different groups in different contexts. Think of Jim's hiring committee—they wanted to define the best candidate for a faculty position in the English department at Boise State University at a particular point in time. In any definition, it is important not to define a *word* but rather to explain a *concept* in terms of how it works in the specific context and for a particular purpose.

In short, to teach kids to define, we have to teach them to identify definitional problems, to group, to analyze, and to distinguish. These are the *crux moves* they must practice and master.

➤ *Writing anchor standard 4*

Why Definition Matters

Definition is central to much of what we do both in and out of school. Virtually every public policy issue involves definition of one sort or another. Is this group made up of terrorists or patriots? Is this species endangered? Is this law discriminatory? Virtually every discipline requires definition. Just type "definition" into the search bar of YouTube—on the first page the following disciplines are represented: law, math, sociology, religion, physics, biology, and music. The takeaway: if our students are to be good citizens, if they are to be successful in any discipline, they have to learn to define.

Model Unit: What Is an Effective Leader?

Essential questions like *what makes a good friend?* or *who is a hero?* or *what is an effective leader?* need to be addressed in an extended definition. In disciplines other than English, any essential question that implies the need for a definition (or ranking or comparison) leads to a unit that will require and reward, support and coproduce the composing of definitions and extended definitions throughout—for example, *what makes a powerful chemical?* or *what were the most influential voyages of discovery?* or *what are the most strategic geographical positions in the world?*

In this chapter we'll highlight a unit Jeff has taught several times on this essential question, *What makes an effective leader?*, which was also framed as two variants: *What distinguishes a great leader from an influential but not so great leader?* and *What constitutes personal greatness and leadership?*

Composing to Plan a Definition

The purpose of composing to plan is to develop knowledge of context and purpose in which the text/thought pattern is important and useful. A focused freewrite about definitions students have previously found useful is a great way to get started. Brainstorming contexts and uses of definition, monitoring how often a thought pattern like definition comes up in a day, and newspaper and Internet "search and finds" are other quick and useful ways to explore context and purpose.

➤ *Lesson idea*

➤ *Writing standards 4 and 7, all grade levels*

➤ *Reading standards 1 and 2, all grade levels*

So that his students could see how definition is important in all disciplines, Jeff recently asked them to leaf through newspapers and identify, by subject area, concepts that might be useful to define. Their list:

Civics/law: What is *guilty*? What is *murder*? What is *terrorism*? What is *pornography*? What are *civil rights*? What is *sexual harassment*? What is *proof*?

History/social studies: What is an *act of war*? What is *terrorism*? What is a *citizen*? What is *patriotism/patriotic action*? What is a *balanced budget*? What is *fair*? What is *treason*? What is *equality*? What is *equality of opportunity*?

Physical education/sports/health: What is an *All-Star*? *All-American*? What is a *team player*? What is a *franchise player*? What is a *slugging average*? What is *healthy teen living*? What is *safe*?

Current events: What is *marriage*? What is a *civil union*? What is *respect*? What is *life*? *death*?

Science: What is *environmental protection*? What is an *ecosystem*? What is *organic*?

Math: What is *statistically significant*?

Personal: What is *friendship*? What is *ethical*? What is *right action*? What is *PG-13*? What is *maturity*? What is *appropriate*?

Students were able to identify defining problems and then relate these to audience needs, the first step in writing extended definitions. With these contexts and purposes in mind, the students continued working in groups and came up with this list of when to embed simple dictionary definitions in compositions:

➤ *Writing anchor standard 4*

- When you are using a term or idea that is probably unfamiliar to your audience.
- When you are using a term or idea in an idiosyncratic (*idiot*-syncratic?) or special way that your audience might confuse with another way of

thinking about that term or idea. For example, "The term *economy* has many meanings; because we are studying leadership and responsibility, we will use economy to mean *personal thriftiness*."

■ When the history of a word (its etymology) is interesting and illuminating to the subject you are writing about.

Here's their list of when to compose extended definitions:

■ When your audience needs to know your understanding of a really important term or concept.

■ When you want to convince your audience that they should accept your definition of a term or concept.

■ When you and your audience need to agree on the definition of something to have a discussion, understand one another, or get something done together.

■ When the term is so abstract or complicated that a simple definition will not do.

Ethnography. There are many other kinds of activities that help us dig deeper into the nature and structure of more complex, less transparent text patterns, particularly those important to acquiring disciplinary knowledge. One is *ethnographic work*, in which students examine their own behavior or the behavior of those around them.

➤ *Lesson idea*

Jeff recently modeled using definition as part of ethnographic investigation by explaining to students that whenever he wanders the hallways, he has to carry with him a definition of *appropriate behavior* so he'll know what student behavior to ignore and what behavior he has to address. He also has to define *cheating* or *creativity* in dealing with student work. Likewise, whenever he grades student compositions, he needs to have a definition of an A paper versus a B paper, and so on. Since Jeff teaches classes in both English and reading, he sometimes has to define for himself, students, or parents what constitutes *English* and what constitutes *reading*.

➤ *Lesson idea*

➤ *Writing standard 7, all grade levels, and collaboration and speaking and listening standards*

He then asked the class to choose some other school activities (drama, sports, academics, etc.) and identify some terms that might need defining. For sports, the kids came up with terms like *varsity, J-V, point guard, center, All Conference, All State*. For drama, they identified *lead, supporting cast, crew, musical, tragedy*. For academics, they talked about the need to define *honors, high honors, AP*, as well as the content of particular classes like environmental science and biology.

➤ *Lesson idea*

Dramatic scenarios. Another way to begin is to have students illustrate key concepts from the unit by composing and performing a scene exhibiting a term or trait.

The assignment requires them to examine what the concept under study looks like in their lived experience. Mining their own thinking and experience (Greene 1991; Ladson-Billings 1994) helps them develop procedural knowledge of substance in both personally and culturally relevant ways. When concepts are represented and named, we have achieved some declarative knowledge of substance. Because students are exhibiting the trait under consideration, they are also grouping, analyzing, and distinguishing and thus beginning to develop procedural knowledge of form. These procedures can be named during discussion, formative assessments, and other kinds of composing to transfer and become declarative knowledge of form.

➤ *See Chapter 3 for more on planning.*

➤ *The crux moves of defining*

A group drama activity we use in the what-makes-a-great-leader unit is presented in Figure 9.1. Conceptual frontloading like this activates students' prior knowledge, brings them into contact with other sometimes complementary or competing ideas, helps them generate ideas for their own definitions of leadership, and introduces them to procedures of defining.

➤ *Lesson idea*

The following activities also help generate conceptual knowledge (resulting in declarative knowledge of substance) while at the same focusing closely on procedures of defining (procedural knowledge of substance and of form). Much of our thinking about extended definition and many of these activities are based on the "defining" (pun intended) work of our colleagues and friends (Hillocks et al. 1983; Johannessen et al. 1982; Smagorinsky et al. 2010).

Ranking models. It's important to teach students what Hillocks calls "enabling strategies," procedures that will help them do what must be done to compose (or read) a particular kind of text. Activities that rank models of the text pattern require students to articulate standards of judgment. In the first few days of most of our units, we share three examples of student culminating compositions or projects from the previous year's unit. We provide three interesting and fairly strong examples of comparable quality, since these models become the baseline for what students must be able to do; and we want there to be a basis for disagreement. Therefore, the models differ in the relative strength of their components. Contested cases always require more thoughtful explanations than clear-cut cases do.

➤ *Lesson idea*

Ranking models focuses students on the criteria of the thought pattern/text structure they will be composing, provides varied models of the structure, gives them ideas about what to include as well as problems to avoid, and helps consider the process of creating this kind of text. We do this activity with pieces of writing, visual displays, video documentaries, PSAs, websites, videos of drama projects—anything students are being prepared to create as culminating projects for the unit.

➤ *Writing standards 2 and 4 plus standards for collaboration, speaking and listening, multimodal presentation*

Figure 9.1   Are You an Effective Leader?

Your mission as a group is to come up with a simulation (skit/role-play scenario) demonstrating in action a concrete example of your group's thinking about what an effective leader is and how she or he acts. Your group may use whatever type of leader you want, but it must be school appropriate. I will be walking around to listen in. If you come up with an idea and are ready to have it approved raise your hands; I will be there as quickly as I can.

In order to accomplish this task successfully within your group you will need to:

1. Decide among the group who will play what roles: leader, assistant leader/side-kick, and followers. It is your choice how the roles are distributed and developed. However, everyone in the group must have an active role to play in the preparation and the performance of the simulation.

2. Once roles have been assigned, your group will come up with a short skit that shows effective ways that leadership is exercised. You can choose situations from daily life or wider-world examples. Feel free to use resources (Internet, books, cartoons, your own life, etc.) for suggestions about situations and roles you may want to portray.

3. The skit must show an example or examples of "effective" leadership (in whatever way your group defines it). The leadership portrayed can be either negative or positive, but it should show or suggest how this leadership behavior affects the other members (assistant leader and followers). You might also include a counterexample of less effective or ineffective leadership, perhaps on the part of the assistant leader or one of the followers.

4. Once your group has your skit prepared, rehearse it a couple of times to make sure it works and makes sense, because you are going to perform it for the class. The class will try to identify how you define effective leadership and how your positive or negative example relates to your definition.

If you have any questions or the group is stuck, I am here to assist you. There will be class time provided to complete this activity. If your group feels you do not have enough time, you may work on this at home. You may also bring in small props and materials that you would like to use during your performance.

Your completed group simulation is due on Thursday. We will have three groups perform on Thursday and three on Friday. Groups will be drawn at random so all groups must be prepared on Thursday!

HAVE FUN AND GOOD LUCK!

This activity results in the articulation of a task analysis, in combination with knowledge of purpose and context, which covers most of what we consider to be composing to plan.

We prefer to use examples from the previous year's students. This adds some reality and gravitas to the project. Our students say: "Oh, that's what last year's eighth graders did. I can do that!" They can't opt out: "That's a professional example and I can't be expected to do that." It's also fun for students to guess about the authors, and since we say that all three examples are pretty good ones, it is a celebration of previous students' work and how such work becomes archival. If you are doing a unit for the first time, it's easy to write your own examples (and sometimes even easier to find student examples on the Internet).

Here are three student models from a ninth-grade inquiry into *what constitutes personal greatness and leadership?* Each student has responded to a subset of the overarching question.

Example A

A great teacher is hard to define. This is because a great teacher is different in different situations and for different people. All teachers instruct. A criterion that all great teachers meet beyond instructing is that they are inspirational. In other words, they make learning fun and interesting and seem worthwhile and important. Another criterion is that they relate to you personally. But what makes something fun and interesting to one person will be different than for someone else. And who anyone likes and feels a relationship with will be different than someone else's likes. So defining a great teacher is really subjective and will be different for different people, but always involves inspiration.

Example B

A great political leader can be defined as someone wielding political power and influence who is inspirational, visionary, communicative, effective (most of the time) particularly in times of crisis, and who works for the common good of not only those whom she serves but for the world as a whole. These criteria are highly interrelated.

It's important to discuss and come to agreement on greatness in leadership so we can evaluate our leaders, decide whether to reelect them, and consider when to call them to account.

For example, Abraham Lincoln was inspirational in that he had a vision of our country as unified ("a house divided against itself cannot stand," "all the soil of this country is American soil"), and as dedicated to equality for all people (e.g., the Emancipation Proclamation). But this was not sufficient to achieve greatness as a leader: he also was an effective communicator and could inspire people to belief and action through his words. His Inaugural Addresses and Gettysburg Address are just a few examples of how he framed the issues facing the country in ways the people could understand and "buy into."

Lincoln's greatness is also defined by the fact that he achieved progress and success even in the face of terrible trials. He kept his cabinet together despite many disagreements. He kept the military funded. He was able to get re-elected, which allowed the country to successfully end the Civil War. He took every opportunity to further his agenda, such as issuing the Emancipation Proclamation after a semi-victory at Antietam Creek, which made the war explicitly about slavery and therefore introduced constitutional constraints to keep England and France out of the war when they were ready to side with the Confederacy.

His emancipation of the slaves, the reunification of the country, and his desire and plans to heal the rifts after the war are all signs of his attempts to serve humanity. And these ends were for a greater good for everyone in the country, for the country itself, and for the world, since ending the slavery and becoming a unified country had positive results and was a positive model for people everywhere.

But consider a counterexample. Hitler was also inspirational, visionary, and communicative. His speeches were spellbinding and envisioned a new Germany emerging from the ruins and humiliation of World War I. He inspired people to make great sacrifices to achieve his vision. He built the Autobahns and gave everyone a Volkswagen and Volksradio. So why is he not a "great" leader? The first and most important reason is that in the end, his vision was unworthy. The Holocaust and a war of conquest were immoral for his own people and hurtful for them and the world. It was selfish and self-serving instead of in service to all. A secondary reason he was defeated is because he overreached. He did not emerge victorious from his trials or his country's trials.

Sometimes, the issue of moral effectiveness is not clear-cut in the near term and we must wait to see what history decides. But moral effectiveness, the ability to raise a people and the world up to greater moral achievement that benefits themselves and others, is the ultimate test of a "great" political leader.

Example C

A great teammate is a great teammate: someone who does whatever is necessary to help the team be better, get along better, and win.

A great teammate is on display when he gives his best every day in practice. A great teammate is when he is sacrificing himself for the team, being willing to sit on the bench, for instance, if another player can help the team more by guarding an opponent or being able to exploit an opponent's weakness. Being a great teammate means staying positive and cheering on teammates and being happy for their personal success since this leads to the team's success. A great teammate buys into the program and can inspire other people to work harder and to strive to be better even if he is not the best athlete on the team.

A great teammate is *not* someone who has great statistics, particularly if the stats are so good because he hogs the ball or deprives teammates of other opportunities. A great teammate is not someone who is talented and a floor leader but is not friendly in the locker room and doesn't say hi to you in the hallways.

Wil Larson is a great example of a good teammate. He cheers on everyone, does whatever the coach or teammates ask of him. He often stays after practice to play one on one with teammates working on certain moves. When he is on the field he is always positive and works his hardest. When he is on the bench he cheers the team on. Wil Larson is the kind of guy who you want to have on your team, even if he is not on the field. That is what makes a great teammate.

We ask students to rank these models from best to weakest and write about the specific reasons that make one superior to the others. We then have students discuss their

➤ *Reading anchor standards 1–9*

➤ *Lesson idea*

➤ *Writing standards 5 and 7, and collaboration and speaking and listening*

rankings—and more important, the reasons for their rankings—in small groups. This leads directly to the creation of class criteria for our own extended definitions.

Student survey. Another great activity for foregrounding definition and the obstacles to it (modified from Johannessen, Kahn, and Walter 1982 to focus more on leadership) is to have students experience the difficulties of defining everyday terms. Individual students provide the best possible answer to questions like:

1. About how many inches of snow would have to fall before you could consider a storm a blizzard?

2. Which of the following are cities, towns, or suburbs? Green Bay, WI; Beverly Hills, CA; Aspen, CO; Boise, ID; Los Angeles, CA; Madison, WI; Beaver Dam, WI.

3. At what age does adolescence typically start and end? Middle age? Old age?

4. What is the average height and weight of an accomplished athlete?

5. How many people in this room have brown hair?

6. How many arts courses and activities does the school sponsor?

7. If a climate is described as "tropical" what would you expect the average temperature to be on a summer's day? What about a climate described as "high desert"?

8. Rank the following activities in terms of how well they demonstrate leadership: daily morning paper route, photographer for the yearbook, lead role in the school play, member of the ski club, vestry at church, volunteer at a hospital, captain of cross country team, student council secretary.

9. How many leaders are there in this classroom?

10. What leadership opportunities are available to you at school and at home?

Then we ask students to justify the thinking behind their answers. As they do so, it becomes clear that there are sometimes several criteria for a concept. The blizzard designation, for example, refers to wind and visibility as much as it does to snow. Who are we referring to when we talk about athletes—high school? professional? runners? basketball players? football players? Don't we need to be more precise? Aren't there different types of athletes? How are we to define *brown*, *teen*, and *the arts*? What are the breadth and limits of each term? Where does each begin and end? How do we formulate and apply clear criteria? How do we relate specific cases and examples to the criteria? How do we differentiate borderline cases?

As students discuss the problems they encounter, they come to grips with the problems that must be addressed while also defining the criteria that makes up a useful definition.

Finally, we ask students to come up with their own survey items requiring definition in general and of leadership in particular and encourage them to ask their parents or friends to answer the questions. They then monitor the answers as well as what obstacles are encountered.

Articulating criteria/rubrics. After the knowledge gained in earlier activities, students can begin articulating criteria for a rubric or checksheet for composing definition. The rubric lays out an action plan for "composing to practice" all that we need to learn to do. As much as possible we assist our students to articulate their own criteria for an effective culminating project. For kids to get good at something, they need the opportunity to practice and to be part of the process. We want our students to be able to develop, articulate, and apply critical standards, so we make it their responsibility to be part of that process of articulating and applying such standards.

➤ *Lesson idea*

Students' reasons for defining and the difficulties they encountered in creating definitions help the class articulate the criteria for a strong extended definition and create a rubric or performance checklist.

We post the rubric and continue to update it through the drafting and finalization stages. Articulated criteria then guides task completion and the application of critical standards throughout practice, composing, and revising. Throughout the process students are grouping, analyzing, and distinguishing in the service of defining, all of this based on specific criteria.

➤ *Writing standards 5 and 7*

The example checklist in Figure 9.2 is from a tenth-grade class. Since they are learning to read and write like disciplinary experts, we incorporate some of the students' phrasings as well as the "terms of art" from the discipline. We also help the students articulate the criteria in the order in which a writer might do things, so the criteria become a kind of task analysis for what they need to learn to do.

Composing to Practice Definition

In this phase, we continue to develop strategies for generating material for the final compositions as often as possible but focus primarily on learning procedures for shaping material into definitions. We continue to revisit and update our criteria. Following are some activities that help us (1) identify the concept generally, (2) generate criteria that discriminate between the target concept (to be defined) and related but essentially different concepts, and (3) generate examples that clarify the distinctions.

Figure 9.2 Definition Checklist

1. Identify something that needs to be defined and explain the importance of defining this concept (unless this is obvious) in a particular context.

2. State the concept to be defined and place it in the "class" or group of ideas to which it most clearly and closely belongs.

3. Gather, generate, and analyze examples, counterexamples, aspects, and forms of the concept.

4. Identify specific criteria (or *bases*) that mark the use of the concept to be defined. Where does the term begin and end? How is it differentiated from others in its class?

5. Provide examples that exemplify these criteria and explain (or *warrant*) how the example concretely demonstrates the criteria.

6. Provide counterexamples so you can show the limits of the concept, and explain how these examples lie outside the term.

7. If things are really sticky, you might want to examine a borderline case and explain what would make that example belong as an example of this concept or of a different related concept.

➤ *CCSS standards for evidentiary reasoning*

➤ *Lesson idea*

Defining the self. We start "close to home" (that is, stick to students' personal experience) by having students write short definitions of themselves—to capture their identity, the absolutely essential qualities of who they are. We have them share this definition with a friend or adult mentor, who suggests things to keep, add, or delete. Generally, students can follow the formula: listing classes of people they belong to as well as how they are unique or different from others in those classes. Here's a model Jeff uses for students to read, critique, and revise:

> Jeff is an athlete. He is an athlete of endurance sports that are silent (nonmotorized). He likes to sea and whitewater kayak, to road bike and mountain bike long distances in remote places, and to do Nordic ski marathoning. He is a thinker too. He is quick-thinking and quick-witted and likes to tell jokes and pull funnies, to make points through humor. He likes to read and write and think about things like how to teach and how to live in more sustainable ways, and he always wants to put his ideas into action. Jeff is a teacher, but not one who purveys information. He likes to teach by creating situations where students do the work through

activities like drama and art and making videos and websites. Jeff is relational. Jeff is only Jeff when skiing, biking, or kayaking with others; telling jokes to others; teaching others through joint activity. Take away Jeff's activity and social relationships and he would no longer be Jeff. Jeff being too quiet would not be Jeff. Jeff lecturing is not Jeff. Jeff skiing alone, slowly, or for a short distance is not Jeff. Activity is his elixir; relationships are his joy.

Biopoems. Another way of making definition immediately and personally relevant is through a biopoem about oneself or about a literary character or historical figure, or of a concept. You and your students should feel free to adapt the formula to fit the needs of the moment, but here are some of the prompts we've used:

➤ *Lesson idea*

First name:
Who is a kind of (member of the class of):

Descriptive words:	Traits:
Who needs:	Friend of:
Who feels:	Foe of:
Who fears:	Lover of:
Who gives:	Who believes:
Who would like to see:	Who gave:
Who is definitely *not*:	Who is considered by others to be:
Who typically:	Who typically does not:
Resident of:	Who acts to/in service of:
Who is like/unlike:	Who contains multitudes of:
Who is made up of/consists of:	Who is caused by:
Who is closely/distantly related to:	Who compares–contrasts with:
Whose relevant history is:	Who is an example of/not an example of:

Last name:

After writing a biopoem about themselves or a character, it's easy to write one about a concept. Here's an example a sixth grader came up with:

➤ *Lesson idea*

Title: Photosynthesis So Finely Defined and Refined and Personified!
PHOTO
Botanical, natural, life-giving, carbon-dioxide sucking
Who needs sunshine to happen

Who feels green and greening
Who fears total darkness
Who gives out oxygen through respiration
Who would like to see the world covered with trees and plants
Essential resident of the breathing pulsing Mother Earth!
Creator of the oxygen in the atmosphere we breathe
SYNTHESIS!

We then have students enumerate what is necessary to the process of identifying and defining themselves, others, or a concept—as unique individuals or ideas—and apply these criteria to our evolving heuristics about defining (and defining identity). We are moving from close-to-home defining of the self to further-from-home defining of concepts. In the context of our unit, students then apply these techniques to leaders they have read about or to effective leadership as a concept.

➤ *Lesson idea*

In-the-style-of poems. Another quick, fun, and useful technique for developing extended definitions is the in-the-style-of poem (see Kenneth Koch and Kate Ferrell's book *Sleeping on the Wing*, for example), where students write after a model, usually in the identifiable style of a famous poet. Emily Dickinson's "Hope Is a Thing with Feathers" is a great example, since it states a metaphor and criteria for a definition of hope and ends with a contrasting example. Our students followed Dickinson's model and created an extended metaphor for loyalty, honesty, flexibility, proactivity, or another trait related to leadership.

➤ *Lesson idea*

➤ *Writing anchor standard 6*

➤ *Writing standards 4, 5, 7, and collaboration and speaking and listening standards*

➤ *Lesson idea*

Video definitions. Our students also enjoy creating YouTube video definitions that visually depict examples and nonexamples of a concept around the inquiry.

The ideas so far relate to all three crux moves. But sometimes we focus more specifically on a single move. What's important is to give the kids enough practice to be successful with the crux move but to move on when they have mastered it.

The pyramid game. Our favorite activity for helping kids identify "classes," or meaningful groupings, is the pyramid game, from Johannessen et al. (1982). To prepare, we come up with ten or so lists of items belonging to a single class. We start with familiar items and then move on to material from our unit—leadership in this case. We also reward different kinds of interests and expertise and therefore encourage learning group teammates to work together. The lists are very easy to make with a simple Google search, and after modeling, students can create their own lists for use by the class. Here are some examples:

Little Debbie	Holding	Mike Krzyzewski
Mudpie	Clipping	Pat Summit
Twinkie	Interference	Billy Martin
Snickers	Offsides	Vince Lombardi
Jolly Ranchers	Grounding	John Wooden

Napoleon	Cleopatra
Grant	Queen Elizabeth
Washington	Margaret Thatcher
Alexander the Great	Hilary Clinton
Julius Caesar	Angela Merkel

To play the game, create teams of four or five students. Uncover the first element of a list and give group 1 the chance to guess the "class" or "grouping." If they abstain, any other group can take a stab. Teams get 3 points for a correct guess and minus 1 for an incorrect guess.

At this point there are two options. One, you can continue uncovering the list to ask for and reward the right answer (or a more precise answer: for example, if students guessed great college basketball coaches for the third list above after seeing Mike Krzyzewski and Pat Summit unveiled, they could be awarded points, but the rest of the list reveals that the list more generally is about the class of great coaches of any sport at any level). Or you can move beyond identifying classes to identify criteria and explain how all uncovered examples fit the criteria. After displaying the complete list we award each team points for collaborative writing that identifies the criteria necessary to being on the list, and that explains how each item on the list meets the criteria they identified. (Students can also write about disqualifying criteria, which lets them practice distinguishing and providing counterexamples.) The pyramid game helps students produce substance related to the inquiry as they practice mastering the procedures of forming definitions. A twofer!

Here's another version: put a contrasting example in each group. For example, in list one, add an apple. Make the game about identifying the class and identifying and explaining the contrasting example. Kids will have to explain how the apple is a sweet snack, like everything else in the list, but is a natural complex carbohydrate, not a manmade concoction of simple sugars. If you can connect the items on the list to ideas students have been studying in other subjects or courses, so much the better (our students had just done a healthy foods unit in health class).

Our students enjoy coming up with their own lists about leaders of particular kinds in a second iteration of the game. We often learn a lot about popular culture from this kind of work, and it gives kids more practice thinking about the concepts of leadership and the procedures of forming definitions.

➤ *Lesson idea*

Name that group. Identifying classes is important but so is knowing the limits of the class. Sometimes students need help naming specific, substantive differences between items that are related but might not fit the same class. A great practice technique here is "name that group" (Johannessen et al. 1982).

Provide groups of students with a collection of objects like seashells, or CD or video game covers, or other concrete objects (or photos of such objects). Ask each group to divide the objects into two groups without leaving any item out. Then ask the group to explain the characteristics of each grouping and how the characteristics are different to distinguish membership in one group or the other. You can quickly move to photos of leaders in different domains like sports, the arts, technology, etc., piles of books about leaders, or newsmagazines that contain stories about leaders. Students will find that there are many different ways to group their items, depending on the criteria they decide to use.

➤ *Writing standards 5 and 7*

As a follow-up, ask students to create groupings for the items in a closet, cupboard, or drawer at home, along with brief explanations of each grouping's common characteristics or violations of the general grouping criteria.

➤ *Lesson idea*

Name that group: The sequel. Up the ante. Have students use the same collection of objects but create elaborate criteria for new classifications: perhaps related to function, appearance, history, material, etc. (this is a direct lead-in to learning about more complex text types like comparison and classification). Model your creation of such criteria for students first. We ask only that at least two items belong to each group and we do allow an item to belong to more than one group. The purpose here is *generating criteria* for differentiating and grouping.

When students have created groupings and characteristic criteria, they can give their items and criteria to another group and ask that group to classify the same set of items according to the offered criteria. This will demonstrate how clear and usable the criteria are for noting important similarities and differences that warrant including or excluding an item from a class of objects. If the criteria aren't clear and usable, students can discuss why and revise their criteria accordingly.

➤ *Writing standards 2, 4, and 5*

➤ *Lesson idea*

Oaths and contracts. For more practice creating criteria, examples, and explanations of how the examples meet the criteria, we have students create oaths or contracts related to a familiar concept or term, then to further-from-home concepts related to the inquiry. Using the model in Figure 9.3, students can fill in their own criteria for friendship in the underlined spaces; use some of the numbered lines and invent others; or start from scratch.

Afterward we ask students to take one of their criteria and compose a specific anecodetal example of how they would meet that criterion. They might also describe a contrasting example and explain how this would be a violation of the criterion.

Students can then create a contract or oath or list of commitments related to a specific leadership situation of their choice, which will help them produce substance for future writing on leadership.

➤ *Writing standards 2, 4, and 5*

Negative examples. To help students develop contrasting examples, we often provide negative examples of leaders or negative models of definitions. Students can also generate or find their own negative models through an Internet research. Students then use the examples to create "how not to" guidelines. On the next page is a set of guidelines a class of tenth graders came up with.

➤ *Lesson idea*

➤ *Writing standards 6 and 7*

Figure 9.3   Creating a Friendship Oath

I do solemnly swear and affirm that for the privilege of being a friend <u>to my friend Dale</u>:

1. I will support my friend in his <u>interests, beliefs, family, and job responsibilities</u>.

2. I will promote his <u>talents and abilities and his becoming his truest self</u>.

3. I will respect my friend and protect <u>his beliefs and reputation</u> with diligence.

4. I will never <u>mislead or judge or get upset with</u> my friend due to <u>unknown and unshared criteria</u>.

5. I will protect my friend's <u>secrets</u> and will expect <u>the same</u> as compensation.

6. I will practice <u>constant communication</u> and avoid <u>offensive conduct</u>; I will <u>believe the best of my friend on all occasions unless proven otherwise</u>.

7. I will never exploit the <u>insecurities and foibles</u> of my friend in public unless the justice of the case demands it.

8. I will not, for idiosyncratic or personal reasons, <u>deny respect or affection</u>.

9. I will personally fulfill <u>the responsibility to help my friend to the fullest of my ability whenever he calls upon me or seems to be in need</u>.

10. <u>I will tell my friend the truth, even if it is hard, especially if it is in his best long-term interest</u>.

How *Not* to Write a Definition: Things to Avoid!

■ Don't define a word by repeating or restating the word or using well-known synonyms.

> "Patriotism is being a patriot." Come on!

Better:

> "Patriotism is acting in ways that serve the democratic ideals of America in ways that serve all citizens, rich or poor, of any religion, background, or ideology."

> "Skin cancer is a bad disease of the skin." How does this clarify anything? Come on!

Better:

> "Skin cancer is a disease of malignant skin cells replicating beyond control."

■ Don't use new terms or complicated words that your audience won't understand and that they are going to have to look up! Really! You are writing this to *help the audience* not cause them more work!

■ Avoid defining with "*X* is when" and "*X* is where" statements. Define a noun with a noun, a verb with a verb, like that, you know!

■ Don't go long if you can keep it shorter! *Shorter is better, baby!*

■ Keep the "class" portion of your definition adequate but focused. It should be large enough to include all members of the term you are defining but no larger.

■ Don't define with just a metaphor: "Patriotism is the last refuge of a scoundrel" can convey something true, but it's not a definition, which is supposed to tell us what *patriotism* is. Metaphors can help a definition, but don't provide one. *Get it?*

■ Don't use personal details that other people won't get like how Wil Larson is a great soccer teammate or how your grandfather exhibits exemplary stinginess. Most people don't know Wil or your grandfather! So this reference won't help them, *donchaknow!*

➤ *Lesson idea*

➤ *Writing standards 2, 4, and 5*

➤ *Lesson idea*

➤ *Writing standards 2 and 4 and multimodality standards*

A variation that focuses on the concepts in the unit is to create a list of how *not* to be a leader with an explanation that relates to each criterion.

Frayer models (see Figures 9.4 and 9.5) are great graphic organizers for helping students think about putting all the crux moves together (except explaining how examples fit criteria, which students can be asked to do after creating the Frayer model).

Figure 9.4   Frayer Model

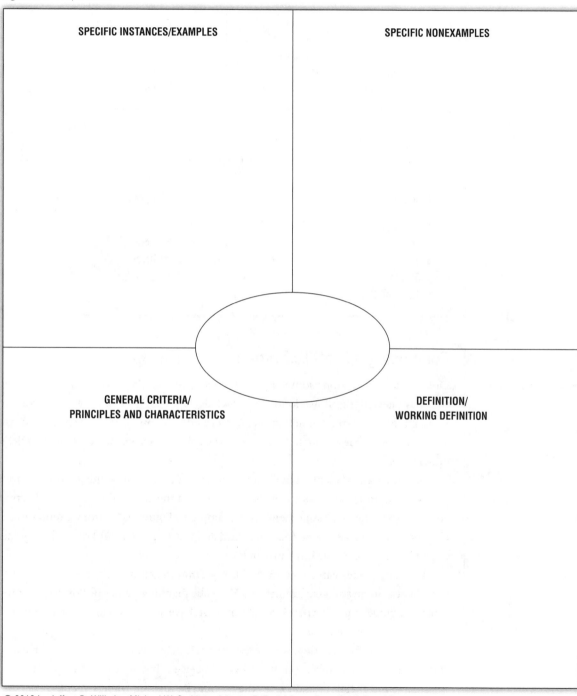

Figure 9.5 Example of a Frayer Model

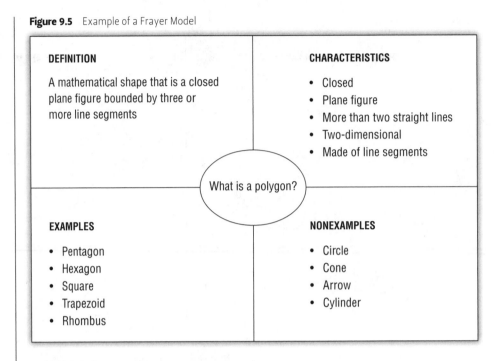

DEFINITION

A mathematical shape that is a closed plane figure bounded by three or more line segments

CHARACTERISTICS

- Closed
- Plane figure
- More than two straight lines
- Two-dimensional
- Made of line segments

What is a polygon?

EXAMPLES

- Pentagon
- Hexagon
- Square
- Trapezoid
- Rhombus

NONEXAMPLES

- Circle
- Cone
- Arrow
- Cylinder

Composing a Draft Definition

➤ See Chapter 3.

Once students have done some of the composing to plan and practice explored here, they have developed all five kinds of knowledge and can now put these into play in writing a formal extended definition. We remind students of the criteria for the assignment and negotiate further changes to the rubric or checklist based on what they have learned.

We often ask students to collaborate to create a planning guide before we proceed with drafting. The guide can also be created at the end of the unit as a reflective composing-to-transfer assignment. The example in Figure 9.6 is from a tenth-grade classroom. (We've also done this with third and fourth graders; although their guide is simpler, it captures the same principles.)

➤ Writing anchor standard 6

Planning guides can be put in the library or on the class website and used by future classes. Some students like making YouTube planning guides or PowerPoint presentation guides for their peers. Sometimes we have students build on and improve guides from a previous year.

To promote peer editing, we use the peer editing guide in Figure 9.7. A guide like this reinforces good collaboration and good peer editing advice and helps students internalize the questions and moves they should be making when self-editing.

Figure 9.6 Definition Essay Planning Guide

1. Identify what needs to be defined and why.

2. Identify the audience and their needs. For example, is it a *general* audience for whom terms must be broken down in simple novice terms, or is it a *specific/specialized* audience who will know technical terms and have other background that will not require further explanation?

3. State the sentence definition (term, class, and distinguishing characteristics):

   • The *term* is the concept(s) to be defined.

   • The *class* is the group or category of similar terms in which the term to be defined is to be placed.

   • The *characteristics* are the essential qualities that set the term apart from all other terms of the same class.

4. Your job is to make the concept clearer in the reader's mind, so plan how to develop your simple definition into an extended one. You will need to do research to develop some of the following:

   • Provide specific examples.

   • Use metaphor, analogy, or comparison.

   • Discuss contrasting ideas that might be confused with this one.

   • Describe parts or subtypes.

   • Put the concept in relation to other concepts—how is lying related to honesty, for example?

   • Provide some history of the term or idea.

   • Describe and commit to any values that may be part of your definition—for example, a leader must be uplifting to his followers and inspire them to healthy action that is of benefit to themselves and others.

   • Apply or look for a test that can be used to determine whether something falls within the concept—an *operational definition*. If so, tell how the test works. For example, a car qualifies as a *zero emission vehicle* if it performs a certain way (does not emit anything other than water, hydrogen, and oxygen) on a particular test (an emissions test).

➤ *Using the planning guide helps students meet writing anchor standards 3 and 4–10.*

Composing a Final Draft Definition

Students now turn their attention to surface-level details, polishing the draft for final submission, public sharing, and perhaps even electronic archiving! As suggested by Smagorinsky et al. (2010), explanations of how examples meet criteria are often weak points in student definitions. To focus students' attention on this move, give a

➤ *Writing anchor standard 7; speaking and listening standards*

➤ *Lesson idea*

Figure 9.7   Peer Editing Guide for Definitions

General Reaction

Read your classmate's piece quickly to understand its ideas.

Then tell the author: What was defined? What class does it belong to and how is it different from other elements in its class?

What are your first impressions about the idea being defined?

In what ways was the essay enlightening and entertaining?

Considered Reaction

Read the piece again. Tell the author:

What is the main point? What is the dominant impression? What stands out the most about this word/concept? How did you see the word/phrase in a new light? How is it different from other similar ideas? How does this definition help you? How might you be able to use this definition in the future?

Consider what to keep:

How has what you as the reader already know or think you know about the word/term been considered and addressed? How have popular misconceptions been addressed?

What particular experiences/examples/metaphors/visuals/etc. helped you understand the term? What counterexamples helped you differentiate the idea from similar ones in the same class?

Consider what to change/move/add:

What clarification do you still need? What experiences/examples/metaphors/visuals/etc. might help you better understand the term and how it is differentiated from other similar ideas?

Consider what to delete:

What is unnecessary in the paper? What words, phrases, or ideas are repeated unnecessarily, or "pad" rather than "add" to the definition.

➤ *Writing anchor standards 4 and 5; speaking and listening and collaboration standards*

minilesson on terms that introduce explanations—*because, owing to, in light of, following from, wheareas, since, for the reason that,* etc.—and have students practice writing explanations using these terms in the context of their writing. (See the example in Figure 9.8.) After this exposure, peer editors should be able to identify places in a paper where explanations are adequate and where they have not been provided or are not clearly connecting the example to the criterion. Then the strategy becomes

Figure 9.8. Explanation Minilesson (based on Smagorinsky et al. 2010)

➤ *Writing anchor standard 4; reading anchor standards 4 and 5*

I'll Show You How

Criterion: An effective leader is proactive versus reactive.

Example: Coach Smith prepared his team to play offense against a full-court press, even though he wasn't sure they would have to.

Explanation: *In light of the fact* that he thought there was a possibility that his team might face a full court-press, Coach Smith decided to prepare them for this instead of waiting and having to react if it did happen. This kind of preparation meets the criterion for proactivity.

Now You Fill in the Blanks

Criterion: An effective leader acts in the interests of those s/he is leading.

Example: President Obama has suggested higher taxes for the rich even though he is wealthy himself.

Explanation: (use your causal transition here) (explanation here).

---

embedded in the students' own writing as they apply what they have learned while they revise their papers.

Composing to Transfer Knowledge About Definition

Daily practice and reflections, exit tickets, and all other formative assessments are forms of composing to transfer, because they inform students' reading and composing of definitions. So are the continually updated criteria guides, planning guides, and peer editing guides that students create and use.

Composing to transfer occurs when students rearticulate heuristics; general purposes, principles and moves; and situations in which they could use definition in the future in school and at home. We have students compose a *process analysis* of how they completed their definition, along with descriptions of challenges and how they met them and how they will use what they have learned in the future (see Chapter 8). If they describe experiencing trouble they could not overcome, we know what students might need more practice on right now or in the future.

➤ *Lesson idea*

Process analyses are often more useful to our assessment of student understanding than the compositions themselves. We often have students read the process analyses of the other members of their learning group and then write a group memo of

➤ *Lesson idea*

➤ *Writing anchor standards 7–9*

advice to us as teachers about what to keep, add, and do differently in our future teaching. The students are thus conducting real-world research and data analysis with an immediate benefit to future students in our school. Reading these process analyses ourselves and looking for patterns is a form of teacher research and reflection that helps us improve our own future teaching as we continually learn from our students how to teach them more effectively.

Comparing and Contrasting

But What's the Difference?

Jeff's in Canada today, in Victoria, on Vancouver Island, as he drafts the introduction to this chapter. *The Globe and Mail*'s cover article is about the crash of a Russian plane that killed all the players on a professional hockey team. The first several pages are nothing but coverage of this tragic event. Whenever Jeff reads a Canadian newspaper, he immediately begins making comparisons to American news coverage, perspectives, and attitudes. In this case, he's wondering how much coverage this event is getting in the U.S., which is much less hockey-crazed than Canada, the home of ice hockey.

After reading about the hockey tragedy, Jeff turns to a feature called Lives Lived, a full obituary of an ordinary Canadian. Today's is about a lifelong elementary school teacher. Jeff can't help but compare this eulogy to the lives of other seemingly normal but heroic people he knows or has known, particularly teachers.

Sometimes a reader doesn't have to compare and contrast on his own. The paper also offers stories that make comparisons and contrasts explicit. The business page has a major feature comparing the Canadian and U.S. economies and their economic policies. Articles in the Life section include a study comparing the attention spans, attitudes, and achievement of students who get less than six hours of sleep a night with those who get nine or more. Another article compares a medical school education in which students begin seeing patients on day one with the more traditional approach that starts with two years of book-learning information before seeing the first patient. (Guess what? The inquiry approach featuring hands-on learning and application is greatly superior to the decontextualized book-learning approach.)

As we're revising this chapter, Michael's department has just had its annual holiday party. Michael finished a disappointing second in the holiday tie competition but he led the talent competition with his parody of "My Favorite Things." (One verse: Department meetings that go on and on / Reading Vygotsky, though he is long gone / Responding to emails / That each hour brings / These are a few professorial things.) No voting is possible without comparing and contrasting. Later Michael went out Christmas shopping for his wife and before he settled on the gold bracelet he bought her he had to make lots of comparisons: 18 carat or 14 carat? bangle, cuff, or link? He drove to the jewelry store with his daughter Catherine, who is a big rap fan. Michael was horrified by some of the lyrics, and Catherine responded by comparing and contrasting what he heard with the lyrics of heavy-metal music.

Comparison–contrast is on full display every winter for a baseball fan like Jim, who wakes up every morning to see which player has been signed by which team. Baseball fans read statistic after statistic comparing players not only on their performance, but also by the salary they make. Fans want to know how adding one player helps one team versus another team, and how that additional salary affects who else may or may not be added to the team. In other words, the comparisons are layered, and the reader of any baseball blog during free agency is likely to see statistics and salaries for teams and for players being compared daily (and even more often).

Why Comparison–Contrast Matters

Just sayin': explicit and implicit comparison fills our lives. It's one of the primary ways we think and make meaning. Think of the work practitioners do in the disciplines. In this morning's *New York Times*, economist Paul Krugman contrasts Keynesian economics with that of the Austrian school. And yesterday physicist Brian Greene wrote about comparing theoretical models and the interpretations that follow to the data gleaned from the Large Haldron Collider. On a more personal note, he compared his excitement about the possible discovery of the Higgs particle to his amazement at discovering in his teens "that mathematical symbols scratched in pencil on a piece of paper could describe things that actually happened in the real world" (Greene 2011, A33), a discovery that began his lifelong love affair with physics.

We learn by comparing the familiar with the new and unknown; we come to terms with new situations and challenges informed by how they seem similar to and different from our past experience; we use the "past made present" to think through current situations and the "past and present made future" to imaginatively rehearse upcoming challenges (Wilhelm and Novak 2011). Beyond question, it's crucial for our students to be able to compare and contrast, both in daily life at home and in academia.

Model Unit: What Influences Us?

This unit addresses the essential question *what influences us?* as it leads to the larger essential question *what is most influential/powerful?* The question could also be framed, *how do we decide and choose?* These essential questions lead in many directions at the unit and lesson level, and can be used with individual stories to explore such questions as *which character/force/idea is most powerful? which setting/idea/force/argument is most influential?* etc. These questions create a context that requires and rewards comparing and contrasting.

In this unit we compare and contrast various influences on particular personal and historical (or current-event) decisions that are related in some way. During our most recent teaching of the unit, the class read *Julius Caesar*, and most of the students composed a culminating essay that compared the influences on a character in that play with the influences they had experienced in their own life.

Composing to Plan: Comparison–Contrast

We've long argued (see Smith and Wilhelm 2006; Wilhelm 2007; Wilhelm, Wilhelm, and Boas 2009) that the best way to encourage our students to develop any skill is to create an inquiry environment that foregrounds purposeful learning for functional results. Any inquiry framed with an essential question involving ranking will involve comparison. What is *the most powerful* chemical? Who is the *greatest* military leader? What are the *most significant* animal adaptations? What are the *most important* mathematical insights/scientific discoveries? *greatest* love poems/movies/buildings? Who are the *greatest* athletes/basketball players/baseball players? *most innovative* musicians/artists/dancers? *most memorable* villains? What are the *most influential* artworks? *most influential* speeches/political initiatives/military campaigns/covert operations?

> ➤ *Unit ideas*

Comparisons depend on describing and defining and often on listing and naming. They can involve any number of subjects, but sometimes they involve only two. Comparison, like any thought pattern, can be the substructure of a longer piece—a sentence, paragraph, section, chapter, or complete text. It can also, like any thought pattern, be the superstructure for a piece. Comparison is used to develop ideas in other kinds of informational writing like description or defining, as well as in narrative, poetry, or argument.

> ➤ *Reading standard 7 for literature and for informational texts at any grade level (all the way back to kindergarten, where this is done "with support")*

As we've noted in previous chapters, *think-alouds* are always a great way to model what to notice and do with a thought pattern, text structure, strategy, or any other

> ➤ *Lesson idea*

process that might be new or challenging to students. In a think-aloud, you think through a reading, writing, problem solving, or performance process, "taking off the top of your head" to make your thinking and decision-making processes and responses visible and available to others.

Think-alouds can be spoken out loud (when we model how to read or write a particular kind of text structure or use a particular strategy), or they can be recorded or written (as when students document their reading "moves" when reading a text). (Wilhelm 2012 is a book-length treatment of using multiple kinds of think-alouds to teach various strategies and text structures.)

Jeff is a member of his high school's movie club. Members pick a movie they want to see, view it, then meet to discuss the film. Choosing the monthly film involves comparing–contrasting. Typically, two or three movies are suggested. Club members compare the movies and make a decision based on their articulated purposes of sharing a meaningful experience, enjoying themselves, and having something substantive to talk about afterward. Comparing two movies aloud is a great way to introduce students to crux moves of comparison. (The crux move of a think-aloud is to name the crux moves as you make them!)

Recently the two movie-club choices being considered were Werner Herzog's *Cave of Forgotten Dreams* and the animated feature *Puss in Boots*. The group had a lively

➤ *Lesson idea*

discussion before deciding on *Cave of Forgotten Dreams*. Jeff later models and thinks through this decision-making process in class to model using comparison–contrast. He covers the following points:

1. Our club had to choose a movie to see. Crux move: *Have a purpose for comparing.*

2. We reviewed our purposes for movie club viewing/discussion. The two movies we most wanted to see were Werner Herzog's *Cave of Forgotten Dreams* and *Puss in Boots*. Both were playing at movie theatres close to the school, important because we had to walk there. We wanted to choose the movie that most of us would enjoy and learn something from and that would give us the most interesting ideas to talk about afterward. This is the second crux step in comparing: *Identify at least two things to compare at this time and in this situation.*

➤ *Writing anchor standard 8*

3. We agreed we would talk to people who had seen one or both of the movies and that we would watch trailers and read reviews from various sources. This is the third necessary move: *Gather data about the items or issues to be compared so we can operate from a rich base of knowledge.*

4. Club members brought in research and grouped interesting points we wanted to consider under the headings genre, topic, reviews, special features, special considerations, rating, and length. Necessary move: *Identify meaningful points of comparison/contrast related to the purpose.*

➤ *Points of contact are included in reading anchor standards 3, 5, 6, and 9.*

5. *We then ranked/prioritized the points of comparison* in order of importance: genre, topic, rating, special considerations, reviews, special features, and length. We put topic, genre, and rating first because we had agreed we would not see certain kinds of movies (like horror) and would not see movies with a rating that might upset parents (R), but would see movies on substantive topics that led to discussion. A movie had to meet these three criteria before we could apply the other points of comparison. Special considerations (including the directors) came next, because it dealt with why the movie appealed to us and might meet our purposes. We then looked at reviews and rankings from sites like Rotten Tomatoes because we wanted to see what the critics thought and avoid seeing a dud. Then came special features and length (length was a factor because we wanted to have time afterward to talk).

6. The next crux move was to *decide how to present the points.* We considered doing one characteristic from *Puss* then the same characteristic from *Cave*, but we thought it might be hard to keep the two movies straight. Therefore we decided to present all the points for *Puss in Boots* first, in order of importance, then all the points for *Cave*, in the same order (parallel structure). We presented *Puss* first because most people already favored *Puss*. Since the final presentation is the privileged position, we wanted to give *Cave* fair consideration.

7. Then we had to *describe and characterize each point of comparison for each item.*

Puss in Boots

Genre: animated action and adventure, prequel to *Shrek* movies, features lots of fairy tale and nursery rhyme figures

Topic: the backstory/origin story of Puss and his adventures before he meets Shrek

Rating: PG

Special considerations: directed by Chris Miller; his most highly rated movie was *Shrek 2*; has directed lots of duds like *Police Academy 4*; seems to specialize in sequels

Reviews: consistently 3 to 4 stars, repeatedly called solid family-friendly entertainment

Special features/recommendations: 3-D, animated, Antonio Banderas gets rave reviews for his voice work, funny

Length: 90 minutes

Cave of Forgotten Dreams

Genre: documentary

Topic: oldest known pictorial creations (the beginning of art?), artistic creation, the nature of time

Rating: G

Special considerations: filmmakers had exclusive access to the cave and its 32,000-year-old paintings in perfect condition; very difficult filming conditions; supposedly needs to be seen on big screen; delivers a "one-of-a-kind art-history lesson"; director Werner Herzog is super-famous, mischievous, countercultural, quirky, and unique

Reviews: solid 4 to 5 stars

Special features/recommendations: groundbreaking content, 3-D, uses the latest in cinematic technology to show how the art uses the contours of the cave for effect

Length: 90 minutes

8. We bulleted the major points and put them on charts displayed next to each other so comparable points were across from each other. This is a further crux move: *Use appropriate graphic organizers to place hold data so it is organized and can be analyzed.*

9. Our final crux move was to *make value judgments and reach some kind of conclusion or choice* based on those judgments.

   Value judgment on Puss: Probably the kind of movie you would watch at home with your family. Lots of opportunities to see it outside of our club. Probably would not lead to substantive discussion about content, form, cinematography, etc.

   Value judgment on Cave: This should give us a lot to talk about as far as content (man's urge to create art), process (the filming and the construction of the film), form (the flipping back and forth from the cave to interviews), the director (who is a narrator/character). This sounds like a unique kind of cinema.

   Decision: Okay, we will go see *Cave of Forgotten Dreams* and we will be happy about it.

After Jeff presents the think-aloud, the class highlights the major moves of the comparison–contrast process and puts them on an anchor chart, agreeing to update the chart as needed to guide their work and provide the basis for a final rubric:

➤ *Crux moves*

- Identify a purpose for comparing.
- Identify at least two things worth comparing (because you have an important choice/decision to make or something important to understand or evaluate) and be able to say why these are worth comparing at this time and in this situation.
- Gather data about the items or issues to be compared so you can operate from knowledge.
- Identify meaningful points of comparison–contrast related to the purpose.
- Rank/prioritize the points of comparison.
- Decide how to present the points.
- Describe and characterize each point of comparison for each item.
- Use appropriate graphic organizers to placehold data so it is organized and can be analyzed.
- Make value judgments and some kind of conclusion or choice that you can justify through the data and evidentiary reasoning.

➤ *Writing anchor standards 4 and 10*

➤ *Writing anchor standard 2*

➤ *Writing anchor standard 3*

➤ *Reading anchor standards 3, 5, 6, and 9*

➤ *Writing standard 4 at any grade level and speaking and listening anchor standard 4*

➤ *Speaking and listening anchor standard 5*

➤ *Reading anchor standards 1–3, 5, and 6*

Next the class connects the think-aloud to the unit's essential question: *What influences us?* What in the movie club's thinking process influenced the final decision and why? How might the influences be different in different situations? Might there have been influences not mentioned in the think-aloud, like Jeff's preference? This reflective activity is a kind of composing to transfer in that it place holds ideas about influence and about comparison–contrast.

For homework the students list some instances when they make comparisons in their daily lives. The next day the class conducts a group think-aloud of a couple of these comparisons (what to have for breakfast or whether to eat breakfast!) and consider what in the think-aloud most influenced their ultimate conclusion.

➤ *Reinforces writing standards 2 and 7*

To further develop knowledge of purpose and context, students brainstorm all the purposes for comparing that they can identify, both in one's personal lives and in the disciplines. (The previous activities frontload and prepare students for success with this activity.) Here's what the class comes up with:

➤ *Lesson idea*

- To make a decision—decide which one is better (like a horse race).
- To help you see that despite differences, there are these similarities (useful for healing, negotiation, fostering agreement).

- To see that despite similarities, there are these differences (useful for slicing things finely, seeing beyond the surface, problematizing and complexifying what seems simple, reframing).
- To persuade someone else about these prior reasonings.
- To evaluate—compare to a rubric/standards.
- To achieve status—differentiate self from the crowd or one group from other groups.
- To highlight and place hold key details, see patterns, create new insights.
- To show difference over time.
- To discover and problem solve: figure out the difference between animal and plant cell structure, for example.
- To understand subtext and implied comparisons (juxtapositions, irony of all kinds: verbal, situational, and dramatic).
- To identify procedural differences: dealing with single verses multiple variable equations—show equations side by side.
- To see multiple perspectives and use them to understand and analyze why and how differences matter.

➤ *Writing standards 2, 5, and 7*

Your students' list needn't be as exhaustive as this one. But such a list shows the wide variety of work comparing–contrasting can do personally and in the disciplines. Creating the list also precludes those ancient and persistent questions *why in the heck do we have to learn this stuff? when are we ever going to use it?* The students have answered these questions for themselves!

Composing to Practice: Frontloading

How do we get the stuff to write a comparison–contrast about a particular topic? And how do we shape that stuff into a comparison–contrast?

➤ *This fits with the CCSS focus on multiple perspectives.*

Conceptual frontloading is a great way not only to activate relevant student background but also to build on it, because different students offer different data and perspectives. Frontloading is also motivating, prompting personal connections to the inquiry and connections from the inquiry back to the world. Finally, frontloading is always a formative assessment, and a template that gives visible signs of accomplishment and progress when returned to throughout the inquiry. Below are some frontloading activities we've used with inquiries into influence. (As always, these activities begin with students' personal experiences and move on to comparisons of ideas.)

Sentence completions. Complete these sentences in any way that rings true for you: ➤ *Lesson idea*

1. I feel influential when _____

2. I feel influenced when _____

3. People with influence should _____

4. People being oppressed by outside influences should _____

5. I'm most influential when _____

6. I'm least influential when _____

7. The most influential person/idea/force is _____

8. The least powerful person/idea/force is _____

Autobiographical writing. Write a journal entry about a time when you felt influ-   ➤ *Lesson idea*
ential and/or persuasive. And/or: Write a journal entry about a time when you felt
persuaded or oppressed by a person or group more influential than you. Reflect:
What do you think persuasion has to do with influence and power? What is the role
of implicit versus explicit forms of pressure and influence?

Opinionnaire. Check the group or individual in each pair who you think is the most   ➤ *Lesson idea*
influential (be prepared to justify your answer):

____ The President   OR   ____ Bill Gates

____ pitcher   OR   ____ batter

____ player   OR   ____ referee

____ women   OR   ____ men

____ actor   OR   ____ script

____ parent   OR   ____ you

____ email   OR   ____ snail mail

____ digital   OR   ____ hard copy documentation

____ Republicans   OR   ____ Democrats

____ president of the
     student body   OR   ____ editor of the school newspaper

___ friends	OR	___ family
___ musician	OR	___ record company
___ Internet	OR	___ TV
___ athlete	OR	___ coach
___ love	OR	___ hate
___ police officer	OR	___ judge
___ comedian	OR	___ politician
___ Armed Forces	OR	___ Congress
___ Supreme Court	OR	___ Congress
___ paintings	OR	___ photographs
___ poetry	OR	___ music
___ individuals	OR	___ groups

Think of some other comparisons between influential people, ideas, or forces you could pose to your classmates.

When they're done, students share answers to the choices they found most interesting. We then ask them to justify their answers to one or two of the choices with a short comparison paragraph that names and assigns features or techniques of exercising influence appropriate to both parties. Students then share their short compositions and identify the comparing "moves" they made and what effects this had on the thinking of the composer and the readers.

You don't need to do all these frontloading activities, though they all provide payoffs throughout the unit. These activities above are flexible. They can be used in various units framed by various questions (*how far are you willing to go to get what you want?* for example, in connection with a deep reading of *Macbeth* or any other text about influence or power or persuasion) or any of the activities can be adapted to work with different inquiry topics. These activities not only develop declarative knowledge but also introduce students to procedural knowledge of substance and form: these are techniques for generating and shaping material they can use in their thinking and composing throughout the unit.

We now ask students to choose a significant experience in their lives that influenced their decisions or behavior in some way, then to identify a current or historical event that influenced someone's decisions and actions in a comparable way.

➤ *Writing anchor standard 10*

➤ *As they compose and read one another's texts, they meet writing standards 2 and 4 and part of 5 and reading standards 1 and 2.*

Composing to Practice: Gathering Substance

As we further practiced and developed our skills in producing substance, we pursued these big heuristic questions for procedural knowledge of substance, applicable to the production of any text structure:

> Where can I find the data (for my comparison, in this case)?

> What data sources are available to me?

> How can I extract the data? What do I have to do to make it available to me?

In doing so they are learning to be researchers—another major thrust of the CCSS. We then have students practice identifying data sources and extracting data. Here's what a group of seventh graders came up with when we asked them how to get the stuff necessary to compare various skateboards. (The research technique that matches each response follows in parentheses.)

➤ *Research is one of the five key design considerations defined on page 4 of the CCSS introduction.*

- Think about my own experience (autobiographical research/narrative inquiry).
- Interview informants/experts (ethnographic interviewing).
- Read thrasher.com, Tony Hawk's biography, *Consumer Reports* (background reading/literature review).
- Search the Internet research: thrasher.com, *Consumer Reports* (background reading/literature review).
- Experiment: test drive different skateboards (experimenting, collecting data).
- Visit visual museum of skateboard development and take notes (studying artifacts and taking notes).
- Watch movies like *Dog Town*, *Z boys*, etc. (studying cultural artifacts).
- Observe and talk to skaters at the local skateboard park (ethnographic observation, taking notes).
- Watch skateboard demos and take notes (ethnographic observation, studying artifacts, and taking notes).
- Look for patterns in data sets (secondary research; literature review; analyzing data to infer patterns, extrapolate, interpolate).

This is a pretty good list. (We're not sure how watching *Dog Town* or *Z Boys* would help the research, but we'll let that go!) The students have suggested data-gathering

➤ *Writing anchor standard 8*

research processes that we can teach them in this context—and that they can then use throughout their lives.

We can't (and wouldn't want to) teach kids everything on this list, but we pick one or two techniques to teach—processes that we think are in the students' ZPD (things students need to know how to do that they can't yet do on their own)—and support as the students gather data. Our teaching is situated, the learning used immediately (and used again and again throughout students' lives).

➤ Writing standards 7–9

Teaching such "enabling strategies" for producing substantive data helps students engage in real research. In this influence unit, students learn to do Boolean searches on the Internet, identify and read about current and historical events with influences comparable to a personal event, watch videos, conduct (usually electronically) an interview with an expert, and take notes to record their findings.

Composing to Practice: Form

Composing to practice also involves shaping the data that we are collecting through our investigations, activities, and readings. These are the heuristic questions we ask about procedural knowledge of form:

- What do we need to do to boil down and form the stuff into a coherent and compelling comparison–contrast?
- How do we choose what stuff to use? What stuff tells *the* central story?
- How do we shape the stuff in a form our audience can understand?

➤ Writing standards 4 (rhetorical stance) and 7–9 (research to build and present knowledge)

Here's what our seventh graders had to say (the earlier composing to plan and conceptual frontloading activities helped them a lot):

- Figure out what is comparable / what is worth comparing (in the context of this inquiry or task).
- Identify key features and corresponding features of the things you are comparing (like cost, performance).
- Differentiate between fact (wide agreement among experts) and opinion (individual thinking)—judge reliability and consistency of data.
- Rank importance of features (prioritizing, selecting data that is best at telling the story or making the case).
- Analyze differences and similarities, their causes and especially their consequences (data analysis).

- Use Venn diagrams, semantic feature analyses (see Figure 10.1), or T-charts to display data, and make sure it's the appropriate way to display that kind of data given your purpose (data display).

- Consider your audience and what evidence is going to convince them (rhetorical stance and evidentiary reasoning).

- Present data through the block method: XXX–YYY or point-by-point method: XYXYXY (data display and representation).

- Present similarities, then differences, or differences, then similarities (data display and representation).

- Make a judgment and explain/justify it in ways that you think will convince your audience (rhetorical stance, evidentiary reasoning, and warranting of data).

Semantic feature analysis. Semantic feature analyses (aka SFAs) are a great tool for organizing data in ways that assist and complement comparing and contrasting. *Consumer Reports* and many outdoor equipment catalogs present data about products

➤ *Lesson idea*

Figure 10.1. Example of a Semantic Feature Analysis

WHO'S THE BEST CUBS BATTER SINCE WORLD WAR II?	HITTING FOR POWER	HITTING FOR AVERAGE	GETTING ON BASE	BASE RUNNING	DEFENSE	DURABILITY	TENURE WITH CUBS
Ernie Banks	X++	X				X	X++
Andre Dawson	X++	X				X+	X
Mark Grace	X	X++	X+		X	X++	X+
Derrek Lee	X++	X	X		X	X+	X
Aramis Ramirez	X++	X	X				X
Ryne Sandberg	X	X	X	X+	X++	X++	X++
Ron Santo	X+	X	X+		X	X++	X++
Hank Sauer	X++		X	X	X	X	X
Sammy Sosa	X++	X	X		X	X+	X+
Billy Williams	X++	X+	X		X	X+	X++

using SFAs. Helping students to read *Consumer Reports* and to compose and place hold data in SFAs is doing them a lifelong favor, in our opinion. To create an SFA, use a chart like this one, listing all the items—issues, people, individual examples or cases that you want to compare—down the left-hand column. Then across the top, list all the criteria, features, terms, or points of comparison you want to consider (in this unit, for being influential—or of effective leadership, of being a good school, and so on). Then simply check off whether each item you are comparing meets a criterion. In advanced SFAs, each individual example can be ranked in terms of how well it meets a criterion, or can get a check plus, check, check minus, or zero to rate how far each individual case meets that criterion. Our students sometimes create visuals for each cell that displays how well and how far each criterion is met. When the SFA is complete, the data patterns are made visible and available to the student inquirer, making comparing and contrasting of different individuals according to different criteria reading available for use, and the comparative data is represented by the SFA in a powerful way to any audience the student may be communicating with. The take-away: the SFA is a powerful data analysis tool for comparing; it's also a powerful way of representing and presenting comparative data.

Composing to Practice: Perspective

To help students identify meaningful points of comparison–contrast related to the purpose, rank/prioritize the points of comparison, describe and characterize the points of comparison, and decide how to present the points (crux moves), we ask students, in small groups, to identify two things they all know a lot about—local bands, pizza parlors, video games, teachers, two stores of the same type, two authors, two influences (friends and parents), and so on. They then list points of comparison, prioritize the importance of these for a particular audience, and describe the important points of comparison for that audience and purpose. Then they switch the audience (from other students to parents, for example), reprioritize, rewrite the description of some of the points to be more friendly and communicative to that audience, and discuss why the revision would be more *influential* with this audience than the first draft, thereby developing more conceptual knowledge.

> *Lesson idea*

> *Writing anchor standard 4*

> *Lesson idea*

An advanced version requires looking at the data from multiple perspectives. After reading about two characters, students, in pairs, identify the similarities and differences of the characters on a T-chart and rank these points on a scale of importance tied to a specific purpose (who is most influential, the best friend, etc.). Next the pairs write a diary entry, speech, dialogue, or interaction (about a specific incident, issue, or topic) in role as these characters, using language, action, tone, attitude, and content that reveals character. The two pieces should be roughly parallel so similarities and differences are apparent.

➤ *Lesson idea*

A *tableau* develops these same capacities multimodally. *Tableau* is derived from the French word for visual presentation. Tableaux help students visualize and explore both the text and the subtext of a narrative, including setting, scenes, situations, characters, relationships, and meanings. Students can also use tableaux to represent vocabulary and create mental models of complex concepts and procedures. In a tableau, four or five students create a "frozen" visual picture with their bodies. Variations allow students to interact then freeze or be unfrozen to speak. Another variation is to draw the tableau (Wilhelm 2002/2012, 2004/2012).

➤ *Writing standard 6 at any grade level*

➤ *Multimodal composing*

In the best/worst or good/poor tableaux variation (Wilhelm 2002/2012), a group of students identify the important points of comparison they want to portray, then brainstorm how to best portray these points through a short action sequence (if they choose) and then through the static positioning of their bodies. They should consider how to convey (or at least be able to explain) a value judgment based on the comparison.

➤ *Lesson idea*

Students could depict a character or historical figure exerting respectfully persuasive influence and then do a contrasting tableau in which the influence is less respectful and more coercive. Scenes could be made up or come from students' reading and research for their culminating project. Likewise students could predict the best and worst possible results of certain situations or actions and present these in tableaux. Whatever the tableau, students should cover the important points from a text or an issue, present them in roughly parallel fashion, and imply some kind of value judgment.

➤ *Literacy in history/ social studies reading standards 3, 6, and 9*

A hot-seat activity (Wilhelm 2002/2012) ratchets up role playing by putting a student, in role as a character, force, or idea, "on the spot": she or he is questioned, addressed, advised, or interviewed by a panel of students also in role as journalists, other characters, interested parties, etc. This technique improves students' ability to analyze characters, infer, elaborate, and think on their feet. A "lifeline" group can assist the person on the hotseat.

➤ *Reading anchor standard 3*

Good angel/bad angel (Wilhelm 2002/2012) is a version of the hot seat in which a character is advised by two "guardian angels," one proffering good advice, the other, bad. Students should make sure that the presentations of the two angels are parallel and cover important points from each perspective. Afterward students can compare and contrast what the two angels had to say (substance), how they said it, devices used (form), which points and techniques seemed to be most influential, etc.

➤ *Lesson idea*

In all of these activities students use the same process: identify meaningful points of comparison–contrast related to a specific purpose; rank/prioritize the points of comparison; describe and characterize points of comparison for a particular audience; and strategically decide how to present the points.

Composing to Practice: Ranking

➤ *CCSS assessments*

The short performance tasks for the next generations of tests, like the PISA, Smarter Balanced, and PARCC assessments, currently require individual writing using provided data. The short and longer performance tasks also incorporate collaborative writing. The longer tasks incorporate multimodal presentations. Both short and long performance tasks require students to reflect on the process they went through to complete the task and justify that process. The activities in this section prepare students for these kinds of sophisticated assessments.

Ranking activities develop students' ability to identify key and corresponding features of the things they are comparing, rank the importance of different features, analyze differences and similarities and their consequences, and make value judgments.

➤ *Speaking and listening anchor standards 1, 4, and 5*

We introduce ranking by giving students information regarding two or three influential bands, speeches, etc., and asking them, in groups, to read the material and put it into a comparative format (perhaps by using T-charts, Venn diagrams, or semantic feature analyses) that will allow them to make a value judgment about which one is most influential.

➤ *Lesson idea*
➤ *Writing anchor standard 9*

We often give kids data from *Consumer Reports* and other resources and ask them to "comparison shop" a cell phone, computer, etc. (see Smith et al. 2012 for more on this comparison technique). We might also provide statistics about baseball or basketball players or teams and ask students to determine which one is the best (see Figure 10.1)—or provide data about recording artists/groups and ask which is the most innovative, influential, significant, etc. Having the data provided makes the task easier for students and helps them focus on using the crux moves before we ask them to find and rate their own data.

➤ *Lesson idea*

If students need still more practice and support, we introduce a more independent activity in which students brainstorm a top-ten list of some kind. If the list fits into the unit's inquiry topic, all the better—knowledge of substance and form will be developed together. A much desired twofer!

Then groups collect their own data about two or three subjects within specified parameters. For example, if a group is researching bands, the members might be asked to visit the band's official website and three independent sources.

We typically conclude the composing to practice phase of any unit with some form of collaborative writing. In this unit, for example, we would ask the group of students researching bands to compare two or three influence-related factors and make a value judgment about which band is most influential—on other performers, music, social consciousness, social justice issues, etc.

➤ *Lesson idea*

If you have time and inclination, students can present their work multimodally through presentation software. We've had students create magazine spreads or a class book ranking items they have researched. Groups read one another's writing and agree on an overall ranking, then write a profile comparing one entry on the list to the one ranked before and after it.

(For examples of top-ten books written by teachers with their students as the result of inquiry units from across the curriculum, please see www.the10books.com /canada/.)

Composing to Practice: Rhetorical Stance

➤ *Lesson idea*

Every act of informative writing involves categorization and is embedded in a meaningful context. Effective writers pay attention to that context by considering the needs, interests, and biases of their audience and how to address them.

Best of Bach activity. To illustrate how audience consideration may affect a piece of writing, we have students compare and contrast pieces of writing that have a similar purpose and content but a different audience. The three sets of liner notes below are for three CDs that contain much of the same music by J. S. Bach but that have been packaged to appeal to different audiences.

➤ *Reading anchor standard 6 and reading standard 9, grades 2–11/12*

Students are divided into groups representing these possible audiences:

- Classical music aficionados/insiders.
- High school musicians with an interest in expanding their musical tastes.
- Parents interested in getting music for themselves and their teenage children.
- Elevator company employees in charge of choosing music for elevators and common areas in various buildings.
- Readers evaluating the liner notes according to the standards of the new CCSS standards for writing.
- English teachers.
- Music teachers.
- Social studies teachers.

➤ *This activity can also be done with movie or book reviews or promotions. Since such texts are meant to "influence" consumers, a twofer is achieved.*

The members of each group discuss, in role, what they will look for in liner notes and contrast these interests and needs with those of the other groups. Then they read all three sets of liner notes, compare and contrast them, and decide which one appeals most to them and why, and then to each of the other audiences and why.

Alternatively, each group could assume the role of the writer of one set of notes and explain his or her perceived audience and rhetorical choices and compare them with the audience and rhetorical choices of the writers of the other two sets of notes.

Here are the liner notes:

The Best of Bach

Classical music has, to borrow a Madison Avenue term, a bad image. Vast numbers of people believe it is only to be enjoyed by those who have been initiated into its mysteries; others are faintly uncomfortable in the society-page setting of symphony or opera house. Still others are frustrated by or impatient with a music that too often takes itself too damn seriously

It needn't be that way. A pretty tune is a pretty tune, whether it's Lennon and McCartney's "Norwegian Wood" or Bach's "Sheep May Safely Graze." A tricky rhythm is exciting whether it is heard in the guitar riff of a Mississippi Delta bluesman or Debussy's "Golliwog Cakewalk." Interesting harmonies are moving and enriching, no matter who fashions them—the Mamas and the Papas' "Twelve-Thirty" is musically as sound as Vivalidi's "Gloria."

Granted there are snobs on both sides of the dispute, including a host of people who should know better. Classical music is not something separate or just for rich people or something to be endured. About all it takes to enjoy classical music is a willingness to listen. Having decided to listen, perhaps while washing dishes or reading the latest *Sports Illustrated*, all you need do is to let your mind wander. The music will conjure up images; it might even help you sort out emotions or events; it might tempt you to wonder and ponder what the composer had on his or her mind when writing the music. Or you might just get caught up in the music. You don't have to know that the Beatles' "Norwegian Wood" is in the mixolydian mode to enjoy it, do you? Then why in heck should it be necessary to know the structure of the sonata format to enjoy Beethoven? If you are convinced, then you are ready to go. We've picked the best of Bach for you. The rest is up to you.

Bach: Cantatas and Fugues

In the spirit of the "sacred concert," the first cantata (No. 146) opens with an overture, which is nothing other than the first movement of the great D-minor Clavier Concerto. The solo part is here played on the organ, as indicated in the score and as Bach himself must have played it in St. Thomas Kirche. It is the most magnificent of his concerto movements, music both deep and spectacular. A leaping germinal theme serves for the *tutti* and as an undercurrent to the solo passages. The episodes for the solo organ are increasingly rich and splendid, employing antiphonal counterpoint, cascading arpeggios, and long sustained pedal-points to unfold the full powers of the instrument. Next comes the slow movement of the concerto, which was also an innovation for the concerto form in its deep, almost tragic seriousness. It consists of a *chaconne*, with a ground bass, constantly reiterated but for interspersed episodes for the purpose of modulation. . . .

Switched-On Bach

The Prelude in E-flat Major is an object lesson in how Bach touches an artistic convention with absolute genius. *Psych!* For three quarters of its length, it behaves like an "arpeggio" prelude, content to make its effect through the building momentum of its characteristic figure. It just keeps on keepin' on. *Truckin'!* Then, just as it has reached an impressive climax, things go awry: the bottom voice seizes the floor for an impressive climax, the characteristic theme flies into a tailspin, and a passionate recitative is required to restore order. *Right on!* You go, Bachster! The fugue (which means "three voices") is notable for the long sixteenth-note scale passages that give it special urgency and passion. *Passion!* That is what Bach is all about, so tune the skull candy, the audio ornaments on the sides of your head, and listen for it. *Just sayin'!*

Students are now ready to try making their own rhetorical decisions regarding audience. We have students practice by asking them to write in-role based on the following scenario, then change the audience for that writing. First, the scenario:

➤ *Lesson idea*

A student presents her teacher with a late paper. It's been previously stated by the teacher, on the syllabus and orally, that no late papers will be accepted and that in the event that a paper is late, that paper will get a failing grade. The student, however, feels justified in submitting the paper a day late because she had two other papers due the same day, as well as a test, and the extra time allowed her to produce a much better paper and actually learn from completing it. The teacher is reluctant to change the policy or make a one-time exception. But without such a move, the student's hard work will result in a failing grade and other negative consequences may follow, like a loss of motivation. Should the teacher's policy be changed or an exception be made?

And now the roles:

Role 1: Write a letter to the teacher as though you are the student explaining why the late policy should be modified or abolished. In order to do so, you'll have to compare and contrast the results of the teacher's policy with the alternative policy solution you propose.

Role 2: Write a brief letter to students as though you were the teacher defending your policy to parents. In order to do so, you'll have to compare and contrast the results of your policy with the results of possible alternatives.

After students have completed the letters, we ask them, as a group, to compare the stylistic choices each writer made to reach his or her audience.

Composing to Draft a Comparison–Contrast

➤ *Lesson idea*

Before they draft, our students create a rubric or set of analytic scales to reinforce what they have learned about good comparison–contrast: substance, organization/ development, audience considerations, language conventions, and anything else they think is important. (Websites like rubistar.com provide digital templates and models of rubrics.)

It's important that students compose the rubric or at least be significantly involved in creating it, because in doing so they demonstrate their own declarative knowledge of substance and form. Once the groundwork of identifying and ranking criteria has been done, all students have to do is flesh out user-friendly descriptions of each criterion. If necessary, we model how to compose usable and understandable benchmark statements and then mentor the students as they compose one or two before having groups compose benchmarks independently. By jigsawing the work, a class can compose a rubric in less than a class period. And it's a twofer: students are practicing specific descriptive writing. For example, an exemplary benchmark for audience consideration might look like this: "The writer has identified an appropriate audience, and the writing addresses that audience's expectations and needs in specific ways, such as in its content, by explaining necessary terms, and through its tone. The tone helps to meet the purpose and get the necessary work done with this audience in ways that will enhance the readers' experience, enjoyment, and understanding, and these moves can be justified and explained."

Then we discuss the model. Does everyone get it? Would a peer editor like an adult mentor get it? Is it usable? Could you point to sections of your paper and explain how the cited criteria are met or not met? If not, how can we revise the benchmark statement to make it more audience-friendly and useful?

Benchmarks are where the assessment rubber hits the road. If benchmarks, which are descriptions of actual accomplishment that meets a criterion, cannot be composed, then students don't have a clear declarative understanding of substance or form. And if they can be composed? Well, this is sufficient proof that students own the declarative knowledge. By meeting the benchmark and explaining how they do so, they show they have procedural understanding. We often tell preservice teachers they don't have to make up tests—the world as well as the classroom is filled with testing situations. If students can use the knowledge we teach them, learning is displayed and demonstrated beyond all dispute.

Once students have developed a rubric, we help them use it. In a procedure we ➤ *Lesson idea*
call a *revision roundtable* or *revision charrette*, we display a student volunteer's draft on the whiteboard; model how we would check the paper against the criteria and benchmarks; and then mentor response by asking the class to help us respond to other features. We can then model responding to and peer editing a second paper, if needed, or provide this option for groups not ready to respond and peer edit without further modeling. We have found that without such modeling, peer editing often does not go well, but after such modeling, subsequent peer editing goes much more smoothly.

We next ask groups of four to conduct revision roundtables in peer editing groups. We model and mentor a spirit of helpfulness and emphasize that we are all working to help everyone write the best possible paper. More and more often, we use ➤ *Writing anchor standards 4, 5, and 6 (collaborative use of technology)*
Googledocs in peer groups, asking peer editors to use the "track changes" feature to note their praise and suggestions for moves, adds, deletes, or changes. This also allows us to note the contributions of each group member.

Composing a Final Draft Comparison–Contrast

➤ *The vertically aligned CCSS language standards lend themselves to this—there are six specific focal areas at each grade level.*

Whenever we teach the phase of final drafts, we choose one or two focal correction areas and teach everyone how to use these specific constructions and how to proofread to correct them. In the context of comparing, our students often need help signaling comparison and contrast without overusing pat transitional phrases (*in contrast, on the other hand, similarly,* and the like) and with punctuating these kinds of navigational signals and alternatives. Through this process, we want students to inquire into how each construction works in the context of comparing. We also typically ask individual students to concentrate on one or two additional focal areas that they have identified as general concerns in their own writing. In this way, they proofread for one or two errors that we focus on as a class, and one or two personal focal errors. This personal focus requires students to inquire into their own writing and the patterns of general weaknesses they tend to exhibit, as well as give them a way to strengthen these issues. We provide folders of corrective strategies for different errors so that students can pursue their personal focal areas on their own or in small groups (see Smith and Wilhelm 2007 for more on how to do this).

We have found that if students have more than two or three areas to proofread for, they often give up on everything. It's cognitive overload. Focus is the first key. Assistance to meet the focal area challenges is the second key.

➤ *Lesson idea*
➤ *Language anchor standard 2*

To address the focal area of providing navigational signals to readers, it's a great idea to have students research how writers signal comparison and contrast (this can obviously be applied to any other text structure). For example, gamers might check out a comparison of gaming systems like this one from *How Stuff Works* (http://electronics.howstuffworks.com/video-game5.htm):

> The Xbox 360's processor is a customized Power-PC based CPU from IBM. It has three symmetrical cores that run at 3.2 gigahertz (GHz) each. This processor has a lot of horsepower, but it lacks the Cell architecture of the PlayStation 3 design.
>
> The Nintendo Wii's processor isn't quite as impressive. It's an IBM Broadway 729 megahertz (MHz) processor. While the chip isn't in the same league as its competitors, Nintendo executives say the processor is more than powerful enough to provide a fun gaming experience.

In these two short paragraphs the author makes three different choices, using a contrastive clause in a compound sentence (*but it lacks . . .*), using a contrastive subordinating clause (*while the chip* . . .), and making a direct comparison (. . . *isn't quite as impressive*).

Once students have collected examples, we name the signals used, and then name and pose possible alternatives. Students then rate the relative effectiveness of each signal. For example the ideas in "this processor has a lot of horsepower, but it lacks the Cell architecture of the PlayStation 3 design" could be written in a variety of ways:

➤ *Lesson idea*

- This processor has a lot of horsepower; however, it lacks the Cell architecture of the PlayStation 3 design.

- Although this processor has a lot of horsepower, it lacks the Cell architecture of the PlayStation 3 design.

- This processor has a lot of horsepower. On the other hand, it lacks the Cell architecture of the PlayStation 3 design.

- This processor has a lot of horsepower, though it lacks the Cell architecture of the PlayStation 3 design.

As we write the alternatives, we explain the punctuation conventions of each, how different meanings are emphasized, and students discuss their preferences. No right or wrong answers here, but students are articulating their standards of judgment. (For more on how sentence combining and different models assist students in making informed rhetorical choices, see Smith and Wilhelm 2007.)

Groups of students then write and rank several versions of some of the sentences demonstrating compare–contrast signals that they have collected. Then, armed with a toolbox of alternatives, they're ready to look at their drafts to make sure they are signaling comparison and contrast both effectively and correctly.

Composing to Transfer Knowledge of Comparison–Contrast

Students produce formative assessments throughout the unit: they compose exit and entrance tickets and write in their journal about how well they are progressing toward reaching the goals of writing their final compositions. We often ask students to evaluate their understanding using the designations *still in harbor*, *leaving harbor*, *setting out to sea*, and *on the high seas* along with explanations of their current state of understanding. We also ask them to provide evidence of progress, designate personal improvement areas, and request specific assistance (see Wilhelm et al. 2009 for extensions of this technique).

➤ *Lesson ideas*

In this unit, we also have students write "reflective notes" (an idea borrowed from law school) exploring their personal reaction to a conceptual issue related to

➤ *Lesson idea*

the inquiry (comparing their personal situation to one encountered by a character in a novel or historical leader, for example) or to a procedural issue related to writing a comparison–contrast.

At the end of the unit, we ask students to write a reflection in response to one or more of the following questions:

➤ *A reflection like this is part of all the Smarter Balanced and PARCC performance tasks currently under review.*

- What helped shape your experience with the comparison–contrast structure (or with your exploration of influence)?
- What have you learned from this experience and what helped you learn it?
- What was the personal meaning of this experience for you?
- What new insights did you gain?
- What future goals might you meet by using what you have learned in this unit?
- What are some topics in your life or in our school and community that could be addressed through the comparison–contrast thought pattern?
- How do your "home funds of knowledge" compare with "school knowledge" in some particular area to which comparing and contrasting could be applied?

Gut Check: How Are We Doing with the CCSS?

➤ *CCSS connections*

Although we've been signaling in the margin how we are meeting the CCSS through our teaching methodology, let's summarize how we're doing. We always nail writing anchor standard 2 on writing informational texts since that is the topic of this book. We hit writing anchor standards 4, 5, and 6 for production and distribution of writing throughout the influence unit, particularly if we do some digital composing and work with Googledocs or other software platforms. The inquiry itself constitutes an extended research project, and shorter research activities, like finding information about a local band, abound throughout the unit. So check off writing anchor standard 7. Students are constantly gathering relevant information from a variety of sources and drawing evidence from these sources that supports analysis, reflection, and research. Writing anchor standards 8 and 9, check and check. Writing anchor standard 10 is nailed as well—the students have been writing every day, for research, for reflection (composing to transfer), for revision (drafting and finalizing).

What about the language standards? We directly address standards 1 and 2 (conventions) in our finalizing phase. Our rhetorical stance activities are all about standard

3: "Apply knowledge of language to understand how language functions in different contexts, to make effective choices for meaning or style, and to comprehend more fully when reading or listening."

We've met the vocabulary standards, because vocabulary has been developed in comprehending the material in the influence-and-power inquiry, in learning and describing the processes of comparing and contrasting, and in composing sentence constructions and transitions useful in the inquiry.

As far as speaking and listening, students are discussing, creating, and presenting (often multimodally) in small groups every day.

Let's turn to reading. We've done some close reading and made inferences from that reading (anchor standard 1) and hit the identification of major themes and their development fairly hard (anchor standard 2). As far as craft and structure, we've hit anchor standard 4 by considering word choice and tone in the stance activities. Since we are exploring text structures in this book, we always solidly hit anchor standard 5, and anchor standard 6 is hammered by assessing persona, perspective, and purpose and its effect on style. As for integration of knowledge and ideas, we've done some multimodal composing to hit anchor standard 7, and rewritten texts and looked at how different texts about similar topics compare (in the Best of Bach activity, for example), so anchor standard 9 goes down. And it all leads to meeting anchor standard 10. Wow, we've done well.

If you read the introduction of the anchor standards, you'll see we've hit some other priorities too: students have been helped to see from multiple perspectives and have developed deep conceptual understanding of the inquiry topic; they've received assistance in multiple ways in learning to be researchers and have been helped to develop audience awareness and other areas of expertise related to rhetorical stance.

In addition, the work here provides specific preparation for the short and longer performance tasks in the drafts of the Smarter Balanced and PARCC tests currently posted online as well as other next generation assessments like PISA.

Not bad!

Classification

The Most Powerful Thought Pattern in the World?

Jeff, by his own admission, is not a particularly "clean" person, but he *is* organized. The refrigerator and pantry at home are carefully classified with a system his family must not completely understand (since they keep putting things away in the wrong places!). His clothes, books and files, skis and ski waxes and outdoor equipment: all classified.

During his recent trip to Canada, Jeff went to the British Columbia Museum of Natural History. The exhibits were classified by type of specimen: herpetology, ichthyology, mammalogy, etc. One of the guides, the resident herpetologist, explained that a large part of his job was preserving and classifying artifacts. He told the group that he maintains a warehouse full of specimens that he likened to "a library, organized according to a careful classification scheme, but it's full of actual physical specimens instead of books." Why? So specimens can be easily located, and so that patterns and evolutions among categories can be seen, studied, and tested.

Why Classification Matters

Modern science is all about classification—all the way from Aristotle through Linnaeus to the current day. The purpose of biological classification is to divide all living things into groups. This enables us to theorize about relationships among the groups. Classification, for instance, was vital to Darwin's developing the theory of evolution.

The elegance and power of the biological system is that it divides all life into a series of ever-smaller groupings until the individual example is reached—human being, for example. In the case of human beings, larger classes such life, domain, and kingdom are followed by:

Phylum: Chordota

Subphylum: Vertebrata

Class: Mammalia

Subclass: Eutheria

Order: Primates

Family: Hominadae

Genus: Homo

Species: Sapiens

Obviously, this classification could continue to categorize human beings into constituent groups according to different bases, all the way down to individual people, but proceeding this way would not answer biological questions. In contrast, the biological grouping does not answer sociological or anthropological questions that begin *not* with the universe of all living things but with human beings. So human beings would be the starting point or "universe" for an anthropological or sociological classification. Your universe also determines what is considered an individual example: if the topic is kinds of living creatures, then an individual species is the most specific case. If your universe is human beings, then individual people would be the most specific case. If your universe was an individual human being, then depending on your purpose for classifying (called the *basis*), ideas like personality traits, interests, affinity groups that the individual belonged to are all examples of what could be the individual case.

All research and data analysis are based on classification. All three of us are researchers, so we do lots of classifying in our work. Classification is implicated in most intellectual breakthroughs and knowledge making.

Classification is so crucial to human activity that the anthropologist Claude Levi-Strauss famously remarked that "man is the classifying animal" (cited in Gardner 1982). Forget the thumb or language, he maintained—what makes us human and allows all uniquely human endeavors is our capacity to sort and categorize. One of Jeff's research professors, upon hearing the Levi-Strauss quote, joked that *"Jeff* is the classifying animal!" One reason Jeff loves literacy research is because it involves classifying data during analysis. Undoubtedly, classification is one of the most powerful intellectual tools of modern humanity.

Since the three of us mostly look at the lived-through experiences of students involved in different kinds of literacy and learning, we've tended to do qualitative research. Our analysis of qualitative data begins with clearly articulating our unit of analysis. That is, we have to divide our data about student experience—with a particular instructional intervention, for instance—into some kind of smaller unit. Doing so is an act of classification determined by our purpose, or what classifiers call *basis*. And when we code those units, we classify again. Even when we do quantitative or quasi-experimental research (in which you can count things)—when we examine the kinds of moves student readers make with different kinds of texts, for example—we still analyze our data by separating it into mutually exclusive categories—that is, by classifying it.

Michael is not as organized around the house as Jeff is (just ask his family), but classification is something he does every day. Michael and his family love *The Sing Off*, the TV show that features a cappella groups. The show's recent Christmas special provoked much conversation about what made some of the songs ("Baby, It's Cold Outside," for example) a Christmas song. Similarly, Michael's been in one book club or another for over twenty-five years and has a definite sense of what makes a "book-club book."

As a kid, Jim used to go on weeklong family fishing trips in northern Wisconsin. The first few days of fishing were enough for Jim, so while the rest of the family continued to sit out on the lake for hours on end, Jim would remain in the cabin with stacks and stacks of baseball cards and magazines. At the time, the lake and cabin were so remote that only the local radio station came in; there was no television, which meant no baseball games. So Jim had hours to himself to organize baseball cards into different categories. He endlessly grouped and regrouped his cards into categories like "former Cubs," "hope the Cubs trade for this player," "left-handed hitting catchers," "best photograph on the front of the card," "best trivia notes on the back of the card," etc. It was all classifying, hour after enjoyable hour.

Classification Defined

According to Berke (2007), classification is a "highly methodical form of analysis and an indispensible condition of systematic thought, for it involves a sorting process that groups things into categories based on similar characteristics." She takes the top-down approach: from general class to most specific instance of it.

Conversely, Mayr (2002) defines classification as bottom-up: "The arrangement of entities in a hierarchical series of nested classes, in which similar or related classes at one hierarchical level are combined comprehensively into more inclusive classes at the next higher level" (170). A class is defined as "a collection of similar entities," where the similarity consists of the entities having attributes or traits in common (retrieved from Wikipedia, November 1, 2011). Both commentators are correct, since classifications can proceed from individual examples up into larger groupings or from the universe or general topic of items down to individual cases.

We have previously written about classification as a basic structure of thought and had this to say: "Classification is an essential intellectual tool in math, the physical and social sciences, and the humanities. Accurate and precise classification is the basis of biological studies and many of our most enduring and explanatory theories. It is essential to all forms of inquiry as the researcher chunks data and is enabled to see new patterns and relationships" (Smith and Wilhelm 2007, 115).

Classification and pattern seeking (seeing repeated patterns and the complex implied relationships among them) are also essential to good reading, particularly of literature. One of the hallmarks of good writing, especially research writing, particularly in the content areas, is the capacity to organize data through classification, which in turn allows the writer to perceive, organize, and express new insights. Yet classification is rarely explicitly taught, causing difficulties for students in both reading and writing this structure (see Smith and Wilhelm 2007, 115–16).

> ➤ *Reading anchor standards 1–3 and 5*

> ➤ *Writing anchor standards 7–9 and writing standard 2a and 2b at any grade level*

In science, categories and subcategories at each level of a classification must be equal, comprehensive (covering all examples at that level), and mutually exclusive. In more informal classifications, produced for theoretical or practical reasons, there is sometimes more latitude.

What characteristics you use as the *basis* of a particular classification are determined by your purpose and interests—any universe or population can be classified in many different ways. People can be classified by sexual orientation, socioeconomic status, interests, ethnicity, politics, and much more, depending on the purpose at hand.

Model Unit: What Are the Types of, Causes of, Effects of, and Solutions to Poverty?

Whenever we devise any kind of instruction, we start with a particular context. We've argued for a long time that the most powerful context for instruction is an inquiry unit built around an essential question. It's easy to ask an essential question that rewards or even requires classification. Berke (2007) identifies the essential classification question as *what are the types of* X? which moves top down. An obvious alternative or subquestion is *what kind of* X *is* Y? which moves bottom up. Another version is *how many kinds of* X *are there (and what are the effects of each)?*

> ➤ *Writing anchor standards 4 and 10*

To accomplish some immediate classification work, we might ask *how many kinds of leaders are there? political ideologies? types of friends?* Such a classification question is often a fruitful subquestion of a larger overarching essential question (see *how essential questions and subquestions form a kind of classification?*). The questions at the beginning of this paragraph evolved from the questions *what makes an* effective *leader? how do political ideologies affect human governance and experience? what is a* good *friend?* Any question that looks at uses, functions, consequences, and effects of different types of something is doing this kind of classification work.

The question *what are the types of, causes of, effects of, and solutions to poverty?* offers a wide array of possibilities for students to analyze and classify data. It's really a subquestion of a larger question: *what are the types of, causes of, effects of, and solutions to major social issues?* This is too big a question to pursue in a unit (or even a career!), but articulating it allows students, after working together in groups, to choose a subquestion of their own—continuing to study poverty, human displacement, environmental issues, the corporatization of America, war, or any other social issue.

Composing to Plan Classifications

Our essential question about poverty is obviously a very important and immediately pressing one. Almost half the world—more than 3.5 billion individuals—live on less than $2.50 a day (www.globalissues.org/article/26/poverty-facts-and-stats). The U.S. Census Bureau (2009) reports that nearly 15 percent of all citizens live below the poverty level, the highest rate since 1997 and steadily growing. Many commentators maintain that the poverty standard is artificially low, and that fully one third of Americans live at a level that could be called poverty.

➤ *Lesson idea*

Conceptual frontloading. To begin activating and building background, we have students mark their agreement or disagreement with the following survey statements:

- Many people in this country don't have a work ethic.
- If you work hard in America, you will prosper.
- Poverty is a sign that individuals aren't taking responsibility and working hard enough.
- The government's purpose is to provide security and a safety net for citizens in trouble.
- Poverty depends on lack of opportunity.
- Poverty stifles hope.

- People can emerge from poverty and achieve success if they get the right help.
- Poverty stifles opportunity.
- People should be responsible for their own economic welfare and not rely on the government.
- We need more equality of opportunity in America.
- Many hardworking people nevertheless live in poverty.
- Welfare and other social programs are an investment that leads to greater social prosperity for all.

Students then list the experiences, beliefs, and attitudes of mind that prompted them to agree or disagree with at least two of the statements.

We take the student lists and model classifying their attitudes, beliefs, and experiences in different ways. We tell students that we will read a variety of texts that address these issues surrounding poverty and that we will ask them to explain how the authors of those texts would respond to this survey.

Analyzing models. Another technique for helping students develop knowledge of context and purpose is to provide some short models of classifications and to ask:

Why: Why did the author choose to classify this particular data? What work gets done or understanding is furthered for the author and for others?

How: How did the author categorize the data? On what basis and for what purpose did the author sort the data into groups?

When/where: In what contexts would this kind of classification be meaningful?

We often use the classification model below (it was written by Leonard Hooper, a lifelong resident of Down East Maine and one of Jeff's favorite Maine Writing Project fellows, during an MWP summer institute):

> You can divide residents of Maine into three groups: the Mainers or "natives," the transplants, and the "folks from away." [Looking closely at each group, Hooper provides a more precise understanding of each:]
>
> 1. The natives, a.k.a. "Mainers" (pronounced *Maine-uhs* by the locals): these are residents who were born in Maine and have lived in Maine their whole lives. These people typically

➤ *Speaking and listening anchor standard 1 and writing anchor standard 1*
➤ *Reading anchor standards 8 and 9 and writing anchor standards 7–9*
➤ *Lesson idea*
➤ *Reading anchor standard 8*

work in the timber, fishery, tourist, or other outdoor-oriented industry or in the service sector.

2. The transplants: these are people who migrated to Maine from somewhere else and have stayed for at least ten years. This longevity has demonstrated their love of Maine and has led to their acceptance by Mainers. They typically come to Maine for a new way of life or employment tied to Maine in some way. They interact positively with Mainers and share their concerns.

3. Folks from away: these are part-time residents, a.k.a. summer people, who have homes or "camps" in Maine. They come and go for a series of short-time stays. They are not perceived as being committed to Maine values of local control, love of nature, and willingness to put up with hardship. Mainers and transplants interact with these folks out of necessity or for economic benefit but in general resent them as outsiders taking advantage of Maine without substantively contributing to the culture. (Smith and Wilhelm 2007, 116)

➤ *Crux move*

Since articulating the basis for categorization is the primary crux move for classifying, we discuss the categories Hooper developed. Some students initially identify the basis as the time spent in Maine, but continued discussion reveals that it is time spent in Maine plus the more important differentiating qualities of commitment and how devoted people are to traditional Maine values.

➤ *Reading anchor standards 1–6, 8, and 9 and writing anchor standards 2, 5, and 7*

This short example demonstrates how a social scientist translates casual local classifications and cover terms (those used by real people) into a more formal, systematic, and complete set of groupings. This work helps us see relationships among groups, explain interactions among the groups, understand culture, and much more. Hooper's classifications helped Jeff understand why some of his Maine students would say "He's from away!" when he said something they disagreed with, and why, when pleased, they might compliment him by saying, "You're our favorite transplant—but just don't go thinking you're something you're not!"

➤ *Lesson idea*

A great follow-up to such an analysis is to ask small student groups to come up with some reasons and contexts in which classifying the students (or teachers or staff!) in your school would matter and then begin such a classification scheme, identifying enough comprehensive categories so that every student (or teacher) would fit into one group but only one group.

We next analyze an article about poverty, "Causes and Effects of Poverty." Here's an excerpt:

➤ *Lesson idea*

The Effects of Poverty

The effects of poverty are serious. Children who grow up in poverty suffer more persistent, frequent, and severe health problems than do children who grow up under better financial circumstances.

- Many infants born into poverty have a low birth weight, which is associated with many preventable mental and physical disabilities. Not only are these poor infants more likely to be irritable or sickly, they are also more likely to die before their first birthday.
- Children raised in poverty tend to miss school more often because of illness. These children also have a much higher rate of accidents than do other children, and they are twice as likely to have impaired vision and hearing, iron deficiency anemia, and higher than normal levels of lead in the blood, which can impair brain function.

Levels of stress in the family have also been shown to correlate with economic circumstances. Studies during economic recessions indicate that job loss and subsequent poverty are associated with violence in families, including child and elder abuse. Poor families experience much more stress than middle-class families. Besides financial uncertainty, these families are more likely to be exposed to series of negative events and "bad luck," including illness, depression, eviction, job loss, criminal victimization, and family death. Parents who experience hard economic times may become excessively punitive and erratic, issuing demands backed by insults, threats, and corporal punishment. (www.cliffsnotes.com/ study_guide/topicArticleId-26957,articleId-26882.html)

The article goes on to describe other effects such as homelessness and a perpetual underclass, which lead to still other effects.

Students answer the same questions:

- *Why* might the author have chosen to classify this particular data? What work gets done or understanding is furthered for the author and for others by doing so?
- *How* were issues sorted? What was the basis of the classification? To what purpose were the effects divided as they were?
- *When and where* would this kind of classification be meaningful? What do we learn here about why and how social scientists classify things?

➤ *Lesson idea*

List–group–label. This activity helps students infer purposes and contexts for classifying while also learning to infer and apply the deep categorization structures implicit in lists of ideas. In our poverty unit, we provided stacks of photographs of people living in poverty, or of impoverished social settings, or of graphs and visual displays of statistics about poverty. The stacks constituted a kind of list. The students then piled groups of photos together that they thought constituted a category related to poverty in some way that they could identify. This was the grouping. Then they labeled each stack of photographs. Voila! A short classification scheme related to poverty. We can then ask questions about their classification of the photos, like: *what does your classification suggest about the causes of poverty? The prevalence of poverty? The effects of poverty? The human cost of poverty?* After a bit, students naturally being to brainstorm their own questions.

Here's another illustration of the activity, using a lesson Jeff and Jim conduct to help teachers see the underlying structures and categories of the CCSS.

➤ *CCSS connection*

We give the teachers strips of paper, each stating a CCSS anchor standard. The strips at a particular table form that group's list of individual examples. (In other situations students can generate their own list or add to a provided list.) We then ask the teachers to group the anchor standards according to underlying purposes (versus conventional groupings already used by the CCSS like reading and writing, speaking and listening, etc.). The groups label the categories they've identified and use the following questions to prompt new insights the categories reveal about the purpose of the CCSS and how to meet them:

- What is the absolute center (basis) of the CCSS curriculum and how do you know? ("The major thrust of the CCSS is. . . .")
- What is the most effective way to meet these standards and why do you think so?
- What theory of teaching and learning is implicitly expressed by the CCSS?

The last time we did this activity, the teachers labeled the following groupings/categories:

- Inquiry/research (learning with purpose and for strategic understanding and use).
- Inferencing (including how conventions, figurative language, local and global structure, contribute to effect and meaning—complex implied relationships, authorial and structural generalizations).
- Argument/evidentiary reasoning.
- Explanatory writing/process analyses—justification/reflection.
- Stance: purpose, voice/perspective, audience consideration, rhetorical choice.
- Reconciling differing perspectives.
- Representation, revision, presentation.

Students can do this with any set of data—lists you provide, lists they generate, advertisements from a magazine, and so on. If the data relate to the ongoing inquiry, so much the better: they will also develop procedural knowledge of substance through the activity. For instance, in a unit focused on leaders, students could be given photos of various leaders in different domains or photos of leaders in action. The deliverable could be to group and then label the components of a classroom museum exhibit on leaders. This activity clearly assists them to generate ideas.

➤ *Lesson idea*

In this unit on the effects of poverty, we follow up on the first activity by giving students a wide variety of WPA photographs from the Depression, including many famous ones taken by Dorothea Lange. We ask them to group and label the photographs and create a class exhibit, justifying the purpose of the exhibit and how the groupings they chose serve this purpose.

➤ *Lesson idea*

To conclude the composing-to-plan phase, we ask groups of students to come up with a definition of classification, including its purpose and contexts of use. Here's one that a group of tenth graders came up with (we provided the italicized labels for their insights, so they would also learn the "terms of art" related to classification):

- Classification schemes group elements or individual examples of a topic group (called a *universe* or *data set*) into different *classes* (groups/categories/families) that share important defining characteristics.
- Classification organizes objects and ideas so they can be easily accessed and so various kinds of relationships, like similarities and differences, can be perceived and explained and then used to solve problems.

- Classifications are used widely in science, math, social sciences, and history to understand large data sets and see new relationships within those data sets.

- We all also use classification in our lives to organize our stuff, our thinking, and our ways of solving problems and getting around.

We also ask students to brainstorm ways in which we can classify causes or effects of poverty that will help our understanding and problem solving, as well as methods and venues for sharing what we come up with. As they plan their culminating classification paper, we want them to consider and carry forward this question in regard to their inquiry: *what do I want to classify (universe) and why (basis)?*

Composing to Practice Classifications

➤ *Lesson idea*

Students now compose *spontaneous classifications* of topics with which they are very familiar: homework, cafeteria food, extracurricular activities, sports, breakfast cereals, junk foods, popular music, video games, television shows, movies, etc. We first frontload as a class by listing all the specific examples of one of these topics that we can think of. Students then chunk and classify (group) the list.

➤ *Lesson idea*
➤ *Reading anchor standard 4 and language standards 3, 4, and 6*

A quick activity a step further from home (and into the disciplines) is a *word sort*. The one in Figure 11.1 classifies vocabulary in a geometry unit. From there, it's a quick step to How to Speak Physics (Figure 11.2); this word sort helps students classify physics by topics and understand how vocabulary, as well as ways of thinking and problem solving around particular topics, helps them enter the discourse community of a discipline.

Figure 11.1 Geometry Word Sort

SEGMENTS	ANGLES	▲
Segment Bisector	Angle Bisector	S.S.S.
Midpoint	Perpendicular	A.S.A.
Reflexive	Vertical Angles	S.A.S.
CPCTC	Linear Pair	A.A.S.
	Supplementary	R.H.L.
	Reflexive	
	CPCTC	

Source: Created by Christine Tarchinski and Blair Covino

Figure 11.2 How to Speak Physics

WORDS TO DESCRIBE MOTION	WORDS TO DESCRIBE GRAPHS	WORDS TO DESCRIBE QUANTITIES
• Object ("It") • Starts • Stops • Moving • Going • Right • Left • Up • Down • Fast • Slow • Speeding up • Slowing down • From rest/at rest	• Straight line • Horizontal line • Parabola • Area • Slope • Y-intercept • Tangent line • Axes • Origin • Steep	• Positive • Negative • Zero • Constant • Increasing • Decreasing • Initial • Instantaneous • Average • Greater than • Less than

Source: Created by Terry Quain and Blair Covino

The next step is to have students begin superordinating and subordinating ideas by identifying subcategories. *Power outlines*, *block diagrams*, and *issue trees* are effective tools for discovering and representing the relationships among various classes and examples and help students organize the entire classification scheme. These tools in turn become scaffolds for writing an explanation of the classification.

➤ *Lesson ideas*

For example, school activities can be organized into the power outline shown in Figure 11.3, in which five levels are needed to get from the universe down to individual examples.

➤ *Writing anchor standard 5*

Figure 11.4 is a block diagram of a classification scheme. Not all classifications will fit neatly into a chart like this. There may be more or fewer subcategories, more levels of subordination, etc. This is not a one-size-fits-all model.

Figure 11.5 is an example of an issue tree. There may be several levels of subcategories to reach the individual examples. There may also be different numbers of subcategories for categories, and different numbers of individual examples for each subcategory.

Figure 11.3

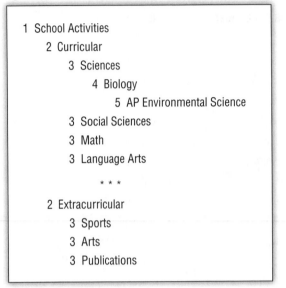

```
1  School Activities
      2  Curricular
            3  Sciences
                  4  Biology
                        5  AP Environmental Science
            3  Social Sciences
            3  Math
            3  Language Arts

                        * * *

      2  Extracurricular
            3  Sports
            3  Arts
            3  Publications
```

Figure 11.4

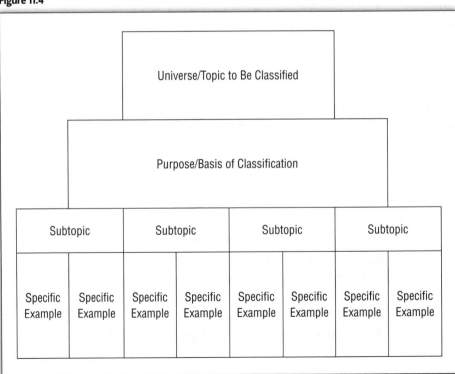

Figure 11.5

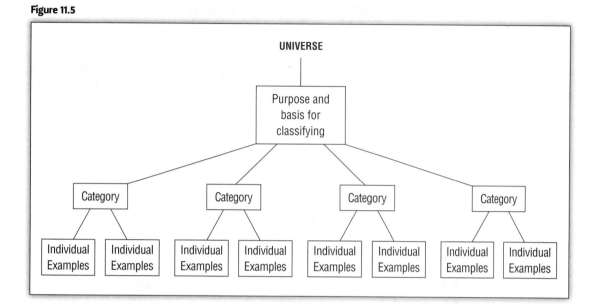

Once students are familiar with issue trees and block diagrams, we give each student one note card on which is written one of these words or phrases:

Ice cream	French vanilla
Vanilla flavors	Cookies and cream
Chocolates and cocoa flavors	Vanilla fudge ripple
Candy and cookie flavors	Praline pecan
Fruit flavors	Cherry
Nutty flavors	Butterfinger
Combination flavors	Chocolate almond
Butter pecan	Rocky road
Black walnut	Chocolate marshmallow
Strawberry	Almond Joy
Vanilla bean	Fudge
Chocolate chip	

We ask them to take the cards and create an issue tree with three categorical levels. They easily identify the universe (ice cream) and the basis of classification (flavor). Then they need to identify subcategories and fit the examples into them. Since the list is not exhaustive, we let them extend the tree for extra credit. To do so, they need to invent new subcategories or split the combination subcategory more finely.

➤ *Speaking and listening standards, 1, 2, and 4*

➤ *Lesson idea*

A slightly more complex activity is to provide some categories and some sub-categories and ask students to create the rest of the classification. Students need to come up with individual examples of each final subcategory and determine whether everything they come up with fits a category/subcategory or whether they need to identify new categories and subcategories.

Below is a partial classification we ask students to complete. We remind them to be sure that they have provided individual examples for each of the final identified categories or subcategories and also that every video game they are aware of fits as an individual example under a branch of categories and subcategories.

Universe: Kinds of video games

Basis: Purpose of game and associated gamer activity

1. Action

   1.1 Shooter

2. Action adventure

3. Adventure

4. Role-playing

   4.1 Multi–role player game

5. Simulation

   5.1 Construction and management simulation

   5.2 Life simulation

   5.3 Vehicle/driving simulation

6. Strategy

➤ *Lesson idea*

➤ *Speaking and listening standards 1, 2, and 4 and language standards 4, 5, and 6*

Textbooks are typically organized through classifications of topic—often very poorly. One year, Jeff's eighth graders complained bitterly about their social studies textbook for world cultures. Jeff asked them to identify all the topics in a chapter about Northern Ireland, and they created the following list. After generating this list of topics, the students classified them using an issue tree and proposed a new way of organizing the chapter.

livelihood	agriculture	population
culture	women and children	religion
social history of Northern Ireland	protestant	the Chieftains
poverty	Catholicism	fairies
Irish language	politics	paganism
education	housing	health
cooking and fuel	diet	dress

potatoes	customs	social habits
storytelling	crime	sports
fairs	Boyle Abbey	Black Church
St. Patrick	British occupation	Easter Uprising
Battle of the Boyne	French invasion of Mayo	priesthood
Sinn Fein	IRA	UPD
Ian Paisley	Parnell	O'Connell
William of Orange	St. Brendan	beers and ales
the Fenians	cider	cream liquors
soda bread	corned beef	potato cakes
soccer	hurling	U2
folk songs	Sinead O'Connor	

As students move toward composing their own classification essays, they need to look at some clear and short examples of the genre. Therefore, we use a technique we call *mystery pot*. We cut up the text in Figure 11.6 into its constituent sentences, scramble the order, and ask small groups of students to resequence the sentences into their original order. Then students circle the cues that lead one sentence to another (transitions, navigational cues, repeated words or ideas), which prompts them to consider the audience's ability to follow trains of thought. (The children's book *Time to Eat*, by Steve Jenkins and Robin Page, is also good example of a classification scheme that can be used for the purposes of this exercise.)

➤ *Lesson idea*

➤ *Mentor text*

There may be different, equally viable ways of reordering a text, but each ordering will provide a different emphasis, meaning, and effect. Students can discuss the choices they made and the effects achieved, which reinforces the notion of rhetorical stance. After the reordering, we ask our students to outline the classification using an issue tree.

➤ *Writing anchor standards 4–6*

Critiquing negative models. Once students have some familiarity with classifying, they have great fun critiquing and writing classifications that violate the rules. We have our students read this great model of an incorrect classification from Jorge Luis Borges:

> . . . a certain Chinese encyclopedia entitled "Celestial Emporium
> of Benevolent Knowledge." On those remote pages it is written
> that animals are divided into a) those that belong to the Emperor,
> b) embalmed ones, c) those that are trained, d) suckling pigs,
> e) mermaids, f) fabulous ones, g) stray dogs, h) those that are
> included in this classification, i) those that tremble as if they were
> mad, j) innumerable ones, k) those drawn with a very fine camel's hair brush, l) others, m) those that have just broken a flower
> vase, n) those that resemble flies from a distance. . . .

Figure 11.6 Example of a Classification Essay

BEN FRANKLIN, MAN OF MULTIFARIOUS GENIUS!
Ben Franklin's accomplishments in four distinct areas show that he was a man of uncommon genius.
His areas of most notable achievement were publishing and writing, inventing, scientific research, and diplomacy.
Publishing and writing, his first area of accomplishment, began when he became apprenticed to a printer, and later took over the business.
He was soon not only publishing newspapers but also immensely popular almanacs, including *The Farmer's Almanack* and *Poor Richard's Almanack*.
He wrote many successful tracts, broadsheets, and books, most famous among them being *The Autobiography of Benjamin Franklin*.
The next area of accomplishment was in the area of scientific research.
Through his many years of travel and research, he is best noted for his research on weather and ocean currents, conducted on his trips to and from Europe, and for his research into electricity, commemorated by the story of his kite flying during a thunderstorm.
This research often culminated in practical ways with the invention of new products for the home and business.
Not content with invention on the page and in the laboratory of life, Franklin also invented functional objects for use in and around the home, which was a third area of accomplishment.

Figure 11.6 *Continued*

BEN FRANKLIN, MAN OF MULTIFARIOUS GENIUS!
The most famous of these inventions was the lightning rod, which greatly reduced home fires.
Another invention was the Franklin stove, which heated the home more efficiently and with less smoke than any previous stove.
Thus, Franklin came into the colonial home through his writing and his inventions!
Finally, Franklin was a diplomat and statesman of incredible acumen.
He was a delegate to the Albany Conference in 1764, which recommended compromising with King George.
Subsequent years in England, though, convinced him that the king could not be reckoned with through compromise.
Thus, when he became a member of the Continental Congress, he urged the congress to declare independence from Britain and assisted John Adams and Thomas Jefferson in writing the Declaration of Independence.
He was then a diplomat to France during the War for Independence, and secured France's much needed financial and military support.
After the war, he served on the Constitutional Convention and continued to serve Pennsylvania and the young United States in many ways until his death.
It is fairly certain that Benjamin Franklin was a man of unparalleled genius in all these areas; he improved our lives and helped to establish not only our country but some of what we might call the American character.

Then we ask them, in small groups, to critique the system and identify the logical classification errors. Finally, we encourage them to commit and name the same kinds of egregious errors by writing a fake classification based on Borges' model. Students can also analyze, explain, and transform their silly, incorrect versions into classification schemes that fit the criteria for a correct one. Students who can successfully do and justify this kind of work demonstrate their understanding of correct classification schemes.

➤ *Writing anchor standard 4*

Through a sequence of activities like these, which include reading and writing from models, students develop a sense of both local and global text structures that will lend purpose and coherence to their writing at the sentence, paragraph, and text levels.

➤ *Lesson idea*

After students have mastered the basic tools of classification, we continue working exclusively with material related to the unit's conceptual inquiry. In our poverty unit, students read profiles of kids living in poverty (provided by aid organizations) or profiles of poverty fighters. They then classify the people affected by poverty, causes of poverty, the effects of poverty on children, kinds of aid, the effects of aid, what they learned about poverty, and anything else they can find to classify.

➤ *Reading anchor standards 7–9 and writing anchor standards 7–9*
➤ *Lesson idea*

During the unit, students also form literature circle groups, give themselves a team name, and read some of the following books (at a minimum, at least one fiction and one nonfiction book):

Fiction

Begging for Change, by Sharon Flake

Uncle Willie and the Soup Kitchen, by DyAnne DiSalvo-Ryan

A Castle on Viola Street, by DyAnne DiSalvo

True Believer, by Virgian Euwer Wolff

Nonfiction

A Kid's Guide to Hunger and Homelessness: How to Take Action, by Cathryn Berger Kaye

Children of the Great Depression, by Russell Freedman

Pitch Black, by Youme Landowne and Anthony Horton

We encourage students to find and read other texts about poverty as well, as part of their free reading agenda, for example. We also distribute short sections of Jeffrey Sachs' *The End of Poverty* and other adult texts about poverty. Such texts are easy to find, and to help students find things to read around specific topics through state

➤ *Writing anchor standards 8 and 9*

library system data searches. We selected our choices with an eye toward exploring deeper, more complex notions of poverty and its causes and effects.

Composing First Drafts of Classifications

To begin our drafting, we ask small groups of students to create a list of dos and don'ts for classification, which also constitutes a formative assessment and a kind of composing to transfer. Here's a guide from one group:

➤ *Lesson idea*

Don't Be Guilty!

- You must stick with the same basis of categorization throughout and for all levels or you are guilty of the logical error of cross-linking.
- Don't oversimplify! Don't fail to consider the different perspectives or types of the subject you are classifying. There are many ways to categorize ideas, intelligence, courage, happiness, loyalty, friendship, leadership, etc. that people might overlook.

Do Be Supersmart!

- Find the story! The story depends on your purpose and on what insights are revealed through the classification.
- Be complete! A place for everything (every individual example) and everything in its place.
- Make sure you get to individual examples!

Figure 11.7 is a more specific guide that Jeff's students came up with during the poverty unit; it can be used when reading, critiquing, or composing any classification scheme.

A technique for getting started with drafts that makes use of classification to assist students is that of outlining in chunks, developed by Anna Daley. When students outline in chunks, they are classifying details and data that they think should go together. This technique helps students to get going with a first draft and is often helpful in overcoming writer's block. (See Figure 11.8.)

After first drafts are composed, we ask pairs of peer editors to read each other's papers and apply the criteria. We also ask them to draw an issue tree of each other's classification paper so that the writer will know if she or he explained it clearly enough for it to be replicated.

➤ *Lesson idea*

Paragraphing. We work on paragraphing by asking pairs of students to study the paragraph breaks in two of the professional classifications they have read and decide

➤ *Lesson idea*

➤ *Reading anchor standard 5*

Figure 11.7   Classification Criteria

A successful classification system will *identify, define, coordinate, subordinate* all the way to individual examples!

Identify topic

1. Clearly identify the subject (the limited topic or universe) of the classification (top level of your issue tree).

Define basis

2. Clearly define and explain the basis (the reasoning for dividing the universe into these particular classes).

   a. Is the basis clearly worded?

3. Identify the purpose of the classification and the explanatory power and work such a classification can do for the audience.

   a. Who is the audience of the classification?

   b. How does the classification meet audience needs and interests?

Coordinate classes

4. List the types (general classes) that will be explained and examined (this will be the second level of your issue tree).

   a. Are all types at any level of equal value? Are they mutually exclusive?

Subordinate classes

5. Each subordinate layer of the classification fits under and is an example of the layer above it.

   a. Are all types at this level of equal value? Are they mutually exclusive?

   b. Do the types at each level of the issue tree comprehensively account for every member of the universe?

   c. Does each descending level of the issue tree reflect an intensifying and specifying power of one?

6. The details (specific examples) are divided in terms of the basis.

7. Paragraphing and headers reflect the organization of the content and helps the reader understand and navigate the text.

8. Transitions and key words are used for coherence and promote text navigation.

9. The examined types (the most specific examples at the bottom of the issue tree) are individual examples and are specifically shown to the reader.

Chant it, curious classifiers: all good classifications *identify, define, coordinate, subordinate* . . .

Figure 11.8   Outlining in Chunks

Now that you've learned to use the Author Says/Does analysis to look at *another* author's text, you have the skills to use this technique to conceptualize your own writing project.

You have an idea for your paper in your head. Consider all of the work you already imagine you'll want or need to get done in this paper. For example, you might already imagine that you could use a personal narrative to begin your paper and that you'll also want to inform your reader of some important historical background. Each of these mini-tasks within your paper can be thought of as "chunks" just like you "chunked" out another author's work in your Says/Does analysis.

So, if you had these parts of your paper in mind, draw a box and inside it write *"Narrative: Personal story about such-and-such."* That's your first chunk of your paper. Notice that you are planning both the content and the form of this section of text.

Your next chunk is that historical background. Draw another box below the first one. Write *"Explain: History of my family immigrating to the U.S. four generations ago and subsequent family moves around the country"* (or whatever).

It might look something like THIS:

Narrative: personal story about my huge family get-together at Thanksgiving.

Explain: history of my family immigrating to the US four generations ago and subsequent family moves around the country. Everyone is spread out but we still come together every year.

Carry on planning your paper in "chunks" until you've exhausted your ideas (for now).

Although Anna's students may be writing a narrative, they use classification—chunking material that goes together—to decompose the task into manageable sections.

the reason or reasons for each break. We then create a list of rules. Next student pairs read each other's paper and see whether these rules are followed. If not, we decide whether we are missing a rule or whether the paragraphing in the student paper should be done differently. We then create a classroom set of rules about paragraphing for use the rest of the year. Here's an anchor chart from a ninth-grade class:

➤ *Language anchor standards 2 and 3 and speaking and listening anchor standards 1–6*

Reasons for Paragraphing

To shift to a new idea or perspective or a new subtopic

To restate a point

To emphasize a point

To provide additional support or explanation

To break things up on the page for the reader, so it doesn't look too long

To make things manageable for the audience

To bring related ideas together and emphasize the relationship by putting them together in a paragraph

In classification, to show we have moved to a new category or subcategory or individual example

To show coordination

To show subordination!

Note Well!

- Textbooks tell us to create a topic sentence and then work to create sentences that build on the topic sentence. But looking at our own writing and that of professionals, we found that real writers don't work that way!!!!

- Paragraphs don't have an independent existence—they are part of the entire discourse, promoting overall understanding and contributing to an overall effect!

(For academic research on paragraphing that shows these students were correct, see Lindemann 2001.)

Composing Final Drafts of Classifications

➤ *Language anchor standards 1 and 2*

As students compose classification papers that explain their scheme, many of them benefit from learning how to use colons (to introduce a list), subordinating conjunctions (for comparing–contrasting categories/classes), and semicolons (for differentiation or coordination). There are extensive models for teaching these moves in *Getting It Right* (Smith and Wilhelm 2007).

Exercises for inductive instruction on how to introduce a classification.

This school offers many different kinds of sports: _____, _____, _____, and _____. (Use as many blanks as you need.)

Ice cream comes in many different kinds of flavors:

Come up with your own example. . . .

Discussion: What do you notice about the language construction? How can you use this construction in your own paper?

Not getting enough education, poor health, _____,
and _____ are all correlated with poverty. (Add
extra blanks as needed.)

Neither _____ nor _____ nor
_____ (use as many blanks as you need) necessarily solves
the problems of poverty.

One can improve his or her upward mobility by _____
or _____ or _____. All of
these are good strategies.

Discussion: What do you notice about each sentence construction? How can
you use these constructions in your own paper?

Exercise for inductive instruction on how to use semicolons in a series.

The first class of curricular offerings at our school are sciences like life,
physical, and chemical sciences; the second class are math areas like basic,
algebra, geometry, and calculus; the third class is social sciences. . . .

Our school offers many kinds of extracurricular activities: those in the visual arts like filmmaking, glassblowing, watercolors, and portraiture; those
in the performing arts like theater, drama, and forensics; those in publishing like. . . .

Discussion: What do you notice about the language construction and particularly the use of the semicolon? How can you use this construction in your
own paper?

Composing to Transfer Knowledge About Classifications

All the units in this book culminate in the application of some kind of social action or
service learning. Those applications are the ultimate compositions for transfer—they
are transfer!

The classifications in this unit serve an even bigger existential question: *what
ways are available to us to address problems and change our local community and world for
the better?* This question leads to social action and service.

In our unit, the final reward for successful learning is that students get to perform
their learning all over again: we ask them to brainstorm a system for classifying what
we can do as citizens to improve our community.

➤ *Lesson idea*

➤ *Writing anchor standards 7–9*

In preparation, we engage in a day of short-term research using both local resources like the Society for New Americans and the Salvation Army and online resources like the National Service-Learning Cooperative's "11 Essential Elements of Service Learning," which emphasizes the need for student voice and student action as an integral part of curricula. The website for Learn and Serve: America's National Service Learning Clearinghouse emphasizes using multimedia and social media to get one's message out and raise awareness.

After reading these resources, the class comes up with a classification scheme of what we could do to improve our community that involves subcategories like (1) working vigorously to deepen our own understanding; (2) listening to one another; (3) raising awareness; (4) providing resources to one another; (5) helping one another directly, face to face; (6) withholding judgments of others and realizing poverty and other issues are much more complicated than we think; (7) actively believing the best of others and expressing this.

The students then brainstorm actual ways and practices to enliven each subcategory of "doing" something to improve our community with regard to poverty and other issues.

Students then choose an activity to pursue. In embodying some of these attempts to changing the community and world, the students go far beyond the classroom requirements. One group camped out in cardboard boxes on the football field for a weekend to both deepen their experience of poverty and raise awareness of homelessness. Another group gave up their lunches for two weeks, instead eating a cup of rice each day, donating their lunch money to a local food bank.

➤ *Lesson idea*

In one piece of reflective writing, students classify what they have learned procedurally, socially, and in other general areas that they did not expect.

➤ *Lesson idea*

In another piece they reflect on their reflections: we introduce students to a system of classifying forms of reflection and ask them to code their own reflections to match those schemes. Boud et al. (1985) propose this classification of kinds of reflection:

Attention to feelings—utilize positive feelings; remove negative feelings

Association—link prior and new knowledge; identify discrepancies between new and old knowledge, feelings and attitudes; reassess prior and new knowledge, decisions, and stances

Integration—seek to understand and connect the relationships between prior knowledge, decisions, feelings, and attitudes and new knowledge, decisions, feelings, and attitudes

Validation—test for internal consistency between new understandings and appreciations and prior knowledge or beliefs

Appropriation—make knowledge one's own; internalize new knowledge and attitudes and stances into one's identity; consider possible applications in one's own life (new knowledge and insights become a force in one's life)

Outcomes—transform perspective; change behavior, prepare to apply, commit to action

In a similar vein, Hatton and Smith (1995) posit four levels of reflection:

Descriptive/nonreflective—descriptive account of events

Descriptive reflection—description with introduction of personal perspective and/or some contemplation of other or alternative perspectives and/or acknowledgment of other perspectives

Dialogic reflection—discussion with oneself and others; exploration of possible reasons and underlying causes; ability to separate oneself from events and actions; engagement with oneself, events, actions, and decisions; logical and integrative commentary

Critical reflection—consideration of the broader social, historical, political, and cultural contexts that influence events, actions, decisions; integration of theory and practice to inform observations and decision making

By using such schemes students both review the process of classification and come to appreciate and sometimes practice various and deeper kinds of reflection.

Conclusion

The classifications throughout the unit are all after something bigger than just classification. They lead naturally to cause–effect and problem–solution thought patterns and text structures, the subject of the next and final chapter.

Problem–Solution and Cause–Effect

So What's the Problem?

We've all been in personal and professional situations in which problems were denied or ignored until too late. Jeff currently is laid up after microfracture surgery on his knee because he failed to recognize the growing pain, swelling, and tightness and proactively address the cause of these symptoms. He also has a student he was worried about but didn't sit down and talk with until after she failed to turn in a paper.

Enrollments are down in Michael's department and he worries that his focus on potential causes that he *can't* control (e.g., teacher layoffs in Philadelphia) have kept him from thinking about potential solutions he *can* control (e.g., doing a better job following up on email contacts).

Jim once taught in a school district in which one of the high schools had to be closed for an entire year because a mold outbreak was not understood to be a problem until health issues for teachers and students became frequent and serious.

In contrast, we want to cultivate—both in ourselves and in our students—a problem-seeking and problem-solving mentality. We want to encourage proactivity versus reactivity: a tomorrow mind instead of a yesterday mind. Denial or just plain avoidance is an all too-human problem—and it needs solving!

As a culture we avoid and deny problems. It is undeniable yet still denied that we are facing problems with global climate change, biodiversity loss, air and water quality, food security, poverty, equality of opportunity, educational policy and assessment, and on and on. Read any newspaper and you can come up with a long list of existing and potential problems (and intimations of hidden, unarticulated ones).

As educators, we need to cultivate a problem-finding and problem-solving spirit and teach our students how to redefine and reframe recognized problems and search for and embrace creative and innovative solutions. Problem–solution and cause–effect structures do exactly this kind of work. These two structures are closely related to each other and much more complex than typically purveyed in school.

Here's an example of that complexity. In *The Globe and Mail* of September 7, 2011, there was an article about the declining number of wild sockeye salmon. Four scientists and their studies were featured. Every scientist agreed that sea lice *may* have an effect on the collapse of the sockeye; none was willing to commit to this. All agreed that sea lice are propagated in salmon farming operations and that they spread from there to wild populations. Every researcher also insisted that the problem of the salmon collapse cannot *solely* be caused by sea lice. As the reporter Mark Hume put it: "All four witnesses replied in the negative when asked if sea lice 'acting in isolation' could have caused the collapse of sockeye salmon stocks." The article concludes that the action required now is to establish some kind of policy that might lead in the direction of a solution, given the murkiness and complexity of the findings in defining the nature of the problem.

This story highlights a major issue: causality and the problem–solution text structure/thought pattern are far more complicated than most people think and far more complicated than our school curriculum portrays them. As one boy in our study of the literate lives of young men (Smith and Wilhelm 2002, 2006) proclaimed: "School takes twisty-twirly ice-cream with sprinkles and turns it pure vanilla!" In other words, school uncomplicates and dumbs things down, and the energy, edginess, and usefulness of what we are teaching is lost.

The cognitive linguist George Lakoff (2008) argues that human beings have various cognitive biases toward simplicity and direct causality that rarely if ever match reality or bear scrutiny. If we want to meet the correspondence concept and really help students develop expert understanding of problem–solution and cause–effect, we must address these biases in direct, wide-awake ways. We begin with problem–solution, because we see cause–effect as a subset of problem–solution and always in service to it. To be precise, we need to be confronted with a compelling problem before we are motivated to understand the nature and causes of that problem.

All Roads Lead to Problem–Solution

All paradigmatic text structures can and often should lead to problem–solution. Problems compel us to understand deeply and use our understanding to solve these problems. Even a text type as simple as a list is undertaken to solve a problem: such as what not forget on a trip or at the grocery store. A recipe solves the problem of how to prepare an unfamiliar dish, as well as the problem of immediate hunger!

One aspect of developing a proactive, tomorrow-minded, inquiring mindset is learning how to see problems even when they exist for others but not for us (this is essential to democratic living). So, too, is learning how to reframe problems so they can be seen in a new way or in a way more amenable to satisfactory solution.

➤ *This ties in with the CCSS emphasis on understanding multiple perspectives, as well as flexibility and creativity in thinking.*

This book addresses problem–solution and cause–effect structures in conjunction with informational/explanatory text because the CCSS refer to these text structures as informational/explanatory. However, unless students are writing about predetermined causes and effects or reporting on already clearly understood problems and established solutions, these texts are not informational but are in fact arguments, often theoretical arguments at that.

We're not entirely against the relatively simple informational research and reporting involved in relaying established information (although using these two text structures as arguments is obviously much more powerful and generative). There is value in reviewing what is already understood about the nature and complexity of understood problems and how solutions address the various aspects of the problem, which would involve summarizing and describing. Likewise, it is important for students to understand the causes of various established effects. Therefore, to be consistent with the CCSS, we introduce these text patterns as informational texts.

That said, it's much more likely that real inquirers and composers will argue for causes and effects that are not yet established or understand problems and possible solutions in innovative and creative ways, in which case this reporting is in service of creating new meanings—and writing arguments. See Smith, Wilhelm, and Fredricksen (2012) for instruction on how to frame and pursue these text structures as arguments.

How the Problem–Solution Pattern Works

Hoey (2001, 123ff.) proposes this problem–solution pattern: (1) a previous *situation*, which provides a context for the problem, (2) the *problem* or "aspect of a situation requiring a response" (124), (3) the *response* to the problem, which must address underlying causes (more on this later), and (4) a positive result or *evaluation*. All these features can be seen in Hoey's humorous fabricated example:

> (1) I was once a teacher of English Language. (2) One day some
> students came to me unable to write their names. (3) I taught
> them text analysis. (4) Now they all write novels. (123)

He also suggests an inappropriate or invalid solutional response in which point 4 is a negative result or evaluation: "This had little effect" (130). In that case, the pattern is recycled until a response provokes either a positive evaluation or a negative one with no possibility of future success (e.g., the teacher is removed from the classroom and sent to professional development boot camp to learn appropriate teaching strategies).

Hoey also distinguishes problem–solution variations (achieving a goal, taking an opportunity, arousing and fulfilling a desire, identifying and filling a knowledge gap) but demonstrates that all these variations can be summarized in the pattern represented as SPRE, in which *S* stands for the situation; *P* for the problem, goal, need of knowledge (depending on the case); *R* for the response, the way of achieving a goal; and, finally, *E* represents a positive evaluation (the pattern ends) or a negative evaluation (the pattern is recycled) (145–69). (See Figure 12.1.)

➤ *Crux moves of problem–solution*

Figure 12.1 Problem–Solution Patterns

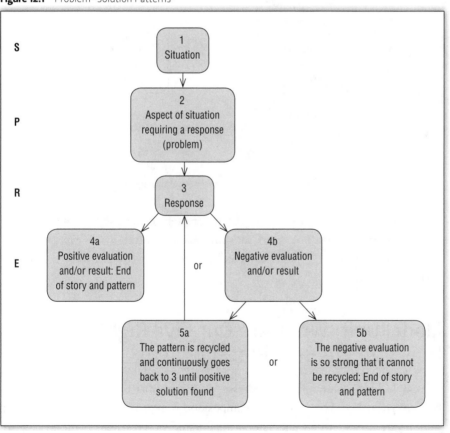

(continues)

Figure 12.1   *Continued*

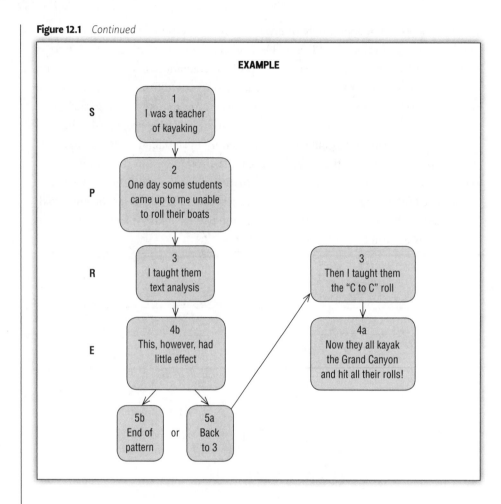

➤ *Writing anchor standard 2, language anchor standards 3 and 6*

According to Hoey, the problem–solution pattern is "lexically signaled" through either "inscribed signals" or direct semantic references (the words *problem* and *solution*). "Inscribed signals" either evaluate (e.g., *unfortunately*) or evoke (e.g., *had no money*) problems (140).

Model Unit: What Are Our Civil Rights and How Can We Best Protect Them?

A good problem–solution paper addresses a problem that is *worth pursuing* and *can be solved practically*. As noted, if the composition is informational, the problem and solution are already widely understood and the student is essentially writing a report.

Composing to Plan Problem–Solution Pieces

We begin by framing the unit as a problem to be solved. The problem is expressed in an essential question that requires students to think with and compose the problem–solution pattern. In this unit, we asked the question: *How can we protect and promote civil rights?*

After identifying a meaningful context for learning, the next step in planning is identifying problems, which often involves calling current situations into question.

We start by tapping into student experience. We ask students to list several groups they belong to in some way—English and other classes, riders of a particular school bus, sports team or fan organization, club, interest group, video game forum, social network, etc. Students then brainstorm as many problems facing each group as they can. (Prompts include *what are the purposes of this group? what problem(s) come up for this group and/or for you as part of this group? what obstacles, inefficiencies, or irritations come up in fulfilling your purposes?*) Students next foreground interventions and solutions to individual problems (*what did or could you do about this problem, obstacle, inefficiency?*) and then attempt an evaluation (*what was or might be the result? what would constitute success?*). (Notice that students are reviewing the SPRE pattern.)

In another great introductory activity, we pose the subquestion *how does our school violate students' civil rights?* (This is an engaging subquestion of our essential question. Ever meet a seventh grader who doesn't think his civil rights are being violated all the time?) Students, in groups, write down ideas, then record them on the board. It doesn't take too long for the whole board to be filled! We have students underline the most compelling problems and circle those to which they think they might be able to provide a practical, workable solution. Students then choose a problem that is both underlined and circled to write about throughout the unit. (Another option is to have small groups of students fill out the problem–consequence chart in Figure 12.2.)

Students' final papers propose solutions to one of our school or community problems that can be supported by historical data related to civil rights. (This is using the problem–solution structure in service to an argument, which is how the thought pattern is typically used.). In pursuing this inquiry students are writing as experts with the knowledge and from the authority of their own experience; they are arguing for solutions to real problems they know about. They must understand the problem, its social context, prior attempts to solve the problem (or similar ones), and be able to explain why the attempts have or haven't worked. This requires research and wide reading, perhaps including interviews with experts.

As students select their individual topics they must consider two crux moves: can they explain the problem and can they propose a justifiable solution to the problem?

➤ *Lesson idea*

➤ *Writing anchor standard 7 (short research)*

➤ *Lesson idea*

➤ *Lesson idea*

➤ *Reading anchor standards 7–9 and writing anchor standards 7–9*

➤ *Writing anchor standards 7–9*

Figure 12.2

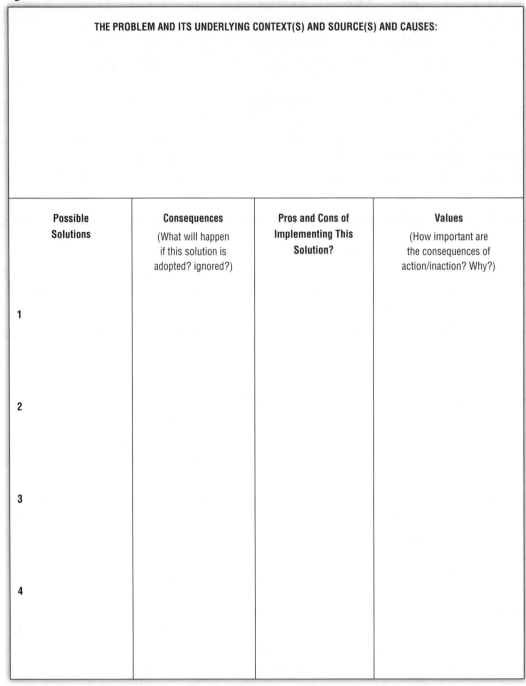

THE PROBLEM AND ITS UNDERLYING CONTEXT(S) AND SOURCE(S) AND CAUSES:			
Possible Solutions	**Consequences** (What will happen if this solution is adopted? ignored?)	**Pros and Cons of Implementing This Solution?**	**Values** (How important are the consequences of action/inaction? Why?)
1			
2			
3			
4			

Before we accept topics from students, we ask them to respond to the following prompts for decomposing the task:

➤ *Lesson idea*

- Develop a rationale for your topic: why it matters, why it's a problem, and why it has been or can be solved. (The brainstorming strategies from the listing/naming chapter help here.)

- Define your initial understanding: summarize and clarify what you know about the problem and what you think you know about potential solutions. (Many of the strategies from the summarization chapter help here.)

- Determine what you need to learn: develop questions to help you begin your research. What data sources are available to you? How will you obtain the data you need? (Some of the process description strategies, like brainstorming a flowchart, help here.)

To teach students how to search for data (observe, take notes, interview) and judge its validity, we emphasize two things:

1. Don't jump to *any* conclusions—*keep all your ideas categorically tentative!*
2. Research, research, research—*and seek out other perspectives!*

Composing to Practice Problem–Solution Pieces

➤ *Writing anchor standards 7–9*

The vocabulary students must notice and use when reading and composing problem–solution patterns occurs in expressions of semantic relationships, particularly in introductions, transitions, and conclusions. Galán and Pérez (2004) found that studying these language cues, which are provided in Figure 12.3, greatly enhances students' understanding of the text pattern and their ability to use it flexibly in composition. Rather than asking students to memorize these cues, we present think-alouds of mentor texts in which students identify and circle these words and record the words and what they signal on anchor charts. In this way they are inquiring into how language works to help readers understand and to get work done.

➤ *Lesson idea*

➤ *Writing anchor standard 7 (short research), reading anchor standards 4–6, and language anchor standards 3–6*

Excellent mentor texts for problem–solution include children's books such as *Should I Share My Ice-Cream*, by Mo Willems; *Pirates Go to School*, by Corine Demas; *Memoirs of a Goldfish*, by Devin Scillian; and many of Kevin O'Malley's books. Problem–solution patterns are also easily found in newspapers and news magazines and on the Internet.

➤ *Mentor texts*

We also ask students to discuss *problem scenarios* and their possible causes and solutions. The following scenario is a good fit with the civil rights unit: *Recently, many*

➤ *Lesson idea*

Figure 12.3.   Vocabulary Signaling Problem–Solution Text Patterns

PROBLEM SIGNALS (PERSONAL)

Adjectives
ashamed, anxious, bold, cheeky, concerned, disgraceful, distressed, disturbed, embarrassed, embarrassing, funny, humiliated, mistaken, nervous, overwhelmed, rude, sad, surprised, worried

Nouns
anxiety, boldness, cheek, concern, disgrace, disrespect, distress, embarrassment, humiliation, insolence, mistake, misunderstanding, nerve, rudeness, sadness, shame, situation, shyness, surprise, worry

Verbs
to be ashamed, to become anxious, to bother, to blush, to be concerned, to confuse, to disrespect, to distress, to disturb, to embarrass, to forget, to humiliate, to mistake, to misunderstand, to show up, to trouble, to undergo, to upset, to worry

SOLUTION SIGNALS (PERSONAL)

Adjectives
cheerful, delighted, grateful, (un)happy, miserable, (dis)pleased, relieved, (un)satisfied, (un)solved

Nouns
attitude, conclusion, consequence, decision, excuse, delight, happiness, idea, reaction, relief, result, satisfaction, solution.

Verbs
to accept, to apologize, to become aware, to cheer up, to conclude, to deal with, to decide, to do about, to excuse, to help, to make up one's mind, to manage, to meditate, to please, to react, to realize, to reflect, to satisfy, to solve, to think out, to work out

Linking Words
after, afterward, consequently, eventually, finally, however, in the end, so, suddenly, then, therefore, thus

---

refugee families have moved to our town. The children of these families lack cultural resources and are often ignored and sometimes called names, threatened, and bullied.

Students research online or elsewhere and present solutions to these problems in multimodal formats, often as homework. They then generate and discuss specific problem scenarios of their own related civil rights. Scenarios brought up by students during the most recent teaching of this unit were:

- Because of suspicion of drug dealing and drug use in schools, student lockers are being searched by sniffer dogs and administrators.
- For the same reason, all teachers and all athletes must undergo random drug testing. Students in other activities are exempt. So are all staff members.

- Because many students have been sleeping at the Occupy Boise camp and coming to school in dirty clothes/clothes proclaiming support for the protesters, the school has created a new dress code requiring students to wear clean clothes free of political advocacy.
- Students using cell phones during class have had their cell phones confiscated until the end of the grading period.
- The school cafeteria often serves food that violates students' dietary restrictions (because of health concerns or religious observances). This particularly affects students who get free lunch.

Alone or in groups, students apply the SPRE framework to each, rank the problems in order of seriousness as a threat to civil rights, and then generate possible actions or solutions, justifying their rationales for success.

As students read a variety of textual materials related to civil rights and complete the classroom activities, they evaluate their solutions against those that have or are being tried in the world (an opportunity for research), refining and/or modifying their own solutions accordingly, sharing their ideas with classmates.

➤ *Speaking and listening anchor standards and writing anchor standard 7*

Activities like these reinforce the SPRE framework and build conceptual and procedural knowledge necessary for the inquiry. Because we want our students to make connections from the inquiry to their own lives and the world, we ask them to scan the newspaper or Internet news/interest sites to identify and analyze problems. Problem-solving prompts like these can help students gather facts and figures and cite their sources and references:

➤ *Lesson idea*

- What is the problem?
- Who says it is a problem? Why?
- What is the context/situation of the problem?
- Does the problem really exist? How can we tell?
- What is the history of the problem, the story behind it? How it has come to our attention?
- Who is affected by the problem? Who is not affected?
- What are the current consequences and possible future consequences if the problem is not addressed?
- Does anyone benefit from the existence of the problem? (adapted from Axelrod and Cooper 1999, 383)

It's also important to consider innovative solutions—to get outside the box. Brainstorming three or more possible solutions to a problem and explaining how

➤ *Lesson idea*

these would address causes is one way. Another is to research solutions that have been tried or proposed and interview experts who might be available in the community or online. (We have found that many experts are happy to exchange emails with students.)

To help students learn to articulate and apply critical problem–solution standards, we ask:

- What solutions would address the causes, or at least reduce the symptoms and effects?
- What first steps could be taken?
- What steps seem most timely, doable, and useful?
- How can approaches be combined?
- What new angles might be possible to try?
- Why and how will your solution work?
- How will you gauge and evaluate success? What will count as progress or success?
- What objections do you predict to your proposal and how will you proactively address objections? (e.g., if people complain that your plan costs a lot of money, how will you explain why it's worth the money or how it can save money in the long run?)

Since resources for solving problems—money, time, people, energy, and technology—are always limited, a good writer needs to establish criteria for picking reasonable solutions. These criteria make the solutions realistic rather than fanciful. (The process description strategies described in Chapter 8 are useful for describing the implementation of a solution.)

It's always important to consider and actively imagine the audience—to think about who they are and their level of familiarity with the problem, how they are implicated in the cause or effects of the problem, their biases toward solutions and objections they might have, as well as how to address these factors proactively. Discussing the audience in small groups and listing possible objections like lack of money, comfort with the status quo, and the like is helpful. Drama activities in which group members play an audience of people resistant to the proposal is often helpful as well (Wilhelm 2002/2012).

Students need to practice identifying and describing the situation/context (the chapter on description can help with this), the nature of the problem, possible/best

➤ *Writing anchor standard 4 (audience consideration and rhetorical stance)*

responses/solutions, and an evaluation of the response in terms that a particular audience will understand and accept.

Composing First Drafts of Problem–Solution Pieces

Students should think aloud as they read mentor texts and keep an anchor chart of what they need to learn about the text pattern during the unit to be successful writing the final composition. They should also use mentor texts to determine criteria for the pattern, articulate critical standards, and create an assessment rubric or checklist. We try to keep criteria to the most important four or five so that instruction, peer response, and the composing process focus on what is most important.

➤ *Lesson idea*

➤ *Reading anchor standards 2 and 7–9*

Here's a rubric prepared by a recent group of students:

- *Engagingly introduces and clearly describes the problem*, including the causes and effects, and the consequences if the problem is not resolved.
- *Clarifies the criteria* that can be used for evaluating and judging options
- *Describes/proposes various alternate solutions* in a logical, coherent way and gives detailed steps for carrying out the "best" solution.
- *Shows how the solution solves/will solve* the problem and address its root causes.
- *Uses language cues* to help the reader navigate the text.

Students should already have had plenty of practice understanding and meeting the criteria in the composing-to-practice phase, so the criteria can now guide them through the steps of writing the paper. The criteria should also help peer groups respond in helpful and substantive ways as students work through multiple drafts. In our unit, we directed that peer responders should:

➤ *Lesson idea*

- Read a draft straight through.
- Record a general impression (two or three sentences).
- Find things to praise (elements of the composition that are particularly effective).
- Read the draft again.
- Ask questions about what needs to be clarified or elaborated.

Peer responders might also see how their own description of the nature and importance of the problem matches the author's conception and point out the reasons

➤ *Reading anchor standards 1–6*

the proposed solution makes sense and the steps for implementing it. If anything is missed, the author knows the writing must be clarified.

Composing Final Drafts of Problem–Solution Pieces

Students are often more motivated to compose stellar final drafts if they are going to share their work publicly. Problem–solution pieces can often be presented to school boards, parent groups, or any other group that might support or be able to use the proposals. At Jeff's school, students hold a "learning fair" every quarter to which the public is invited. Civil rights presentations can to made to school administrators and local legislators. Students may also take part in public service awareness campaigns about civil rights issues facing members of the community. Rehearsal, feedback, and proofreading are all very important before a public presentation.

> ➤ *Multimodal presentations meet the CCSS standards for multimodal composing and public presentation.*

Jeff has two great presentation stories. During a unit on *what is teen health?* one group of students became very interested in sleep deprivation research, going so far as to interview a Mayo Clinic sleep researcher. They found that researchers agree that high school students need to sleep in and that it makes much more sense for elementary school to start earlier in the day and high school to start later. The school board agreed to hear their presentation, which included a number of multimedia data displays. The presentation was well received, but in return the students got a lesson on bus schedules, sport schedules, credits for graduation, and much else! They learned that the problem was much more complex than they had thought and went back to rethinking their solution!

In another case, students in an alternative program being considered for elimination because of poor attendance made a presentation to the school board about why the program should be retained. Attendance was perfect during the three weeks in which the students researched and created their presentation about solving the problem of poor attendance. The students gave a fantastic presentation, and the school board voted unanimously to retain the program. The next day, not one of the students came to school! Once this highly meaningful and compelling problem had been solved, they decided to take a break!

Composing to Transfer Knowledge of Problem–Solution Pieces

> ➤ *Lesson idea*

Students can write an analysis of the process they went through to compose their paper and/or presentation. They can do a PQP of their own work, *praising* what they think they did best and what went well, raising *questions* they still have about composing problem–solution patterns, and identifying what they are *prepared* do in the future.

Or students can write a short, one-page reflection on what they learned about their topic from the thought pattern, as well as what they learned about using and composing the pattern. We ask students to explain what helped and contributed to their learning—what did they learn by reading, planning and practicing, drafting, using and revising criteria, receiving peer response, and reflecting? how does problem–solution make use of other patterns like description and definition?

We also ask students to consider the nature of problem–solution patterns and policy proposals in the world. Why are they important personally and socially? What contributions do they make to society? In what situations are they most useful? Students thus develop metacognitive awareness of their own learning process and can plan future, more independent ventures using problem–solution patterns.

And we always foster immediate transfer by having students review the problem solving they are doing in other classes and identify and use the strategies they have learned in this class. (See the problem sort for physics in Figure 12.4 and part of a math think-aloud in Figure 12.5 for examples of how to reinforce the crux moves of problem–solution in the context of local level disciplinary learning.)

Figure 12.4 Problem Sort

Physics 400	Names: _____	_____
Whitepapering WS	_____	_____

For each box, fill in what you think were the **crux moves and main ideas** that you should have learned and applied in the context of solving each problem. Explain briefly how these moves/ideas were used in solving the problem and justify this use.

Problem 1:	Problem 2:	Problem 3:	Problem 4:

Problem 5:	Problem 6:	Problem 7:	

(continues)

Figure 12.4   *Continued*

CATEGORIZE PROBLEMS:

Now, looking at the overall worksheet, please sort (classify) the problems into different categories. Think about what problems shared in common. You may include a problem in more than one category. Also indicate how, when looking at a problem, you may determine if a problem will fit into this category:

Category:				
Problem #s that fit this category				
How you can determine if a problem will fit a category				
What steps did you do to solve this problem?				

Source: Created by Stephen Zownorega and Blair Covino

Figure 12.5

Algebra 300   Name:_____

Solving Word Problems with Two Variables

1. The Bears fans for a home football game bought five times as many tickets as the visiting team fans. The total number of tickets sold was 1440. How many tickets did the home team fans and the visiting team fans buy?

    Identify   x: _____

                     y: _____

Equation 1:
Topic: _____ Equation: _____

Equation 2:
Topic: _____ Equation: _____

Think aloud about how you identify the kind of problem and how you know what data, ideas, and moves are necessary to "solve the system" and how you apply these:

Answer: _____

Figure 12.5 *Continued*

2. The perimeter of a rectangle is 26 meters. The length is 3 meters more than the width. Find the length and width. Identify x: _____ y: _____	**Equation 1:** Topic: _____ Equation: _____ **Equation 2:** Topic: _____ Equation: _____ Think aloud about how you identify the kind of problem and how you know what data, ideas, and moves are necessary to "solve the system" and how you apply these: Answer: _____
3. A rectangular plot of land has a perimeter of 196 feet. The length is 18 feet longer than the width. Find the length and width. Identify x: _____ y: _____	**Equation 1:** Topic: _____ Equation: _____ **Equation 2:** Topic: _____ Equation: _____ Think aloud about how you identify the kind of problem and how you know what data, ideas, and moves are necessary to "solve the system" and how you apply these: Answer: _____

Source: Created by Terry Quain and Christine Tarchinski

The Cause–Effect Thought Pattern

As human beings moving at the speed of life, we are constantly confronted with problems for which we must consider causes. Just today, there were bubbles in the glasswork Jeff's wife Peggy pulled out of her kiln. She needed to know what had caused the bubbles: her kiln shelf, moisture in the kiln, the temperature, the glass? Jeff's back bike tire was losing air. Was the tube bad, or the valve? Did he have a goathead pricker in the tire? If that was the cause, could the problem be solved by tightening the valve and extracting the goathead and applying goo?

Michael just got back from a meeting with his financial advisor. Their discussion focused almost exclusively on what's causing the current market volatility. He came home to find that some of his holiday decorations had fallen down. In order to decide what to do, he had to determine whether the fault lay with the way he put them up or with the many years of wear-and-tear they had endured.

Jim spent some time with friends brainstorming the causes of the Cubs long World Series drought—the longest in the major leagues. More positively they discussed the possible effects that might follow from the hiring of a new general manager and some recent trades.

In all the above cases, we needed to identify the cause of a problem and its effect before we could experiment with solutions leading to a different desired effect.

Cause–effect essays are concerned with *why*: why things happen (causes) and what happens as a result (effects). The effects typically constitute some kind of problem, which is why cause–effect is usually a subset of problem–solution and often embedded in that pattern. When we are trying to avoid certain effects in the future, we go from asking *why did that happen?* to *how can we keep that from happening?* Conversely, we may be proactively trying to improve a situation, so that our positive actions can be causes for reformed effects.

➤ *Crux moves*

How the Cause–Effect Pattern Works

Cause–effect is about asking why. To define the cause of something, ask yourself why. Ask yourself what, and you will determine the effect. That's good as far as it goes, but it gets considerably more complicated than that:

> Determining causes and effects is usually thought-provoking and quite complex. One reason for this is that there are two types of causes: *immediate causes*, which are readily apparent because they are closest to the effect, and *ultimate causes*, which, being somewhat removed, are not so apparent and may perhaps even be hidden. Furthermore, ultimate causes may bring about effects which themselves become immediate causes, thus creating a *causal chain*. For example, consider the following causal chain: Sally, a computer salesperson, prepared extensively for a meeting with a client (ultimate cause), impressed the client (immediate cause), and made a very large sale (effect). The chain did not stop there: the large sale caused her to be promoted by her employer (effect). (Rosa and Eschholz 1998, 211)

So an initial problem is establishing causality. (See Figure 12.6.)

Figure 12.6   Cause and Effect Brainstorming Chart

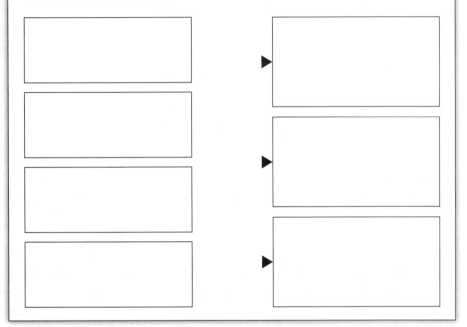

CAUSE AND EFFECT

Please list the causes and the effect in appropriate boxes. Then draw an error from the possible multiple cause(s) to the possible multiple effect(s). Some effects may have multiple causes; some causes may have the same effect or several effects—use your arrows to help us see all the connections you see. Causes on the left, effects on the right. You may also create a kind of flow chart to show how an effect could become a new cause, etc.

The Web Center for Social Research Methods (www.socialresearchmethods.net) maintains that three criteria must be met to establish evidence of a causal relationship: temporal precedence, covariation of the cause–effect, and no alternative explanation. These are crux moves then for establishing causality.

> ➤ *Crux moves for casuality*

Let's take the temporal precedence issue first:

> First, you have to be able to show that your cause happened *before* your effect. Sounds easy, huh? Of course the cause has to happen before the effect. Before we get lost in the logic here, consider a classic example from economics: does inflation cause unemployment? It certainly seems plausible that as inflation increases, more employers find that in order to meet costs they have to lay off employees. So

it seems that inflation could, at least partially, be a cause for unemployment. But both inflation and employment rates are occurring together in an ongoing basis. (www.socialresearchmethods.net/kb/causeeff.php)

The authors go on to explain that this kind of cyclical situation can involve processes that influence one another, making it very challenging and complicated to establish a causal relationship. Does inflation cause unemployment? Or does unemployment cause inflation? Or is there a more complex relationship between these factors and even other factors?

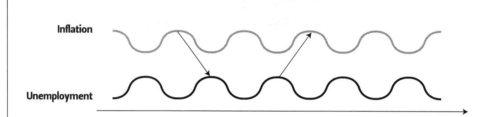

CYCLICAL FUNCTIONS

Before you can show that you have a *causal* relationship, you first have to show that you actually have a relationship. This requires establishing covariation—or continuity over time and situation. For instance, consider the statements *if* X *then* Y and *if not* X *then not* Y. If you observe that whenever X is present, Y is also present, and whenever X is absent, Y is too, then you have demonstrated that there is a relationship between X and Y. A relationship that has continuity.

Let's illustrate this pattern using a teaching problem. If we teach close reading through think-alouds of particular text types, our students improve in their capacity to read that kind of text. If we do not model close reading of a particular text type through think-alouds, our students' capacity to read these kinds of text is not improved. This provides evidence that the intervention and the result are related and continually so.

Here's another test:

if more of the intervention then more of the improvement

if less of the intervention then less of the improvement

However, the existence of the relationship doesn't provide evidence that the teaching intervention (think-alouds in this case) *caused* the outcome—there might be other factors involved. Demonstrating a relationship does not demonstrate cause. This is sometimes referred to as the "third variable" or "missing variable" problem. It is also the difference between demonstrating correlation and demonstrating causality. So it is necessary to demonstrate sufficiency of your considered cause to produce the effect on its own, and to brainstorm all alternative explanations for the observed effect and rule them out:

Berke (2007) also describes various criteria for establishing causation: (1) uniformity (two events, *X* and *Y*, are "so closely and conditionally connected that one cannot occur without the other" [205], which subsumes temporality and covariation) and (2) sufficiency (the cause or number of causes explored are sufficient to explain all the effects). Add the criterion that there are no other possible explanations, and Berke is in agreement with the social science research.

We have combined these insights into a series of crux moves for establishing causality, TCSNO: time (temporality)—continuity (covariation)—sufficiency—no other explanation.

Model Unit: How Can We Really Establish the Truth?

This unit followed the unit framed with the essential question: *what are our civil rights and how can we best protect them?* since in that unit students became very interested in how to establish the truth.

Students generated a number of subquestions: *What causes people to lie, twist the truth, and tell the truth? What are the effects of lying, twisting the truth, and telling the truth in different situations? How does situation and perspective affect what seems "true"? What are obstacles to perceiving the truth?* During the unit, we read excerpts from Kathryn Schulz's fascinating book *Being Wrong* (2010), along with Elie Wiesel's *Night* and Avi's YA book *Nothing but the Truth*. The culminating essay explored the causes and effects of deception, delusion, and persistent attempts to find the truth in a novel, movie, or historical case.

➤ *Writing anchor standards 4 and 5 and reading anchor standards 1–3*

Composing to Plan Cause–Effect Pieces

We began by having students brainstorm situations in which they needed to identify the cause of some effect—why someone was angry with them or why their grades were going down. Students then kept a daylong log in which they observed the purposes and possibilities of discerning cause–effect relationships. Based on their logs,

➤ *Lesson idea*

they made an anchor chart of purposes and contexts that rewarded or even required understanding causality.

Using what they learned in the civil rights unit, students brainstormed what the causes might be for bullying and other civil rights abuses. The following activities provide both conceptual frontloading (how to establish truth) and procedural frontloading (how to identify causes and effects). They connect students to the inquiry personally, build motivation, highlight different perspectives, and help students begin to generate ideas about cause and effect.

➤ *Reading anchor standards 4 and 9*

➤ *Lesson idea*

Autobiographical response establishing truth. Students respond to the following journal prompts and then share their writing with each other to foster discussion (thanks to teacher Kaidi Stroud for her work creating these activities):

> It has been said that there are at least two sides to every story. What do you think this means? What could possibly be the underlying causes behind different versions of events or situations? Refer to specific life experiences where there were different versions of events.

> Think of a recent disagreement you've had with a friend, family member, or teacher and tell the story. What was the situation? What caused the disagreement? What was your side of the story? What was the other side? What might have caused the differing perspectives? What problems were caused as a result of the disagreement? What were the effects? What possible solutions might there be to reconciling the problem? How would you evaluate an effective response?

> Are there really two (or more) sides to every story or is one side the real truth and the other sides just wrong?

➤ *Lesson idea*

Ranking truthfulness. Students complete the following exercise:

> Each of the following scenes describes an attitude toward truthfulness that is held by a character you will meet later in our unit reading. Read each scene and rank them, from the scene that best fits your ideas, beliefs, and values about responsibility to truthfulness (1) to the scene that least captures your ideas, beliefs, and values about truthfulness (3). Make sure you can support your opinions

about what constitutes responsibility to truthfulness in each situation. Be sure to identify perspectives you have a problem with, the possible causes and effects of such a perspective, and how that problem might be resolved for you. You'll be sharing your responses in groups and then with the whole class as we discuss what we think our responsibility is to ascertaining the truth.

_____ A. Jennifer Stewart, the education reporter for the *Manchester Record*, was eager to cover a story about a local student who was suspended from school for singing the national anthem during the tape-recorded playing of it over the school's loudspeakers. While Ms. Stewart interviewed the student in question, two other persons were present who often interrupted the student or answered questions in his place. When Ms. Stewart felt she had an accurate representation of the student's story, she attempted to contact the school superintendent, principal, assistant principal, and the teacher in question. They were unwilling or unable to answer her questions. Despite her inability to fully fact-check the story from all perspectives, she decided to run the story.

_____ B. Old Horse (called this because of his looks) was a veteran algebra teacher. He was known among the faculty and students to have a sharp tongue. Part way through the school year, Old Horse got a new student in his class. His classmates nicknamed the new student Rabbit because of his buck teeth and hare lip. Old Horse stayed after school with Rabbit to help him catch up on algebra, even though he knew becoming friends with the boy would make him more of an outcast. Then one day Old Horse embarrassed Rabbit in front of the class. Shortly thereafter, Rabbit made new friends. Old Horse never told anyone why he treated Rabbit so meanly, but it would appear he had a master plan for Rabbit.

_____ C. Tom lived down the street from Walter, who had inflammatory rheumatism (a disease that causes joint pain). Tom was surprised that Walter didn't have to go to school but fished any day of the week he wanted. One day, after Tom spotted Walter by the water on his way to school, Tom's legs and back began to hurt. He decided that he had inflammatory rheumatism as well. Tom told his teacher he ached all over and she sent him home right away. Since Walter had the illness and went fishing all day, Tom decided that fishing was the most logical way for him to spend his time, too. Though there was no medical diagnosis of inflammatory rheumatism from a doctor, Tom did feel better fishing instead of going to school.

Nothing but the truth. Students complete the following opinionnaire:

Identify whether you agree (A) or disagree (D) with each statement. Then choose one statement that you feel particularly strongly about and write a brief comment about what in your experience of the world causes you to feel this way. Then choose one statement you disagree with strongly and do the same. We will discuss what problems are avoided or caused by adhering to different statements.

_____ 1. Telling the whole truth is *always* the best.

_____ 2. It is okay to stretch or hide the truth *sometimes*, especially to protect or help someone.

_____ 3. There is only one real truth.

_____ 4. There are many real truths.

_____ 5. Truth is absolute—it is what it is and it never changes.

_____ 6. Truth is malleable—it can change and bend over time, with context and perspective, depending on who is looking at it.

_____ 7. Knowing the truth is an intellectual (thoughtful) process.

_____ 8. Knowing the truth is an intuitive (emotional) process.

_____ 9. It is not possible to fully know the truth about something.

_____ 10. It is okay to ignore facts or evidence if it interferes with your truth.

_____ 11. Almost everything we think we know is actually stuff
we believe.

_____ 12. There are not different realities, but there are different
ways of perceiving reality.

Reading newspaper articles or monitoring news reports on various forms of electronic media about situations involving personal, group, local, and global problems also helps students consider and plan what they might want to write about related to discerning or inferring cause–effect regarding the topic of truth. Daily newspapers are filled with disagreements about various issues, articles describing people telling the truth, speaking truth to power, being delusional or in denial, or just lying like crazy. We have students compose journal responses to the news stories they've been following, rating how well causality is established and even ranking how well authors establish causality, listing both strengths and weaknesses in their approaches.

➤ *Lesson idea*

➤ *Reading anchor standards 5 and 6*

Before leaving the planning phase, students identify potential topics for their culminating composition. They consider the unit inquiry, their interest, the interest of an audience, the importance and possibility of establishing causality (or the lack of it), what they already know, and data sources for finding out more. If they can satisfactorily address all these aspects, they put the topic on their list of possibilities.

➤ *Lesson idea*

➤ *Writing anchor standard 7*

Composing to Practice Cause–Effect Pieces

The crux move here is establishing causality. How *do* we establish a cause–effect (causal) relationship? It is rare that there is a single cause for an effect, particularly with complex personal, social, or content-area problems, so it is important to practice speculating about many possible causes. For example, we might present a cause and ask students, in role (as authorities at an inquest or some other group of experts; see Wilhelm 2002/2012), if this single cause is sufficient to explain the effect. If it isn't, students brainstorm other possible causes.

Berke (2007) suggests having students respond to and judge the causality in morals or parables, such as this Sufi one:

➤ *Lesson idea*

> "What is fate?" the Mulla Nasrudin was asked.
>
>   "An endless succession of intertwined events, each influencing the other."
>
>   "That is hardly satisfactory. It does not accommodate cause and effect."

"Very well," said the Mulla, pointing to a procession. "That man is being taken to be hanged. Is this because his parents neglected him which leads him to anger, or because someone gave him silver that enabled him to buy a knife with which he committed the murder, or because someone saw him do it and witnessed against him, or because nobody stopped him, or for some other reasons?"

Evaluating causality helps students distinguish ultimate and immediate causes, as well as explore different ways of establishing causality. As they test out what they think are the causes, they can apply the TCSNO criteria.

➤ *Lesson ideas*

While we were writing this book, a popular series of advertisements for DirecTV played on extended causal chains. "You get your cable bill. The numerous surcharges make you angry. Your wife thinks you have anger management problems. She leaves you. You become single. You adopt a cat for companionship. You grow a scraggly beard and never wash. You never go out and begin eating cat food. You adopt numerous cats for companionship. Don't become a stray-pet-collecting person: switch to DirecTV." Similar causal chains end with "don't end up lying in a roadside ditch" and "don't be a person whose grandchildren wear dog collars." Students have fun critiquing the causal chains presented, and in proposing their own causal chains emanating from a single ultimate cause.

In this unit, we encourage students to read and watch mysteries and spy thrillers, which afford many opportunities to consider how the truth is both obscured and ascertained, and to consider causality, particularly in the domain of human motivations.

We also ask students to create flowcharts that identify causes (why, because of) and reasons for certain effects and lead to possible solutions or corrections, connecting the causes, reasons, effects, and solutions with arrows. (See Figure 12.7.) Students consider primary or immediate causes as well as ultimate or necessary causes. We remind students that effects are often the problem in a problem–solution paper. When they have completed the flowchart, they apply the TCSNO criteria to see whether they have reasonably established causality between certain causes and effects.

➤ *Lesson idea*

Composing First Drafts of Cause–Effect Pieces

It's always helpful for writers to decompose the task and make a schedule—setting goals in the order they need to be achieved, perhaps even establishing a due date. We ask students to use what they have learned through planning and practice to articulate critical standards and criteria.

Figure 12.7 *Example of a Student Cause–Effect Flowchart*

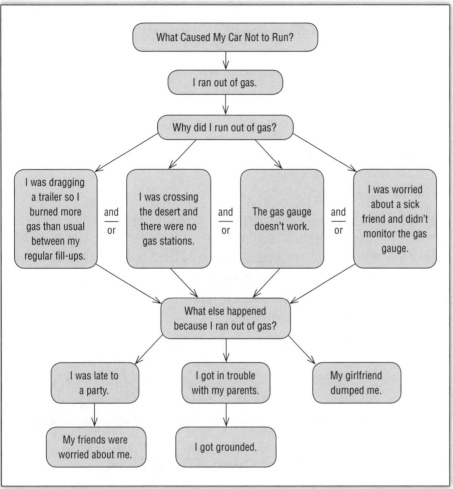

Here are the criteria for a cause–effect essay that a group of seniors came up with:

- States the cause–effect relationship being examined in the introduction (for a control claim) or in the conclusion (for a culminating claim).

- Focuses on an important subject involving causality *and* illustrates the relationship between causes and effects; distinguishes between a cause and an effect.

- Establishes causality according to criteria of time, covariation, uniformity, sufficiency, and elimination of alternatives.

- Provides an effective organizational strategy (cause-to-effect, effect-to-cause, or cause–effect chain of events), one that is clearly best suited for the topic, purpose, and audience.
- Uses appropriate transitional words and phrases throughout the writing to keep relationships among ideas clear; things flow.

➤ *Lesson idea*

➤ *Writing anchor standards 2, 4, 5, and 7–9*

Peer responders can follow a protocol like this:

- Read the draft.
- Relay your general impression, identifying an aspect of the paper that seems particularly effective.
- Reread the draft.
- Say how the introduction orients and guides you throughout your reading.
- Explain how you know that you have or don't have enough background information. Point out places where those less knowledgeable than you may need more information or explanation.
- Say how the author makes the topic important and compelling and how she or he can do this even better.
- List the causes and effects that are explored.
- Identify compelling and convincing relationships between causes and effects (that met the TCSNO criteria); suggest relationships that may have been missed or that may be coincidental.
- Point out how the author establishes her or his authority and credibility.

Composing Final Drafts of Cause–Effect Pieces

➤ *Lesson idea*

Have students identify transitions and other navigational devices (see Figure 12.8) as they read and create anchor reference charts. Then have them use these transitions and other devices to help navigate the reader and justify and demonstrate relationships among causes and effects.

Have pairs of peer proofreaders look for particular problems related to cause–effect writing. For example, have them circle repetitions of any kind (needless repetition is a problem our student writers suffer from), as well as of transitions like *the reason is because* or *the reason for* and use variations like *what follows is*. The author may justify using the repetition for effect, or together the pair can brainstorm possible variations to eliminate needless repetitions and provide variety.

Figure 12.8. Cause–Effect Transitions

PURPOSE

for the purpose of	in the hope that	for fear that	so that
with this intention	to the end that	in order to	lest
with this in mind	in order that	so as to	so

CAUSE/REASON

for the (simple) reason that	being that	for	in view of (the fact)	inasmuch as
because (of the fact)	seeing that		owing to (the fact)	
due to (the fact that)	in that		forasmuch as	since

CONDITION

on (the) condition (that)	granted (that)	if	provided that	in case
in the event that	as/so long as	unless	given that	
granting (that)	providing that	even if	only if	

EFFECT/RESULT

as a result (of this)	consequently	hence	for this reason	thus
because (of this)	in consequence	so that	accordingly	
as a consequence	so much (so) that	so	therefore	

CONSEQUENCE

under those circumstances	then	in that case	if not
that being the case	if so	otherwise	

Sometimes students need help presenting numerical evidence. The website http:// lilt.ilstu.edu/gmklass/pos138/datadisplay/sections/goodtables.htm, among others, has great suggestions for presenting numerical data, particularly for cause-and-effect essays. Numerical data can establish patterns that support causal relationships across cases, one of the crux moves of establishing causality, particularly through

➤ *Language anchor standard 3*

covariation. We also used excerpts from *Damned Lies and Statistics* (Best 2001) to help our students explore how numbers can both express and obscure the truth.

Composing to Transfer Knowledge of Cause–Effect

Students can use process analyses to create a flowchart or how-to protocol for establishing cause–effect or for using cause–effect patterns in thinking, problem solving, or composing. Students can always use a variation of the PQP format to assess their learning, recording what *pleased* them, what *questions* they still have about cause–effect, and what they are now *prepared* to do in the future, as well as when they anticipate using the structure and how they will try to improve their use of it in future disciplinary and personal work. They can also write in their journal about what they learned about a particular topic—an aspect of establishing or approaching truth, or a cause of deception, and how that might be useful and applicable in new situations, as well as about what they learned about using this particular thought pattern.

Axelrod and Cooper (1999) suggest that students should also critically reflect on establishing causation. How comfortable are they when dealing with possibilities versus certainties, with theorizing versus establishing causality? Is there any difference in their comfort level prior to the unit and after it? How might their own prior knowledge, biases, and values have influenced the causes and effects they decided to support? Who benefits from the causes and effects they established, if accepted by others? Who might not benefit or even be harmed? What contributions does speculating about causes make in the disciplines, in our personal lives, and in society that other patterns of thinking and writing cannot make?

➤ *CCSS multimodal emphasis*

We have students design a multimodal version of their reflection and present it to a small learning group. Students also often respond to one another's reflective writings on the class wiki.

If students can do all these things, they demonstrate all five kinds of knowledge and they're ready to take their show on the road—transfer what they've learned to new composing situations as well as to thinking critically and incisively about causality in their own lives. This, in turn, will help students use all of the thought patterns and text structures explored in this book to be more independent and expert problem solvers and meaning makers, the goal of all our instruction.

Bringing It All Together

Working Toward Opportunity and Possibility

We've been making the argument that the real power of the informational thought patterns and text structures is in their *telos*: in the *work* they can get done and the problems they can serve to circumvent or solve. When we categorize, organize, analyze, and come to understand categories and patterns of data, as the patterns and structures explored in this book help us to do, we are ultimately able to see problems and causes, see effects and propose solutions, make and evaluate arguments, and as a result, change our understandings and transform our behaviors in wide-awake ways.

As for our own telos, the three of us have dedicated our lives to teaching literacy and developing and promoting the most powerful contexts and methods to help students, particularly struggling ones, read and compose in more potent, useful, and transformative ways. Above all, we want our work to *matter*—to teachers and to the students they are shepherding into new ways of thinking and being.

That's why we promote the context of inquiry for all reading and composing—because reading and composing are then in service of understanding and dealing with important and compelling problems. As we recounted in the first chapter, the research supporting inquiry, construed as rigorous apprenticeship leading to expertise, is compelling and unrivaled.

When it comes to any kind of learning, we want our students to go beyond what is already understood and to reframe problems, see new causes or complexity of causes, propose creative new solutions, and evaluate innovative effects. We want them to internalize and apply critical standards for concept, procedure, and genre. We want them to compose in ways that do not repeat what is already known but that create new meanings and possibilities. We want them to resist simple and accepted explanations and ways of doing things. We want them to cultivate a sense of personal and civic agency. We want them to embrace a dynamic growth mindset (Dweck

2006). We want them to apply their passion and imagination to the problems facing themselves and the world.

In that world, problems abound, and the knowledge and methods to solve many of these problems have not yet been applied, conceived, or created. As we argued in the previous chapter, we need to cultivate a tomorrow mind versus a yesterday mind in all our students.

Jeff particularly enjoys books by Malcolm Gladwell, because Gladwell is so good at complicating and reframing problems so they can be understood and sometimes solved in new ways. Right now, Jeff is reading Francis Lappé Moore's *Ecomind*, in which she argues that we misconstrue at least seven causes of our current ecological dilemma; that if we reframe our understanding we'll see that these supposed causes are in error; and that this will lead us to new framings, new understandings, new hope, and new solutions.

Michael is going to his book club tonight to discuss Lou Ureneck's *Cabin: Two Brothers, a Dream, and Five Acres in Maine*. The book contains lots of description, both of physical details and processes. Lots of analyses of causes and effects. Comparisons of urban and rural life and of different kinds of wilderness. Michael anticipates a rousing discussion, focusing especially on whether the building of the cabin was indeed a solution to the dislocation the author was feeling and whether analogs exist for the club members.

Jim is spending considerable time reading research on teacher induction and the kind of teacher talk that helps teachers learn from one another. He is interested in applying these insights to his work with both preservice and inservice teachers.

So it is: our favorite informational authors help us see the world in a new way, often shocking us and directly addressing our misconceptions or simplified understandings of phenomenon to deepen our understanding and lead us to reformed ways of thinking and of living. This is what we want for our students.

Setting the Task Before Us

In his book *The Genius in All of Us* (2010) David Shenk reviews recent research in cognitive science and neuroscience. His major points can be summarized thus: talent is a process. It is learned. The causes of talent are interactive and dynamic, as expressed by the formula $G \times E = T$: genetics times experience leads to talent. Expertise is a specific response to environmental demands. Expertise comes from the power of process and practice. Expertise comes from assistance, "deliberate practice," and nurturance over time.

In other words, all of our students can become more expert composers and readers of informational texts if we provide purposeful contexts for using informational texts, assistance over time, and lots of feedback that covers the five kinds of knowledge and the five kinds of composing.

Research by the famous Anders Ericsson (Ericsson and Lehmann 1996, for example) established that ten thousand hours of practice is necessary to gain expertise, based partly on his finding that practice animates neurons and builds neural pathways through the brain, which builds ever-evolving new capacities. Ericsson also established that technical facility must be abetted by creativity. True expertise adds something innovative from the self. According to Ericsson expertise always involves risk taking and cultivating intellectual adventurousness.

He further asserts that expertise is a flexible mental representation of knowing what to do in specific situations and having the facility to do it. Expertise therefore requires complex adaptations and control mechanisms. This in turn requires elaborate preparation and the use of anticipatory cues and flexible *heuristic* thought patterns. This is what we have attempted to provide and cultivate in this book both for teachers, in terms of instruction, and for students, in terms of getting the necessary reflective practice with crux moves to read and compose with informational thought and composing patterns.

To summarize Ericsson: talent is the result of acquired skill. Acquired skill requires taking a long and incremental view, constant practice, reflection, and the willingness to take risks and innovate. Think of the lessons of this research for us as teachers and for our students. Think of the promise of the CCSS if teachers K–12 work on the same few generative anchor standards for reading and composing informational text throughout the twelve years of a students' schooling, putting their own insights and innovations into play in service of this project. Our students just might get enough practice to develop competence and proceed toward expertise!

➤ *CCSS connection*

Einstein once famously protested that he should not be called a genius: "I just stay with problems longer than most people" was his explanation for his insights. What if we stuck with the most generative problems throughout our careers? What if we helped our students stay with problems and processes until deep understanding and facility were achieved?

In this regard, it's important to note that the Common Core State Standards are part of a systemic educational movement, but they are only one part. They provide solid and generative goals but not the contexts for reaching them or the necessary methods for achieving them. This is what must be determined by professional teachers in the contexts of their own classrooms, where we will all need to cultivate motivation, provide assistance and prodigious amounts of guided practice, and engage our students in experiencing the rewards that come from visible signs of actual accomplishment and from doing significant work together.

In short, we think that through effective instruction the goals of the CCSS and much more can be achieved. We hope this book gives you ideas about how to devise that effective instruction. And even if the CCSS evolve or are not adopted in your state, the instructional models and methods we develop as a result of their influence are still apposite and useful.

Working Toward Democracy

Teaching is at once immensely challenging and tremendously sublime. At its heart, teaching is immensely hopeful work. All three of us are committed to creating learning situations and instructional assistance that actualize all of our students' potential, particularly those students who often struggle in school. Further, we are committed to helping them participate in the life of our democracy in mutually beneficial ways.

In this book, we have presented both theory and instruction devoted to developing competence not only in literacy but also in life. We know from our own experience that using the five kinds of knowledge / five kinds of composing heuristics develop general, task-specific, and especially text-specific processes of reading, composing, and learning. Further, the instructional model shared here develops generative habits of mind: motivation, engagement, curiosity, creativity, problem solving, flexibility, willingness to take risks, fortitude and endurance, joy in the challenge, nameable competence, and reflectivity. Never have these habits been more essential than they are today.

We believe that nearly anything is possible for our students if we are respectful of them and offer them meaningful opportunities and assistance to meet important challenges. This is not just an ethereal belief. Benjamin Bloom, at the end of his career, committed himself to studying human potential (1976, 1985) and found that any student could achieve the next available goal if provided with the right assistance in a meaningful context of use.

We believe in providing instructional opportunities to all our students, and we believe that if they receive the right instruction, they will thrive and grow no matter their backgrounds or challenges, no matter how they (and we) are assessed and measured. These beliefs put schools and teachers at the center of the democratic enterprise. And this is where we think all of us truly belong.

Anna's Food Unit

by Anna Daley,

member of the Boise State Writing Project CCSS Implementation team

Cover Sheet

Unit Title: Food Unit Essential Question: What is the effect of food and its production on people and the environment?

Unit Description (Overview Narrative): The final unit of a Concurrent Enrollment Senior English course, this unit is designed to reinforce research skills, to *review the reading and composing of several informational text structures*, and to allow students a greater amount of flexibility and independence as writers than they have experienced thus far in the course. Food is an incredibly universal and relevant topic with many personal connections and social action implications, as are issues of food and personal health, food production and environmental damage, and food security. In this unit of study, students explore the essential question and narrow their writing focus by writing about food through a disciplinary lens of their choosing. Several skills that students are using independently in this unit have been carefully scaffolded in previous units. For example, students have been supported in developing facility in using and responding to informational texts through various frontloading and planning activities, practicing through a variety of discussion protocols, writer's workshop protocols, Author Says/Author Does analyses, annotation skills, drafting through outlining, using criteria guides, revision and proofreading tools. Finally, it is implied that students are given in-class time to discuss and/or reflect on each of the activities listed in this unit sequence, either with their home groups or as a whole class. This reflection may take as little as 5 minutes or as long as 30 minutes, but no activity occurs without this composing to transfer, which serves as feedback for the students and a form of formative assessment for the instructor.

Grade(s)/Level:	12
Discipline:	Language Arts
Course:	Concurrent Enrollment Senior English
Author(s):	Anna K. Daley
Contact Information:	daleyanna@hotmail.com

SECTION 1: STANDARDS MET IN THE UNIT

A. College and Career Readiness Standards (CCR) for Grade Level: 11–12

Number	CCR Anchor Standards for Reading Grade: 11–12
1	Cite strong and thorough textual evidence to support analysis of what the text says explicitly as well as inferences drawn from the text, including determining where the text leaves matters uncertain.
4	Determine the meaning of words and phrases as they are used in a text, including figurative, connotative, and technical meanings; analyze how an author uses and refines the meaning of a key term or terms over the course of a text (e.g., how Madison defines faction in Federalist No. 10).
5	Analyze and evaluate the effectiveness of the structure an author uses in his or her exposition or argument, including whether the structure makes points clear, convincing, and engaging.
7	Integrate and evaluate multiple sources of information presented in different media or formats (e.g., visually, quantitatively) as well as in words in order to address a question or solve a problem.
10	By the end of grade 11, read and comprehend literary nonfiction in the grades 11–12 CCR text complexity band proficiently, with scaffolding as needed at the high end of the range.
Number	**CCR Anchor Standards for Writing Grade: 12**
2	Write informative/explanatory texts to examine and convey complex ideas, concepts, and information clearly and accurately through the effective selection, organization, and analysis of content.
4	Produce clear and coherent writing in which the development, organization, and style are appropriate to task, purpose, and audience. (Grade-specific expectations for writing types are defined in standards 1–3 above.)
5	Develop and strengthen writing as needed by planning, revising, editing, rewriting, or trying a new approach, focusing on addressing what is most significant for a specific purpose and audience.
7	Conduct short as well as more sustained research projects to answer a question (including a self-generated question) or solve a problem; narrow or broaden the inquiry when appropriate; synthesize multiple sources on the subject, demonstrating understanding of the subject under investigation.
10	Write routinely over extended time frames (time for research, reflection, and revision) and shorter time frames (a single sitting or a day or two) for a range of tasks, purposes.
Number	**CCR Anchor Standards for Speaking and Listening Grade: 12**
1	Initiate and participate effectively in a range of collaborative discussions (one-on-one, in groups, and teacher-led) with diverse partners on grades 11–12 topics, texts, and issues, building on others' ideas and expressing their own clearly and persuasively.
4	Present information, findings, and supporting evidence, conveying a clear and distinct perspective, such that listeners can follow the line of reasoning, alternative or opposing perspectives are addressed, and the organization, development, substance, and style are appropriate to purpose, audience, and a range of formal and informal tasks.

SECTION 2: ASSESSMENT

A. Summative Writing Assessment

Background: This course is a portfolio design course. As such, students will submit a culminating composition for each unit. At the end of the course, students will select from among the multiple culminating unit compositions those pieces they would like to submit in the Final Writing Portfolio. Those compositions that are selected by the student for the Final Portfolio will undergo a final round of revisions and reflection on the writing and students' writing processes.

Culminating Composition Prompt (Including Essential Question): (What is the effect of food and its production on people and the environment?)

Write an informative/explanatory **problem–solution** or **cause–effect paper** to examine and convey complex ideas, concepts, and information **about food** from **a disciplinary approach**, attending to the norms and conventions of the discipline in which you are writing.

B. Ongoing Formative Assessment (Composing to Transfer)

Time: Daily

Prompt: Students will be asked to compose class exit and entrance tickets recording what they have learned that class period about the substance of the inquiry into food and its effects, and/or what they have learned about informational text structures that they will want to make sure to use in their culminating project. These will sometimes take the form of Muddy/Marvy sticky notes; sometimes will be the In Harbor–On the High Seas. Formative assessments will also include the daily work of the students, which will indicate what concepts about food and what techniques of reading and composing informational text have been mastered and which require more attention and assistance. Finally, we will use the changes in understanding concentric circles at the end of each week.

SECTION 3: THE INSTRUCTIONAL LADDER

5 Kinds of Knowledge	Instructional Strategies	Common Core State Standards	See Page
What are the students getting after in terms of the 5 kinds of knowledge?	*What strategies and what sequence will apprentice students to the culminating writing task?*	*Which Common Core State Standards are being taught?*	*Where in this book can one read more about a specific strategy?*
	MODEL AND MENTOR		
Knowledge of purpose and context

Procedural knowledge of substance | **Write exploration 1: Personal reflections on food and personal relationship with food.**

In this exploration, students are exploring their personal relationship to food, reflecting on their choices, food culture, a favorite meal, what others might eat but they cannot consider to be food, beliefs, and values about food. They are encouraged to write freely as they *describe* their reflections. As part of our debriefing of this exploration, special attention will be paid to genre features of effective descriptions. | CCSS writing standard 2

CCSS writing standard 7

CCSS writing standard 10

CCSS speaking and listening standard 4 | Composing to Plan, Chapters 4 and 5

Description, Chapter 8 |
| Procedural knowledge of substance

Procedural knowledge of form | **Write exploration 2: What is "good food"?**

For this in-class activity, I have students complete each step on a new page of notebook paper, writing the text structure (*definition, listing, classification,* etc.) across the top of the page. This is a visible cue to encourage students to see that the purpose and structure of their writing is shifting with each step. First, students *define*: What is "good food"? Then, they *list* everything they have eaten in the past 24 hours.

Next, students *classify* that list of food into categories based on different possible definitions of "good" (or "not so good") food. Following this, students write a *description* of each of the categories and the foods/meals they classified in those categories.

Finally, students write an *extended definition* of "good food" using their food categories as examples or nonexamples. | CCSS reading informative texts standard 1

CCSS reading informative texts standard 4

CCSS writing standard 2

CCSS writing standard 10

CCSS speaking and listening standard 4 | Definition and Extended Definition, Chapter 9

Listing, Chapter 6

Classification, Chapter 11

Description, Chapter 8 |

(continues)

(continued)

5 Kinds of Knowledge	Instructional Strategies	Common Core State Standards	See Page
	MODEL AND MENTOR *(continued)*		
Declarative knowledge of form Procedural and declarative knowledge of substance	**Jigsaw short food readings:** *What informative or explanatory work is getting done?* In this activity, students are given a choice of short texts to read. (See the bibliography of readings, selected for their variety of approaches to food and variety of informational text structures.) Since I print only four copies of each article, I know a variety of texts (and text structures) will be read. Students read their selected article independently, conducting an Author Says/Author Does analysis, looking for informative structures in particular. Halfway through their reading, I'll interrupt students and have them report out on what informative text structures they are finding, in terms of both superstructures and substructures. If I need to, I'll suggest names for other text structures to support students in naming what they might be seeing in their readings. Then, students configure into groups based on common readings to discuss their findings for 10 minutes. As a group, they must compose an accurate summary of the content of their article. Then, they must be able to point to and name all of the informative text structures they found in the article. Finally, they must identify the disciplinary lens used in their article. This group work allows students to see a variety of disciplinary approaches to food, to see a variety of text structures in use, to make approximations and learn from their peers before reporting out to the whole class, and to practice summary and listing. Groups then report out to the whole class on the document camera, sharing their summaries, listing of text structures, and citing of disciplinary lenses. **Listing: Anchor chart of informative/explanatory text types/ purposes.** As groups report out, I act as record keeper of the informative text structures they noticed in their readings. We place a star next to the "big" superstructure informative text structures (the ones that provide the overall framework for the article like problem–solution or cause–effect). This way, students begin to see the relationship between the embedded text structures, like dictionary level definition, and how they are in service of the bigger work that is getting done in each reading.	CCSS reading informative texts standard 1 CCSS reading informative texts standard 4 CCSS reading informative texts standard 5 CCSS reading informative texts standard 10 CCSS speaking and listening standard 1 CCSS speaking and listening standard 4 CCSS speaking and listening standard 1 CCSS speaking and listening standard 4	Composing to Plan and Practice, Chapters 4 and 5 Summary, Chapter 7 Listing, Chapter 6 Compare and Contrast, Chapter 10 Composing to Transfer, Chapters 4 and 5 Listing, Chapter 6

(continues)

5 Kinds of Knowledge	Instructional Strategies	Common Core State Standards	See Page
	MODEL AND MENTOR (*continued*)		
Knowledge of purpose and context Procedural knowledge of form Procedural knowledge of substance	**Write exploration 3: Holiday food writing** In this exploration, students *describe* their holiday food traditions from a disciplinary perspective. This is a time for students to "try on" disciplinary approaches in a writing environment where they may take the risk of not yet quite getting it right. Students will practice an important component of the culminating writing project here and get feedback on mistakes and misunderstandings during their in-class discussion of the exploration.	CCSS writing standard 2 CCSS writing standard 5 CCSS writing standard 10 CCSS speaking and listening standard 1	Composing to Practice, Chapters 4 and 5 Description, Chapter 8
	MENTOR AND MONITOR		
Declarative knowledge of substance Procedural and declarative knowledge of form	**Jigsaw long food readings: *What informative or explanatory work is getting done?*** In this activity, students are given a choice of long texts to read for homework. (See the bibliography of readings, selected for their variety of approaches to food and their variety of embedded informative text structures.) I print only five copies of each article to ensure a variety of informational content and text structures. Students read their selected article independently, having practiced for this assignment in class using our short readings. Again, students conduct an Author Says/Author Does analysis, looking for informative structures. And again, students are to write an accurate summary of the content of the article. In class, students are grouped based on common readings to discuss their general reactions to the articles. The home group summarizes their article, including a review of the article's definition of food, and process description of effects on people and environment that proceed from various eating habits, farming practices, food security measures, etc.	CCSS reading informative texts CCSS reading informative texts standard 1 CCSS reading informative texts standard 4 CCSS reading informative texts standard 5 CCSS reading informative texts standard 10 CCSS speaking and listening standard 1 CCSS speaking and listening standard 4	Composing to Practice, Chapters 4 and 5 All informational text structures, both overarching and embedded Jigsaw Activities Review Listing, Chapter 6 Summarizing, Chapter 7 Describing, Process Description/ Explanation, Chapter 8 Classification, Chapter 11 Process Description, Chapter 8

(*continues*)

(continued)

5 Kinds of Knowledge	Instructional Strategies	Common Core State Standards	See Page
	MENTOR AND MONITOR (*continued*)		
Declarative knowledge of substance Procedural and declarative knowledge of form	Then, in mixed jigsaw groups, they share summaries and compare the use and effect of different text structures in each article, and create a classified issue tree of major ideas about food and its effects across all articles. Students then reconfigure into their home groups so that each group member has a different article. Each group member reports out by summarizing the content of the article from the jigsaw group and describing the informative or explanatory work that was done and how it got done through the use of different text structures. Finally, they present their issue tree of major ideas. **Revise anchor chart of informative/explanatory text types/ purposes.** As a class, we revisit our anchor chart, adding any text structures and reorganizing them visually to depict the large, overarching structures like *problem–solution* or *cause–effect* and the embedded, supportive structures like *definition* or *description* as they are found in these particular articles.	CCSS speaking and listening standard 1 CCSS speaking and listening standard 4	Classification, Chapter 11 Composing to Transfer, Chapters 4 and 5
Procedural knowledge of substance and form	**Write exploration 4: A tale of two meals** In this exploration, students select two recent meals that differ in preparation, context, nutritional value, etc., and describe the processes of preparing and eating these meals and then **compare and contrast** those **process descriptions**.	CCSS writing standard 2 CCSS writing standard 10	Composing to Practice, Chapters 4 and 5 Process Description/ Explanation, specifically Memory Description, Chapter 8 Compare and Contrast, Chapter 10

(continues)

5 Kinds of Knowledge	Instructional Strategies	Common Core State Standards	See Page
	MENTOR AND MONITOR (*continued*)		
Procedural and declarative knowledge of substance	**Word web 101: All things food!** This in-class brainstorm is intended to help students identify and refine the topics they are considering writing about in their culminating composition. As a class, we will brainstorm 101 possible food-related topics. Students start by brainstorming a list of topics independently. Then, students share their list with their home groups. On the whiteboard, I've written our EQ: What is the effect of food and its production on people and the environment? inside a circle. Groups document their brainstormed list by writing it on the whiteboard, drawing connections to other ideas from other groups where they see them occurring. If we do not get to 101 different ideas after this first round of brainstorming, groups are sent back to brainstorm additional ideas.	CCSS writing standard 2 CCSS writing standard 7 CCSS writing standard 10 CCSS speaking and listening standard 1 CCSS speaking and listening standard 4	Composing to Plan, Chapters 4 and 5 Listing, Chapter 6
Knowledge of purpose and context Procedural and declarative knowledge of substance Procedural and declarative knowledge of form	**Begin write exploration 5: Writing to plan your paper.** In this exploration, students home in on a paper topic of interest to them. They situate their topic as befitting either a problem–solution paper or a cause–effect paper depending on their purposes. They consider the purpose and function of their work, both personally and in the discipline they choose. They also write to connect their approach to the academic disciplines, a key move for these future college writers. The exploration also asks students to reflect on their purposes for writing and the text structures that might help them achieve these purposes. Students consider issues of rhetorical stance: their purpose, the audience/discourse community of the chosen discipline, format, vocabulary, and the like.	CCSS writing standard 2 CCSS writing standard 4 CCSS writing standard 5 CCSS writing standard 7 CCSS writing standard 10	Composing to Plan, Chapters 4 and 5 Task Decomposition, Chapter 5
Knowledge of purpose and context Procedural and declarative knowledge of form	**Research a model text.** This homework assignment tasks students with finding a model text for their writing by researching in academic databases. Students will often narrow their search by searching for databases within the academic subject they've selected as an approach to food. The model must exhibit a problem–solution or cause–effect superstructure.	CCSS reading informative texts standard 4 Reading anchor standard 7 CCSS speaking and listening standard 4	Composing to Plan, Chapters 4 and 5 Composing to Practice, Chapters 4 and 5 Composing to Transfer, Chapters 4 and 5

(*continues*)

(continued)

5 Kinds of Knowledge	Instructional Strategies	Common Core State Standards	See Page
	MENTOR AND MONITOR *(continued)*		
Knowledge of purpose and context Procedural and declarative knowledge of form	**Complete exploration 5.** Once students have identified a model text, the exploration prompts them to examine the disciplinary purposes, content, and structures (textual, visual, and other) of the article. Students identify other situations in which these purposes, this content and these text structures would be useful.	CCSS reading informative texts standard 4 CCSS reading informative texts standard 5 CCSS writing standard 10	Problem–Solution and Cause–Effect, Chapter 12
Knowledge of purpose and context Procedural and declarative knowledge of substance	**Report out on paper topics.** After composing their thoughts on a short reflection worksheet, students report out to their home groups on their selected paper topics, purposes, text structures they plan to use as super- and substructures, and intended audience. Then I ask for volunteers to report out to the whole class. During this time, I focus my comments to reinforce the problem–solution or cause–effect structure, the selected disciplinary approach, including likely norms and conventions of that disciplinary writing and to question, challenge, or encourage an appropriate level of complexity for the final writing project.	CCSS writing standards 4, 7 CCSS writing standard 10 CCSS speaking and listening standard 1 CCSS speaking and listening standard 4	Composing to Transfer, Chapters 4 and 5 Composing to Plan and Practice, Chapters 4 and 5 Problem–Solution and Cause–Effect, Chapter 12
Procedural knowledge of substance and form	**Compose rough draft or outline in chunks.** Students compose their "messy first draft." They are given the option of either writing a rough draft or an "outline in chunks," a form of early composing taught in previous units. The point is that they have options to choose from—whatever will help them most to get their ideas down on paper without holding back, revising as they go, or succumbing to writer's block.	CCSS writing standard 2 CCSS writing standard 4 CCSS writing standard 5 CCSS writing standard 7 CCSS writing standard 10	Composing as Drafting, Chapters 4 and 5 Classification, Chapter 11
Declarative knowledge of substance and form	**Workshop 1: Drafting and revising for global revisions** In their home groups, students workshop for global revisions, like content and form. Students focus on the purpose of the paper and based on this, the embedded text structures that would support the writer's purposes in proposing solutions or establishing causality. Peer editors use Keep, Add, Move, Delete, and Change protocol.	CCSS reading informative texts standard 4 CCSS speaking and listening standard 1	Composing as Drafting, Chapters 4 and 5

(continues)

5 Kinds of Knowledge	Instructional Strategies	Common Core State Standards	See Page
	MENTOR AND MONITOR (*continued*)		
Procedural knowledge of substance and form	**Compose global revisions, conducting additional research as needed.** Based on workshop comments, students revise for these global issues as homework, including conducting additional research as needed to provide additional data, to more fully explicate their topic, to clarify concepts, etc.	CCSS writing standard 2 CCSS writing standard 4 CCSS writing standard 5 CCSS writing standard 7 CCSS writing standard 10	Problem–Solution and Cause–Effect (Chapter 12)
Declarative knowledge of form and substance	**Write two letters of feedback to two members of your group.** Students respond to two members of their home writing groups in a letter of feedback. In these letters, students compose their response as an audience member at an academic forum. These letters also give students a place to practice their declarative knowledge of the assignment before they write the reflective cover letter. Letters will follow the Praise, Question, Suggestion format.	CCSS reading informative texts standard 1 CCSS reading informative texts standard 4 CCSS reading informative texts standard 5 CCSS writing standard 2 CCSS writing standard 4 CCSS writing standard 10 CCSS speaking and listening standard 4	Composing as Drafting, Chapters 4 and 5 Composing to Transfer, Chapters 4 and 5
Declarative knowledge of form and substance Procedural knowledge of form and substance	**Workshop 2: Additional global revisions** Students again focus on global issues, this time commenting on the success of the revisions the writer has made. Students also note final places where additional research is advisable. **Revise, conducting additional research as needed.**	CCSS reading informative texts standard 4 CCSS speaking and listening standard CCSS writing standard 2 CCSS writing standard 4 CCSS writing standard 5 CCSS writing standard 7 CCSS writing standard 10	Composing as Drafting, Chapters 4 and 5 Composing to Transfer, Chapters 4 and 5

(continues)

(continued)

5 Kinds of Knowledge	Instructional Strategies	Common Core State Standards	See Page
	MENTOR AND MONITOR (*continued*)		
Procedural knowledge of form	**Workshop 3: Composing to finalize. Revisit local writing goals and conduct quick revisions.** In class, we review our local writing goals (from CCSS language standards), examining focal correction area examples of navigational structures and transitions. Students are directed to find places in their drafts where these structures might help to clarify or tighten their language, to more clearly demonstrate cause and effect or problem–solution and to conduct "quick revisions" right then.	CCSS writing standard 4 CCSS writing standard 5 CCSS writing standard 10 CCSS language standards 1, 2, 3	Composing as Drafting, and Finalizing, Chapters 4 and 5
Procedural knowledge of form	**Workshop 4: Local revisions (and additional global revisions)** In this workshop, students are looking to correct spelling, grammar, punctuation errors, and other local writing issues.	CCSS reading informative texts standard 4 CCSS speaking and listening standard 1	Problem–Solution and Cause–Effect, Chapter 12
	MASTERY		
Procedural knowledge of form and substance	**Compose the final draft, revising locally and globally as needed.**	CCSS reading informative texts standard 4 CCSS writing standard 2 CCSS writing standard 4 CCSS writing standard 5 CCSS writing standard 7 CCSS writing standard 10	Composing to Finalize, Chapters 4 and 5
Declarative knowledge of form and substance	**Write reflective cover letter.** In the reflective cover letter, students describe their process for developing the substance and form of their paper. They describe their perceived strengths of the paper and what they would do differently if they had more time or tools to do so.	CCSS writing standard 2 CCSS writing standard 4 CCSS writing standard 10	Composing to Transfer, Chapters 4 and 5

Ideas for sequencing from Wilhelm (2007); Smith and Wilhelm (2002); Wilhelm, Baker, and Hackett (2001).
Ideas for Model, Mentor, and Monitoring from Wilhelm (2007); Wilhelm, Wilhelm, and Boas (2009).

Reflection Narrative

As mentioned in the overview, this unit is the final unit of a portfolio-design Dual Enrollment course. It is important to note that following the submission of this Culminating Unit Writing Project, students would undergo the process of selecting papers for submission in the Portfolio and then revision and reflection upon their selected writings. If students selected their paper on food, they would subject their writing to yet additional rounds of workshop, revision, and reflection.

It is also important to note that the relatively light level of teacher support (of skills, routines, procedures and thinking heuristics, etc.) is due to intentional scaffolding of those skills, routines, procedures, and heuristics in units leading up to this one. In this unit, students are demonstrating more independence as writers. Were I teaching to younger students, I would build much greater scaffolded support for students in terms of using more readings, which would be done with greater social support, such as think-alouds, and much more specific guidance toward practicing, in informal low-stakes ways, the composing of particular text types, and specific features of those text types. (I would also eliminate language from the prompt referring to "disciplinary approach of choice.") The culminating writing project would not be so broad, but instead have clearer, shared goals and fewer options (while still maintaining some choice for students' writing). However, because this is a college-level composition course, it is important to designate the responsibility of matching forms to purposes upon the student, with ever careful guidance along the way to apprentice students into practicing those forms.

Works Cited

Anderson, R. C., R. J. Spiro, and W. E. Montague, eds. 1984. *Schooling and the Acquisition of Knowledge.* Hillsdale, NJ: Lawrence Erlbaum.

Arnold, J. 1997. "Teams and Curriculum." In *We Gain More Than We Give*, edited by T. S. Dickinson and T. O. Erb, 443–59. Columbus, OH: National Middle School Association (NMSA).

Axelrod, R., and C. Cooper. 1999. *Reading Critically; Writing Well.* 5th ed. Boston: Bedford/St. Martin's.

Bereiter, C. 2002. *Education and Mind in the Knowledge Age.* Mahwah, NJ: Lawrence Erlbaum.

———. 2004. "Reflections on Depth." In *Teaching for Deep Understanding*, edited by K. Leithwood, P. McAdie, N. Bascia, and A. Rodriguez, 8–12. Toronto: Elementary Teachers' Federation of Ontario (EFTO).

Berke, J. 2007. *Twenty Questions for the Writer.* New York: Harcourt Brace.

Best, J. 2001. *Damned Lies and Statistics.* Berkeley: University of California Press.

Binet, A. [1909] 1975. *Modern Ideas About Children.* Ann Arbor: University of Michigan.

Bloom, B. 1976. *Human Characteristics and School Learning.* New York: McGraw-Hill.

———. 1985. *Developing Talent in Young People.* New York: Ballantine.

Boud, D., R. Keogh, and D. Walker. 1985. *Reflection: Turning Experience into Learning.* London: Kogan Page.

Bransford, J. D., and M. K. Johnson. 1972. "Contextual Prerequisites for Understanding: Some Investigations of Comprehension and Recall." *Journal of Verbal Learning and Verbal Behavior* 11 (6): 717–72.

Brophy, J. E., and T. L. Good. 1986. *Educational Psychology.* 3d ed. New York: Longman.

Brown, A., and J. Day. 1983. *For Summarizing Texts: The Development of Expertise.* Technical Report No. 27QS. Champaign-Urbana: University of Illinois.

Brown, J., A. Collins, and P. Duguid. 1989. "Situated Cognition and the Culture of Learning." *Educational Researcher* 18: 32–42.

Bruner, J. 1986. *Actual Minds, Possible Worlds.* Cambridge, MA: Harvard University Press.

Carr, E. 1972. *Fresh Seeing.* Toronto: Clark Irwin.

Celce-Murcia, M., and E. Olshtain. 2000. *Discourse and Context in Language Teaching.* New York: Cambridge University Press.

Chall, J. S. 1983. *Stages of Reading Development.* New York: McGraw-Hill.

Damasio, A. 2010. *Self Comes to Mind: Constructing the Conscious Brain.* New York: Pantheon.

Davids, A. 2010. "The Power of a Name: The Power of Naming." Retrieved August 28, 2011, from myjewishlearning.com.

Diehl, M., and W. Stroebe. 1987. "Productivity Loss in Brainstorming Groups: Toward the Solution of a Riddle." *Journal of Personality and Social Psychology* 53 (3): 497–509. DOI: 10.1037/0022-3514.53.3.497.

———. 1991. "Productivity Loss in Idea-Generating Groups: Tracking Down the Blocking Effect." *Journal of Personality and Social Psychology* 61 (3): 392–403. DOI: 10.1037/0022-3514.61.3.392.

Dweck, C. 2006. *Mindset: The New Psychology of Success.* New York: Random House.

Edmiston, B. 1990. How Far Have You Travelled? Unpublished doctoral dissertation, Ohio State University, Columbus, OH.

Elliott, R. 1960. *The Power of Satire: Magic, Ritual, Art.* Princeton, NJ: Princeton University Press.

Ericsson, K. A., and A. C. Lehmann. 1996. "Expert and Exceptional Performance: Evidence of Maximal Adaptation to Task Constraints." *Annual Review of Psychology* 47: 273–305. DOI: 10.1146/annurev.psych.47.1.273.

Folk, S. 2004. "Understanding Understanding." In *Teaching for Deep Understanding*, edited by K. Leithwood, P. McAdie, N. Bascia, and A. Rodriguez, 21–24. Toronto: Elementary Teachers' Federation of Ontario (EFTO).

Fredricksen, J. E., J. D. Wilhelm, and M. W. Smith. 2012. *So, What's the Story? Teaching Narrative to Understand Ourselves, Others, and the World.* Portsmouth, NH: Heinemann.

Friend, R. 2001. "Teaching Summarization as a Content Area Reading Strategy." *Journal of Adolescent & Adult Literacy* 44: 320–29.

Galán, A., and C. Pérez. 2004. "The Problem–Solution Pattern: A Tool for Writing." *BELLS: Barcelona English Language and Literature Studies* 12. (Ejemplar dedicado a: The Teaching of Foreign languages in Higher and Adult Education: Barcelona, Spain.)

Gardner, H. 1982. *Art, Mind, and Brain.* New York: Basic Books.

Gladwell, M. 2000. *The Tipping Point.* New York: Little, Brown.

———. 2009. "Enron, Intelligence, and the Perils of Too Much Information." In *What the Dog Saw: And Other Adventures*, 151–76. New York: Little, Brown.

Goodlad, J. 1984. *A Place Called School.* New York: McGraw-Hill.

Graham, L. 2009. The Power of Names: Religion and Mathematics. Speech presented to the New York Council of the Humanities, November 11.

Graves, M. 2009. *Essential Readings on Vocabulary Instruction.* Newark, DE: International Reading Association.

Greene, B. 2011. "Waiting for the Higgs Particle." *New York Times*, 15 December, A33.

Greene, S. 1991. "Mining Texts in Reading to Write." Occasional paper 29 (October 1991). Retrieved November 30, 2011, from www.nwp.org/cs/public/print/resource/724.

Grimaldi, D. A., and M. S. Engel. 2007. "Why Descriptive Science Still Matters." *BioScience* 57 (8): 646–47.

Halverson, C. 2002. "Activity Theory and Distributed Cognition." *Computer Supported Cooperative Work* 11: 243–67.

Hardy, B. 1977. "Towards a Poetics of Fiction." In *The Cool Web*, edited by M. Meek, A. Warlow, and G. Barton. London: The Bodley Head.

Haskell, R. 2000. *Transfer of Learning: Cognition, Instruction, and Reasoning*. San Diego, CA: Academic Press.

Hatton, N., and D. Smith. 1995. "Reflection in Teacher Education: Towards Definition and Implementation." *Teaching and Teacher Education* 11 (1): 33–49.

Hillocks, G. 1983. *Research on Written Composition*. Champaign-Urbana, IL: National Council of Teachers of English (NCTE).

———. 1986. "The Writer's Knowledge: Theory, Research, and Implications for Practice." In *The Teaching of Writing* (85th Yearbook of the National Society for the Study of Education, Part 2), edited by A. Petrosky and D. Bartholomae, 71–94. Chicago: National Society for the Study of Education.

———. 1995. *Teaching Writing as Reflective Practice*. New York: Teachers College Press.

Hillocks, G., E. Kahn, and L. Johannessen. 1983. "Teaching Defining Strategies as a Mode of Inquiry: Some Effects on Student Writing." *Research in the Teaching of English* 17 (3): 275–84.

Hoey, M. 1983. *On the Surface of Discourse*. London: Allen and Unwin.

———. 1986. "Overlapping Patterns of Discourse Organization and Their Implication for a Clause Relational Analysis of Problem–Solution Texts." *Studying Writing Linguistic Approaches*, edited by C. R. Cooper and S. Greenbaum, 187–214. London: Sage.

———. 1991. *Patterns of Lexis in Text*. Oxford, UK: Oxford University Press.

———. 1993. "A Common Signal in Discourse: How the Word *Reason* Is Used in Texts." In *Techniques of Description: Spoken and Written Discourse*, edited by J. Sinclair, M. Hoey, and G. Fox, 67–82. London: Routledge.

———. 2001. *Textual Interaction: An Introduction to Written Discourse Analysis*. London: Routledge.

Horwood, R. 1988. "Explanation and Description in Science Teaching." *Science Education* 72 (1): 41–49.

Johannessen, L., E. Kahn, and C. Walter. 1982. *Designing and Sequencing Prewriting Activities*. Champaign-Urbana, IL: National Council of Teachers of English (NCTE).

Kintsch, W., and T. A. Van Dijk. 1978. "Toward a Model of Text Comprehension and Production." *Psychological Review* 85 (1): 363–94.

Koch, K., and K. Farrell. 1981. *Sleeping on the Wing*. New York: Random House.

Kuhn, T. 1962. *The Structure of Scientific Revolutions*. Chicago: University of Chicago Press.

Ladson-Billings, G. 1994. *The Dreamkeepers*. San Francisco: Jossey-Bass.

Lakoff, G. 2008. *The Political Mind*. New York: Penguin.

Levitin, D. 2007. *This Is Your Brain on Music*. New York: Penguin.

Lindemann, E. 2001. *A Rhetoric for Writing Teachers*. New York: Oxford University Press.

Mayr, E., and W. J. Bock. 2002. "Classifications and Other Ordering Systems." *Journal of Zoological Systems and Evolutionary Research* 40 (4): 169–94. DOI:10.1046/j.1439-0469.2002.00211.

McKenna, M. C., D. J. Kear, and R. A. Ellsworth. 1995. "Children's Attitudes Toward Reading: A National Survey." *Reading Research Quarterly* 30: 934–55.

McTighe, J., E. Seif, and G. Wiggins. 2004. "You Can Teach for Meaning." *Phi Delta Kappan* 62 (1): 26–31.

Newman, F., and Associates. 1996. *Authentic Achievement: Restructuring of Schools for Intellectual Quality*. San Francisco: Jossey-Bass.

Newman, F., and G. Wehlage. 1995. *Successful School Restructuring: A Report to the Public and Educators by the Center on Organization and Restructuring of Schools*. Madison, WI: Board of Regents of the University of Wisconsin System and Document Service, Wisconsin Center for Education Research.

Nickerson, R. 1985. "Understanding Understanding." *American Journal of Education* 93: 201–39.

Niiniluoto, I. 1993. "The Aim and Structure of Applied Research." *Erkenntnis* 38: 1–21.

Nystrand, M., A. Gamoran, R. Kachur, and C. Prendergast. 1997. *Opening Dialogue: Understanding the Dynamics of Language and Learning in the English Classroom*. New York: Teachers College Press.

Oz, M., and M. Roizen. 2012. "Do You Suffer from the Doorway Effect?" *The Idaho Statesman*, 9 January, L2.

Pace, D. 2010. From Description to Prediction: The Paradigm of Science, the Role of Ecology. Blog post from Sat., November 20, 2010—17:59. Available at www.oceanomaredelphis.org/drupal/node/75.

Perkins, D., and G. Salomon. 1988. "Teaching for Transfer." *Educational Leadership* 46 (1): 22–32.

Peters, E. 2005. Ways of Knowing. Journal Entry 6. Retrieved August 17, 2011, from http://mason.gmu.edu/~epeters1/Journal_Entry_6.htm.

Rabinowitz, P. 1998. *Before Reading*. Columbus: Ohio State University Press.

Rosa, A., and P. Eschholz. 1998. *Models for Writers*. 6th ed. New York: St. Martin's.

Sagoff, M. 1970. *ShrinkLits*. New York: Workman.

Schank, R. 1990. *Tell Me a Story*. New York: Scribner's.

Schleicher, A. 2009. Presentation on the comparative strengths and weaknesses of education in the United States at the 2009 SAS Global Forum, Washington, DC, March 24.

Scholes, R., and N. Comley. 1981. *The Practice of Writing*. New York: St. Martin's.

Schulz, K. 2010. *Being Wrong*. New York: Ecco.

Shenk, D. 2010. *The Genius in All of Us*. New York: Random House.

Siegel, D. 2007. *The Mindful Brain*. New York: W. W. Norton.

Smagorinsky, P. 1995. "Constructing Meaning in the Disciplines: Reconceptualizing Writing Across the Curriculum as Composing Across the Curriculum." *American Journal of Education* 103: 160–84.

———. 1997. "Artistic Composing as Representational Process." *Journal of Applied Developmental Psychology* 18: 87–105.

Smagorinsky, P., and M. W. Smith. 1992. "The Nature of Knowledge in Composition and Literary Understanding: The Question of Specificity." *Review of Educational Research* 62: 279–306.

Smagorinsky, P., V. Pettis, and P. Reed. 2004. "High School Students' Compositions of Ranch Designs: Implications for Academic and Personal Achievement." *Written Communication* 21: 386–418.

Smagorinsky, P., M. Zoss, and P. Reed. 2006. "Residential Interior Design as Complex Composition: A Case Study of a High School Senior's Composing Process." *Written Communication* 23: 295–330.

Smagorinsky, P., L. Johannessen, E. Kahn, and T. McCann. 2010. *The Dynamics of Writing Instruction*. Portsmouth, NH: Heinemann.

Smith, M. W., and J. Wilhelm. 2002. *"Reading Don't Fix No Chevys": Literacy in the Lives of Young Men*. Portsmouth, NH: Heinemann.

———. 2006. *Going with the Flow: How to Engage Boys (and Girls) in Their Literacy Learning*. Portsmouth, NH: Heinemann.

———. 2007. *Getting It Right*. New York: Scholastic.

———. 2009. *Fresh Takes on Teaching the Literary Elements*. New York: Scholastic.

Smith, M. W., J. D. Wilhelm, and J. E. Fredricksen. 2012. *Oh Yeah?! Putting Argument to Work Both in School and Out*. Portsmouth, NH: Heinemann.

Sternberg, R. 2007. *Wisdom, Intelligence, and Creativity Synthesized*. New York: Cambridge University Press.

Tharp, R., and R. Gallimore. 1990 *Rousing Minds to Life: Teaching, Learning and Schooling in Social Context*. Cambridge, UK: Cambridge University Press.

U.S. Census Bureau. 2009. *Income, Poverty, and Health Insurance Coverage*. Washington, DC: U.S. Department of Commerce.

Van Dijk, T. A. 1977. "Complex Semantic Information Processing." In *Natural Language in Information Science*, edited by D. E. Walker, et al., 127–63. Stockholm: Skriptor.

———. 1979: "Recalling and Summarizing Complex Discourse." In *Text Processing*, edited W. Burghardt and K. Holker, 49–118. Berlin: De Gruyter.

———. 1980. *Macrostructures*. Hillsdale, NJ: Erlbaum.

Van Dijk, T. A., and W. Kintsch. 1983. *Strategies of Discourse Comprehension*. New York: Academic.

Van Dijk, T., W. Kintsch, T. Mandel, and E. Kozminsky. 1977. "Recalling and Summarizing Complex Discourse." *Memory and Cognition* 5 (5): 547–52. DOI: 10.3758/BF03197399.

Wiggins, G., and J. McTighe. 2005. *Understanding by Design*. 2d ed. Fairfax, VA: Association for Supervision and Curriculum Development (ASCD).

Wilhelm, J. 2002/2012. *Action Strategies for Deepening Comprehension*. New York: Scholastic.

———. 2004/2012. *Reading IS Seeing*. New York: Scholastic.

———. 2007. *Engaging Readers and Writers with Inquiry*. New York: Scholastic.

———. 2008. *"You Gotta BE the Book": Teaching Engaged and Reflective Reading with Adolescents*. New York: Teachers College Press.

———. 2009. "Teaching with a Sense of Urgency." *Voices from the Middle* 16 (2): 54–57.

———. 2012. *Improving Comprehension with Think-Aloud Strategies*, 2d ed. New York: Scholastic.

Wilhelm, J., T. Baker, and J. Dube. 2001. *Strategic Reading*. Portsmouth, NH: Heinemann.

Wilhelm, J., and B. Edmiston. 1998. *Imagining to Learn: Inquiry, Ethics, and Integration Through Drama*. Portsmouth, NH: Heinemann.

Wilhelm, J., and P. Friedemann. 1998. *Hyperlearning: Where Inquiry, Technology, and Learning Meet*. York, ME: Stenhouse.

Wilhelm, J., and B. Novak. 2011. *Teaching Literacy for Love and Wisdom: Being the Book and Being the Change*. New York: Teachers College Press.

Wilhelm, J., P. Wilhelm, and E. Boas. 2009. *Inquiring Minds Learn to Read and Write*. Oakville, ON: Rubicon.

Index